A SEXUAL ODYSSEY

From Forbidden Fruit to Cybersex

A SEXUAL ODYSSEY

From Forbidden Fruit to Cybersex

KENNETH MAXWELL

PLENUM PRESS • NEW YORK AND LONDON

Library of Congress Cataloging in Publication Data

Maxwell, Kenneth E., [DATE]
  A sexual odyssey: from forbidden fruit to cybersex / Kenneth Maxwell.
     p.   cm.
  Includes bibliographical references and index.
  ISBN 0-306-45405-X
  1. Sex customs—History. 2. Sex role—History. 3. Computer sex. I. Title.
HQ12.M378 1996   96-9675
306.7'09—dc20   CIP

ISBN 0-306-45405-X

© 1996 Kenneth Maxwell
Plenum Press is a Division of Plenum Publishing Corporation
233 Spring Street, New York, N.Y. 10013-1578

An Insight Book

10 9 8 7 6 5 4 3 2 1

Printed in the United States of America

PREFACE

Sex is no longer simply the perennial target of moralists intent on taking the fun out of bedtime sport. The problems and pleasures of sex have become serious studies of medical doctors, psychologists, psychiatrists, sex therapists, sociologists, sexologists, demographers, and teachers. To these are added the contributions of writers described as experts in a steady stream of essays on the art of love, dating from the works of Ovid in first century Rome to the present.

If sex has a future, it is rooted in the past—more than 3.5 billion years ago when young Mother Earth cradled a microscopic form of matter endowed with the miraculous qualities we call life. The first forms of life were invisible, even if there had been eyes to see them. As the evolutionary clock ticked away—ticks measured in millions of years—diverse forms managed to survive in the harsh and dangerous young world. These microscopic organisms, still hardly big enough to cast a shadow, made an astounding discovery that was to determine the state of the living world forever. They found that sex, that is, the transfer of genetic material between consenting microbes, gave them a leg up on survival in an ever-changing hostile environment. Sex remained a dominant force through the millennia. How we manage sex in the future is destined to change our habits, social structure, and above all, the quality of life in astonishing ways.

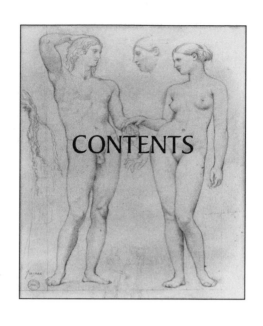

CONTENTS

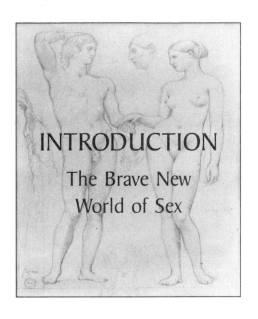

INTRODUCTION
The Brave New World of Sex

We've seen in less than a generation a swift revolution in human sexual behavior, attitude, and consequences so dramatic that some people are left in a state of stunned dismay and the public at large in aimless confusion. Much of the trend, if you can call a revolution a trend, is fueled by, or at least made possible by, technological innovations dating back to the middle of the twentieth century. The birth control pill opened the gate to promiscuity with little fear of pregnancy; marriage became an annoyance; divorce became an opportunity; two working parents became a necessity; and teenage sex became nearly as socially acceptable as holding hands or going to the movies. The copulation explosion resulted in a spiraling epidemic of children giving birth to children, many of them on welfare. Girls seeking relief through abortions were sometimes forced to have their unwanted offspring despite the inevitability of some of them living in poverty and a desperate dead-end environment of squalor and crime. Some misguidedly wanted babies and ended up the same way. To top it all, discipline became a lost art, leaving schools and neighborhoods infested with gun-toting, knife-wielding teenage delinquents—even in middle-class areas—who engaged in contests to see who could get the most girls knocked up.

The chaotic state of fornication, mating, and birthing may be a throwback to the past. In ancient Rome there were several categories of marriage having different and confusing legal status. Divorce was easy, often with no more formality than the husband's declaration that the marriage was ended. The system encouraged promiscuity, and because of the uncertainty of fatherhood, the practice was to name children after the mother's side of the family as that was the only surname of which they could be certain. The present method of naming children after the mother in Spanish-speaking countries is a legacy of Roman times.

In the brave new world of the twenty-first century, traditional weddings will continue to be popular but marriage itself will decline in some circles as an unnecessary and outdated formality, although modified ceremonies will remain as nostalgic reminders of ancestral rites. Two separate trends in social mores will tend to accelerate substitutions for traditional marriages: gay and lesbian couples who want official and legal recognition of a binding relationship, and older heterosexual couples who for financial or other reasons do not want the binding legalities of marriage. Optional cohabitation contracts will replace formal marriages, and will allow easy, economical, and quick separation—formerly called divorce. Premarital contracts will continue to be useful in many cases.

The contract ceremony will be more than simply signing a document before a notary public. Bonding of male and female is a ancient practice predating recorded history, and people love pomp and ceremony, especially in celebration of an event that may last a lifetime. Whether heterosexual, homosexual, or elderly, solemn vows of love will be exchanged, followed by congratulations, feasting, and dancing depending on traditions of the group, often with religious formalities but without the trappings of judicial sanction.

The modern attitude toward sexuality is believed to have had its roots in the thinking of early Greek philosophers who espoused the dualistic nature of mankind, and had an impact on subsequent generations, especially those of the early Christian era. Pythagoras, who lived in the sixth century BC, taught that people should not be dominated by the flesh. The dualism of human existence was most emphatically expressed by Plato, who believed in the overriding existence of two principles, Ideas and Matter. Ideas, he said, were immutable truths, without beginning or end, revealed only to the mind. On the other hand, matter, the material world, existed only insofar as it represented the Idea, but could never achieve perfection. Plato thought of love as dualistic: the sacred and the profane—the former of the mind, the latter of the body. True happiness could be achieved only through the nonphysical, the higher form of love. Other philosophers, as well, argued that pleasures of the senses were of no lasting virtue and were harmful; Lucretius advised men to avoid sex completely.

The theme of restraint was carried into religion by others, especially Philo, a Jewish philosopher in Alexandria of the first century BC, and Plotinus, writing on Christian matters in the third century AD. Early Jewish law was probably derived from Babylonian law, encoded by Hammurabi and the main features written in stone by Moses. Two of the ten commandments relate to sex: adultery and coveting a neighbor's wife. Adultery was the sin of infringing on the property of another man, and coveting was what led to that crime. In contrast to our own time, harsh conditions and high mortality made it imperative to maintain the flow of new members into the family, clan, and nation. It was customary for a man to have as many wives and mistresses (concubines) as he wanted, a practice that persisted for centuries. No father or other members of the family would let rape go unpunished. Whores were so numerous in Jerusalem that they had their own marketplace, comparable to a modern red-light district.

Christianity tightened the noose on sex and expanded the definition of sin. The Christian religion had strong elements of submission, guilt, masochism, punishment, sacrifice, and denial. One sect took the Jew's circumcision ritual a step further by castrating themselves. Another Christian sect went so far in their evangelical zeal that they castrated any guest unlucky enough to fall in with them.[1] Saint Augustine, a monk sent to England in the sixth century to convert the people there to Christianity, was one of the most influential Christian writers on sexuality and marriage. He had been converted from Manichaeanism, a sect based on the teachings of the prophet Mani, who was crucified in Babylonia in the third century AD. The most ascetic members of the sect, the Adepts, refused to have sexual intercourse, but Augustine never became an Adept. He lived with a mistress before his conversion, and struggled constantly with his conscience. He decided that although celibacy was the highest good, and sexual intercourse was merely animal lust, sex was justified, but only for the purpose of procreation. There followed declarations by successive Christian theologians and rulers on what was sinful and what the punishment should be.

In twelfth- and thirteenth-century England, churchmen made valiant attempts to crack down on sin. They denounced everything they could think of that was pleasurable: racing horses, the theater, dancing, and muttonchops. Their most urgent mission was to restrict sexual intercourse. For starters, they wanted to limit the act to only one position, later called the missionary position. "Canino," presumably the dorsal–ventral position thought to be the most primitive and exciting, and therefore the most barbarian and horrible, called for seven years of penance. Sex was made illegal on Sundays, Wednesdays, and Fridays, and was made illegal for 40 days before Easter, 40 days before Christmas, and 3 days before communion. Sex was also prohibited from conception to 40 days after childbirth. Clerics denounced masturbation. Thomas Aquinas, a thirteenth-century theologian and forceful monitor of sex, declared masturbation a greater sin than fornication. Sodomy, especially anal intercourse and bestiality, and all forms of "unnatural" sex were among the worst sins.

The modern world's view of sex ranges from restraint to tolerance to "the more the better," especially if the result is more children. Still, the sex scene is on the verge of new developments in the Western world. In some places and in some societies there will be little observable change in the immediate future, but a strong undercurrent of change will have global effects by the end of the century, and we will see a vastly different level of living standard in parts of the world where people are now suffering. Change will be brought about by the control or manipulation of sex-related developments and activities, especially population control and care of pregnant women and children. Some things may get worse before they get better, and changes will be accompanied by acrimonious debate and prolonged disputes. But the long-term trend will be a vast improvement in the quality of life.

The world of sex is at the threshold of trends amounting to a twenty-first-century revolution, bringing about the most dramatic changes in sexual relationships, habits, health, pleasures, pains, and living standards the world has ever seen during the half million years or so of human existence on earth.

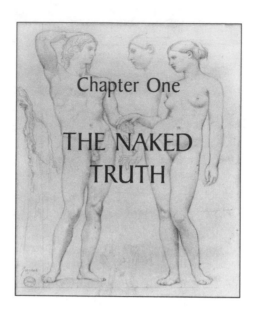

Chapter One

THE NAKED TRUTH

We're born naked. In Western societies our baby nakedness is quickly covered with pretty clothes. Small children are often allowed to run around naked at home, but by the time they're about three years old they've been carefully taught to keep their private parts covered. While they are not yet aware of the fact that the genitals are for reproduction and fun, not just to pee with, they've learned that it's wrong to display them in public.

The puritanical view that public nudity is sinful, and in most places criminal, stems from the time Eve fell for the snake's spiel about how it would make her and Adam like gods if they ate the forbidden fruit. Adam and Eve at first, we're told, "were naked . . . and were not ashamed." But after they ate the forbidden fruit that gave them knowledge of good and evil, "they knew that they were naked; and they sewed fig leaves together, and made themselves aprons."[1]

The humiliation of being seen naked is described in a story told of Noah, grandson of Methuselah, and a direct descendent of

Adam. Noah, who owned a vineyard, had imbibed too much wine when one of his sons, Ham, walked into the tent and saw his father naked in a drunken stupor. Ham told his two brothers, who entered the tent backward with a robe over their shoulders to cover their father. When Noah sobered up and learned of Ham's violation of the sancrosanct taboo, he was so incensed that he condemned Ham to a life of servitude, a "servant of servants."[2]

Historian Hugh Lester describes early nudism. Probably the first nudist cult anywhere in the world was established by the Egyptian pharaoh Amenhotep IV and his wife, Queen Nefertiti, who were avid sunbathers. Amenhotep IV, at the age of 24, was crowned in 1375 BC, and moved the capitol from Thebes to a new location he named Akhtaton. The young king was an exceptionally independent thinker, and he had the support of his wife. He established a new religion based on the worship of only one god, which he called Aton, meaning "Disk of the Sun," and changed his name to Ikhnaton, meaning "pleases Aton." Unlike the panoply of gods of previous Egyptian and other religions, Aton, the one and only god, was everywhere in nature, and the sun's rays were Aton's symbolic presence. Ikhnaton and Nefertiti and their seven daughters went naked in the palace, the gardens, and even, it is said, into the streets. They had temples built with exposure to the sun where their followers could worship in the nude and let their naked bodies be bathed in the sacred, life-giving rays of Aton.

The deposed priests of the old religion of Amon-Re were understandably furious. When Ikhnaton died, the throne went to a son-in-law, Senkenre, who after a few years was succeeded by another son-in-law, Tutankhaten, now known as "King Tut." The priests prevailed on Tut to move the capitol back to Thebes, change his name to Tutankhamen, and to get rid of the hated revolutionary Aton cult. There is speculation that remnant followers of the monotheistic Aton religion may have influenced Moses during his formative years in Egypt. A portion of Ikhnaton's *Hymn to Aton* is said to be in Psalm 104 of the Old Testament.[3]

In ancient Greece, appreciation for the beauty of the human body was an obsession, as seen in their sculptures. Nakedness was

Bathers, by Auguste Renoir. Courtesy of the Fogg Art Museum, Harvard University Art Museums.

a way of life in sports. Olympic athletes performed completely naked. The first Olympic festival of record was held in 776 BC. Irrepressible physical fitness buffs, they built and used gymnasiums, from the Greek word *gymnos*, meaning "naked." Gymnasiums were also centers of learning and general education where pupils typically went nude. The Spartans were physical fitness fanatics, and because the young people were encouraged to go with little clothing and no artificial adornment in public, Sparta was, in effect, a clothing-optional camp. Women of Crete wore attractive clothing, but it was stylish to leave the breasts uncovered. They used cosmetics liberally, including the practice of enhancing the beauty of their breasts by applying lipstick to the nipples. The Romans copied many of the Greek customs, including the practice of exercising in the nude, and indulging communally in the famous Roman baths. They participated in Greek games, adopted the gymnasium for games and physical fitness, and acquired some of the aesthetic fascination for the beauty of the human body that had reached a peak of perfection with the Greeks.

Jesus was crucified nude ("They parted his garments, casting lots") in accordance with the Roman custom of executing people in public as cruelly as possible and in a way that deprived them of all dignity.[4] With the coming of Christianity to the West, the human body became associated not with beauty, but with sex, an increasingly sinful preoccupation, justifiable only for procreation or to be avoided altogether by the truly devout. Exercise was to be obtained through hard work or fighting, for which clothing was required, and anyone contemplating the unthinkable act of bathing nude in the sun would be guilty of the double transgression of immorality and sloth. However, one of several nudist cults was a group of early Christians, the Adamiani, a sect based on *The Gospel of St. Thomas* that flourished in northern Africa during the second and third centuries AD. They went naked to religious services as well as often during everyday life. Their spiritual descendants, the Adamites, calling themselves "brothers and sisters of the free spirit," came into existence in Germany and Holland in the Middle Ages. They believed in ritual nakedness and were severely persecuted for it. In most segments of the Greco-Roman world during the early Christian era, nudism and physical fitness became unfashionable or officially prohibited. The Christian Roman Emperor Theodosius padlocked the gymnasiums throughout the empire about 395 AD, and his successor, Justinian, abolished the Olympic Games, declaring them pagan ceremonies. Obsession with evils of the body led one of the Popes to order drapes painted over Michelangelo's figures on the lower panels in the Sistine Chapel. Fortunately, the ceiling panels were too high to be conveniently reached.

The ancient Cretan custom of upper-class women exposing their breasts was revived during the seventeenth century in Europe with formal wear that barely covered the nipples. Women who could not compete with the more spectacularly endowed beauties simply took satisfaction in their higher level of modesty and decorum. Hugh Lester tells the story in *Godiva Rides Again* of the Victorian period when missionaries went all over the world trying to get natives to cover their nakedness. The Emperor of Japan, eager to adopt European culture, decreed that everyone must cover their pubic area when swimming. His subjects, taking the Emperor's order literally, disported on the beach in the nude as usual, and dutifully slipped on trunks before going in the water.

Modern nudism, as a fashion, first appeared in Germany during the 1920s, where organizations conducted exercise classes, similar to today's physical fitness centers except the members, male and female including children, performed as a group under strict discipline, and in the nude. Outdoor nudism also flourished, attracting thousands of people to organized nudist parks and selected beaches where clothing was optional. Meanwhile, the Scandinavians were quietly continuing their venerable habit of taking steam baths in the nude, and astonishingly to the uninitiated, adding the additional stimulation of cooling off quickly, naked, in the snow or jumping into the icy water of a lake.

Nudism for physical fitness did not catch on quickly in southern Europe, England, or the United States, but it did make a hit more recently on a few beaches, the most famous of which is Saint-Tropez on the French Riviera, where thousands of locals and tourists flock to feast their eyes on the beauty of topless and nude sunbathers.

The first nudist park in the United States opened in 1930 near Spring Valley, New York, by a small group that called themselves the American League for Physical Culture, founded primarily through the efforts of a German immigrant, Kurt Barthel, who had experienced *Freikorperkultur* (free body culture) in Germany. The group grew so fast that later the same year they moved to a larger site near Dover, New Jersey. Among those who joined the League was a preacher named Ilsley Boone. The Reverend Boone was a man of remarkable vitality and talents, who had a distinguished record of achievements as a theological scholar, author, and promoter of education using innovative visual aid techniques. Known to League members and followers as "Uncle Danny," the Reverend Boone created his own organization, which he called the International Nudist Conference, and started a magazine called *The Nudist*, with airbrushed pictures to cover the genital anatomy of people otherwise in the nude. The magazine was a success, partly because of publicity from the howls of protest about its being shameless and obscene.

Nudists in the United States realized from the beginning that they would have to conduct themselves in a way that would avoid public antagonism. Most of the parks screened applicants to determine if they were serious about the health values of nudism, and if they were the type of people who would be discrete. But, despite everything, nudist parks were frequently raided by sheriffs and their deputies, usually accompanied by cameramen and often by news reporters. Raids were sometimes preceded by aircraft surveillance, usually in response to citizen complaints of what they imagined was going on. More than once, members were handcuffed and hauled off to jail. In one case a fully dressed woman was ordered by police to undress so photographers could take her picture naked. She refused. In Michigan, a sheriff raided a newly opened park called the Sun Sport League, and arrested everyone there. Two fishermen had appeared at an opportune time along a small stream that ran across the property, open to fishing but virtually unfishable, making it possible to indict the nudists for "indecent exposure." The owners of the club, Mr. and Mrs. Ring, were found guilty and sentenced to a $300 fine plus 60 days in jail. The Michigan Supreme Court upheld the conviction, so the Rings went to jail, the first martyrs to nudism in the United States.[5]

When nudist organizations started publishing magazines containing photos of participants, officials of the U.S. Post Office saw it as their duty to protect the country from immorality. Anthony Comstock, a special agent for the U.S. Postal Service, started in 1868 an unrelenting crusade against "smut" during which he confiscated many classical literary and pictorial works by writers and artists. In what was intended to be a crippling move against nudist magazines, the Post Office under Comstock's guidance refused to send nudist literature at a rate lower than first-class mail. The Postal Service conducted a series of hearings over a ten-year period to build a case against what they viewed as obscenity. The courts generally supported the organizations' right to publish their magazines, but some of Comstock's rulings remained in force many years after his death.

Meanwhile legislators were not idle. In 1934, the Catholic League of Decency sponsored a bill to outlaw nudism in the State of New York. The bill was enthusiastically supported by Governor Al Smith, who was about to make a run for the presidency of the United States. Although not acted on until the administration of Governor Lehman, and signed by him, the antinudist law was known as the Al Smith Law. A similar law was defeated in Michigan. Still, law enforcement officers were usually able to find a legal reason, no matter how remote, for raiding nudist parks.

The early nudist clubs were formed by courageous types who were willing to flout convention because they were devoted to nakedness on principle as a healthful and wholesome way to enjoy relaxation and play. They had nothing in common with nudity in nightclubs and topless bars, the sole purpose of which was and is to titillate, and especially in nude bars where men, and occasionally women, go for a quick voyeuristic thrill, and where touching is forbidden for fear of "incidents." Women who perform in nude bars generally do not get naked for the fun of it, but for money to make a living, some of them being single mothers. In a good location, they can do quite well on tips. Most of them say they do not do "tricks," but it's reported that some of them do.

A historical counterpart of the nudist clubs was the Esalen-type encounter group which introduced nudity as group therapy. These groups take nakedness a step further by encouraging closeness and touching as a means of discovering sensuality in self and others. The Esalen Institute was founded in 1962 by Michael Murphy, whose grandfather, a Salinas physician, had purchased in 1910 a 300-acre tract on the wild and rugged Big Sur coastline 150 miles south of San Francisco with the idea of creating a health spa made possible by the natural endowment of hot mineral springs. The name Esalen comes from the Esalen Indians who once occupied the area. It is part of the Esalen belief that the power of touch in fostering empathy, understanding, and friendship, as well as having a therapeutic effect, is a valuable but often ignored human resource. Freud encouraged psychological nakedness to reveal our deepest, most hidden thoughts and longings. Besides, as Alex Comfort, author of *The Joy of Sex*, pointed out,

> Social nakedness has always had ritual value and nakedness in general has had magical value. Though the ideological nudist, who undressed on principle, is being replaced by people who simply undress because they feel like it, we may elect to keep nudity for special places and occasions in order to preserve its ritual and bonding value.[6]

Some things writers write about can be experienced personally. Public nudity is one of them. It's easy physically but there can be psychological obstacles. When I decided honesty required me to experience nudity, I thought of several ways I might get by with less than honesty. Then I thought of the carefree days of my youth when the gang would go skinny-dipping in any available isolated pond, of the days when we went in our own pool out on the ranch, sans shorts, not caring who peeked, of the days in later years when I always went swimming nude in our own pool unless visitors were around to be shocked, and how the exhilaration of being free and unfettered made clothing unthinkable except when demanded by social convention.

Descriptions and locations of nudist clubs and nude beaches

can be found in several publications.[7] For years, I had known of several "nudist colonies" on the West Coast. I decided to visit one of the remote ones, the Sierra Sunburn Club, although that's not its real name, and was introduced to an official host, whom I shall call Jim, who offered to escort me on a tour of the club. The Club is not clothing optional. For an agonizing moment I tried to decide which would be more embarrassing, to strip naked or cut and run. I was relieved when my host said, "You can leave your clothes on until two o'clock." After that, no oddballs.

We took our tour in a golf cart over paved roads, past a swimming pool, tennis courts, volleyball and basketball courts, softball diamond, picnic area, horseshoe pits, rows of rental trailers, RV spaces with full hookups, an area for tent campers, and a nondenominational chapel. We drove past a convenience store and stopped at the clubhouse and pool area where there are two pools, one indoors and heated, an outdoor spa, and a sauna. We walked through the communal showers where a lone woman, exceptionally attractive I noticed, was taking a shower. The only gender segregation I could see were separate male and female restrooms.

"The membership," my host continued, "is about 75% or more married couples, roughly 15% singles, and probably 5% children. There's no discrimination."

We walked into the café and sat at a table with a soft drink on the house. I noticed an open area.

"Dancing?" I asked.

"Saturdays, and with a live band on holidays and special occasions."

"Must be exciting," I said.

"Most wear casual clothes," he explained.

"No alcoholic beverages are served on the grounds," he told me, "but members can bring beer, wine, or liquor with them if they want to, or buy beer and wine at the office.

"But there are some rules the members agree to. Married men and women must be accompanied in the club by their spouses if they are not members. No cameras or videocameras except for official club photographers covering special events. And if you're around the pool and recreation areas, no glass containers, bicycles or dogs, and no radios without earphones."

The Club says it has the support of local law enforcement, and is a long-time member of the local Chamber of Commerce, as well as a participant in activities such as the March of Dimes Walk-A-Thon and Business Expo.

My host takes a dim view of nude beaches. Unlike most private nudist clubs and parks, where members participate under established rules and customs, and in any case have the privacy of their own environs, public nude beaches or so-called "free" beaches are frequented by people of diverse interest and motives.

Later, I drove down the coast to a place south of San Clemente, and hiked to a sandy beach protected by high, treacherous cliffs. Although nudity is prohibited, the spot is frequented by nude beachers, too isolated for authorities to bother about unless someone complains. I recalled what Aileen Goodson wrote about her first experience in group nudity—in 1964 at the Swallows nudist resort near San Diego:

> Up until that time I had seen very few nude men, and those mostly in sexual situations, so I spent the rest of the day being fascinated by various kinds of male and female bodies and the tremendous variety in genitals.

I don't know why I was surprised to see that Goodson was right. After skinny-dipping as a kid, and showering in open gym showers innumerable times without having any particular interest in appraising genitals, I was vaguely aware of the fact that the dimensional differences in genitals are greater than those of any other part of the human anatomy. But there in a relaxed state of contemplation, I noted an astonishing range in size and shape of primary and secondary sexual parts of both the male and female body, from nearly invisible to, let us say, impressive. Surely, I thought, some enterprising graduate student must have thought of making a mathematical study of human genital variations with genetic correlations. But I'm not aware of any, other than studies of doubtful statistical validity.

The legal status of nudism generally is poorly defined, and

nudists are vulnerable if outside the confines of a private club. Beaches may or may not be safe. The legality varies from state to state. In most states, "indecent exposure" is a serious offense, labeled a "sex crime." For example, since a 1969 California law, mere arrest *before* conviction can lead to listing as a sex offender, and filing the offender's description and fingerprints with the State Bureau of Criminal Identification and Investigation (Penal Code Section No. 314 and Section No. 11112). If convicted, the criminal is required to register as a sex offender and file fingerprints with the chief of police of the city. Offenders are also required to file photographs, other personal information, and any change of address for the rest of their lives unless released from the penalty by a court. Thus, it is extremely risky to strip naked in a public place such as a beach frequented by the general public, no matter what the motive might be. That is one reason nude sunbathers have always sought out isolated, usually hard-to-reach, woodsy places or beaches. Some of the beaches are either far from cities or accessible only over treacherous rocky trails or from high cliffs. On the more popular nude beaches, police typically maintain surveillances from the beach bluffs, usually with the aid of binoculars. They make an occasional close-up inspection and sometimes an arrest for illegal behavior.

Over time, an understanding developed between nude beachers and authorities that nudity would be permitted at certain isolated beaches. A scattering of nude beaches are now recognized along the California coast and elsewhere, which in the aggregate are frequented by tens of thousands of nude beachers, semi-nude beachers, and fully clothed voyeurs, with and without cameras. Leon Elder, in his book *Free Beaches*, includes a map showing the locations of a dozen such beaches along the California coast. Writer Elder and photographer Tim Crawford say they know of nearly 50 nude beaches between San Francisco and San Diego, but many of them are "problematical—parking, access over private property, in view of homes, highways or railroads or adjoining open land that will be a condominium development tomorrow." Some of the nude beaches are parts of state beaches unofficially set aside for the purpose. Most nude beachers express resentment at

A nude beach in an isolated part of the California coast, sparsely occupied on a cloudless December day.

voyeurs who refuse to take off their clothes, although there is toleration of first-timers, so-called virgins, who can't work up the courage to expose it all.

Sociologist Jack Douglas, who wrote *The Nude Beach* with the help of coauthors Paul Rasmussen and Carol Flanagan, devoted days and months, apparently years, on a project of research— voyeurism and talking with nude beachers, primarily at Eden Beach, near San Diego, where as many as 10,000 or 20,000 congregate on a sunny day.[8] Gays tend to congregate in a certain area of Eden Beach. Although Douglas maintained that sexual activity at the nude beach where he spent most of his time was uncommon, he tells of men walking around with erections, displaying or confronting women with it, a guy masturbating to the giggles of young girls, and the inevitable cruisers looking for an excuse to strike up a conversation with a hot number, hoping to line up a date for a score. One might assume from this that a nude beach is the backdrop for a sex scene. But that is not the impression most people get. A casual visitor might not see any of it. According to Douglas, direct sexual contact is almost invariably in the most secluded spots. Says Douglas,

Time after time, people have told us how they heard it was a wild sex scene, and believed that until they went to see it. Rather than being shocked at seeing a sex orgy, they are slightly shocked at seeing "a perfectly ordinary beach scene." . . . One young woman, a doctor's wife, commented at a dinner party that she found it *depressingly* normal.

FUTURE NUDES

During the past few decades, America has seen one of the most massive migrations in history. With an increase in abundance and leisure, people in droves have left behind the harsh winters of the North and interior to settle near the warm coastal areas of the Southeast, the Gulf, and the Western shore. Where before there was plenty of sand and surf, accessible beaches have become increasingly crowded with bodies wanting to expose their skin to the sun. Surf and sun worshippers are a motley crowd—surfers with and without wet suits depending on location and time of year, children energetically building sand castles and energetically tearing them down, groups of all ages gathered together for family picnics, young women vying with each other to expose the most legally allowable skin, young hunks eager to be titillated, "dirty old men" trying to recapture their vanished youth, and the hardy souls who are there to indulge in the invigorating pleasure of the surf. Most of these people would resent intrusion by nudes as indecent and obscene.

A custom as ancient as civilization is to keep the genitals protected from public view. The semilegal description "private parts" is a reflection of this nearly universal understanding. Anyone who violates the rule is engaged in deviant behavior that is shocking to all but a small fraction of society. Exposure of the sex organs in private or in communal one-sex showers such as in school gymnasiums or the military is socially acceptable, but exposure in public areas or in other inappropriate places is "indecent exposure," usually an offense that invokes immediate arrest, incarceration, and a criminal record. Copulation in public is even a more shocking violation of the longstanding rule of privacy, and

Despite the warning, beachers bask in the nude unmolested in an isolated part of this park.

anyone who ignores it is deviating seriously from the centuries-old perception of the human norm. Masturbation is by common understanding a private activity, and a deviant form of behavior in public. Nudity, though never an acceptable condition in everyday modern civilized life except in approved activities, has a complicated history that reflects the ambivalence of human nature stemming from the societal pressure to conform and the yearning for individual freedom. In much of the world, especially in rural areas, it is more than improper—it is disgusting—for either males or females to expose any flesh beyond the hands and face. In contrast, there is very little prudery about nudity in Scandinavia where, historically, men and women have shared steam baths and other public baths. In Oslo at the Vigeland sculpture garden, there is a giant phallus rising 56 feet made up of entwining nude figures and surrounded with family groups in the nude.

Nudity is the expression, to various degrees in different people, of deeply ingrained human qualities. It is a way of gaining freedom from the oppressive restraints of society and to become one with nature; it is an expression of defiance; it is freedom from ambition and greed; and it is a great equalizer. Valerie Tamis, writing about behavior in a Finnish sauna, gives advice to businessmen in the thick of sensitive negotiations: "Get what you want in writing before accepting your host's invitation for a traditional late-day sauna." She quotes an American engineer who was flying back to the States, "When you're sitting there buck naked, you're no longer in the driver's seat."[9]

At the same time, nudity is a way to attract attention, and for that reason is a stimulus to stay in top form; and it is a mildly erotic pleasure providing an awareness of the mystery of the human body. A full body tan is both a personal satisfaction and the envy of those who are compelled to hide most of their paleness with clothing. Lack of clothing does not stop nude beachers from using personal adornments to make themselves more attractive or noticeable. An extreme case described by Douglas was a man who wore what he called a "prick ring."

Partial nudity can be more erotic than complete nudity. The skillful use of clothing to reveal some, but not all, of the body's attractions leaves it to the power of imagination to arouse the eroticism of virtual nudity. Partial nudity may invoke strong erotic sensations of a clearly sexual nature. This is the predominate perception of people who see nudity as sinful, even though complete nudity is apt to be less sensual than partially revealed body parts.

Where does all this leave the future of nudity in parks or at the beach? Young people are increasingly libertarian in their view of life and their idea of having fun. This is partly the product of freedom from the economic stranglehold of previous generations, and this, in turn, has given them time to experiment and engage in creative and less restrictive activities that encroach on traditional taboos. There is no reason to think that this trend will not continue, subject to the braking power of careless sex that runs the risk of rampant disease.

Sociologist Douglas observed a high rate of turnover of nude beachers. As new ones joined the nude scene, older ones dropped out for activities more pressing for their time: family, work, political activity, social obligations, or other interests. Some people may heed the warnings of physicians and others about the danger of skin cancer, especially in view of predictions that erosion of the ozone layer will cause an increase in ultraviolet radiation in the future. But there is no obvious reduction in the number of beach visitors, and with inevitable growth in population, and continued migration to warm climes, more people will want to shed their clothes in the warmth of the sun. They will want the privacy of nude beaches—and more of them. At the same time, more people will want the privacy of "straight" beaches, aggravating a conflict of interest that already exists. Fundamentalists, beach home-owners, law enforcement authorities, and politicos will have the upper hand, and will almost certainly force nude beachers to be prudent or go elsewhere. There are still some isolated private coves known only to a few lucky explorers, and they are careful not to publicize them.

In any serious dispute between nude beachers and "straights," the vote of politicians is predictable, making it extremely risky for the nude beachers to engage in demonstrations or any other action that might arouse contrary public opinion. At the same time, law enforcement officials usually caution against any political move to crack down on the nude beachers because even if cities, counties, and states pass laws prohibiting nudity on isolated beaches, they doubt that convictions for exercising the constitutional guarantee of freedom of expression could be sustained in court. In most jurisdictions, the police are wary of making arrests unless there is lewd conduct. If they make arrests at all, it is usually for "disturbing the peace," a less serious offense and one that is easier to prosecute. But even that will be enough of a threat to convince most nude beachers to restrict the sexual enjoyment of their private parts to their private parties. They'll use the nude beaches for sunning and skinny-dipping.

Aileen Goodson makes a strong case for the value of nudity in sex therapy.[10] Sex therapists have increasingly seen nudity, touching, and learning to be comfortable with the naked body—both the client's and his or her partner's—as an important part of therapy. When William Masters and Virginia Johnson teamed up in pioneering sex therapy in connection with their Reproductive Biology Research Foundation, they made a splash by introducing what they called "sensate focus" training—sensitivity to a partner in nongenital body touching, including exercises in locating and caressing nongenital, sensitive areas. They emphasized the "relationship" problem of the marital couples rather than the individuals themselves. Masters and Johnson introduced similar treatment of singles by using surrogate partners during which the first step was a social evening at which time the client and surrogate could become acquainted over dinner, and eventually come to think of each other as friends in anticipation of becoming sexual partners.

According to Aileen Goodson, William Hartman and Marylin Fithian had started work in sex research and therapy before Masters and Johnson's *Human Sexual Response* was published in 1966. At their Center for Marital and Sexual Studies in Long Beach, California, they do not appear nude with their clients, as some therapists do, but their sex therapy training of students includes experience in nudity. They believe that if therapists are uncomfortable with their own nudity, the discomfort will be projected onto their clients. Exercises and videotapes are part of the therapy regime. Multi-Media, part of the National Sex Forum in San Francisco, produces films showing people engaged in various sexual activities for use as teaching guides. Some of them include explicit sex.

Psychotherapist Barbara Roberts is believed to have been the first to establish a sex therapy practice using a trained staff of surrogate partners, both male and female. In her Center for Social and Sensory Learning in Los Angeles, Roberts emphasized nudity as an essential part of the treatment. Aileen Goodson quotes Roberts:

> It's amazing how many people seeking sex therapy have never seen a naked adult of the opposite sex. Even in long-time marriages, I found couples who had never been completely nude together. It was "turn off the lights, get undressed, hop into bed, and close your eyes." . . . intimacy is limited if shame gets in the way.[11]

A consensus of therapists is that nude body acceptance is an important contributor to self-esteem, which, in turn, is one of the most important components of a healthy and gratifying sexual relationship.

Despite recognition of the role of nudity in acceptance of one's body in achieving self-esteem, important gains are still to be made with nudity, both in developing normal relationships and in therapy of sex-abused children and the physically disabled. Psychotherapists Frederick Shotz and his wife, Linda Shotz, at their Intimacy Disorders Foundation in Florida, have done pioneering work in these areas. Aileen Goodson tells of a surrogate, Patricia Pearlman, who found that she had a desire and talent for treating patients with various forms of physical disabilities—therapy that calls for a great deal of tact, understanding, patience, and innovative adaptability. She has them help undress her from the very beginning. She is nude first, and the two of them are nude together for discussions on the first day.

Probably the most controversial, but to some, the most promising, gains in nude therapy are to be made in the treatment of sexually abused children. Having been deeply traumatized almost beyond comprehension, they may think of their bodies as in constant danger, or as contaminated and filthy, or both. Because their body gets them into trouble, it is not safe for it to be seen. And the sight of a man's body might be uncontrollably threatening. Treatment that would make them come to love and respect their bodies and to see that the nudeness of others is natural and normal could restore their self-esteem and transform their lives.

We've seen that nudity has been a form of expression for thousands of years, symbolically and physically liberating people from oppressive strictures of civilization. But the more "civilized" people became, the more they came to view nakedness as sinful, to be kept from public view under pain of severe penalties. Consequently, in a fully clothed society, nudity and partial nudity are highly effective, and commonly used, as a way to titillate and stimulate erotic excitement. Devotees of public nudity are a mixed bag, ranging from voyeurs to exhibitionists and sex-seekers. But many are folks who simply enjoy the freedom from public restraint and presumed healthfulness of being naked in an ordinary, open-air environment. Freedom from social demands is overwhelming when naked. It's hard to be a bare-assed hypocrite. The most revealing of the nude activities is the finding that nudity has proven therapeutic value for treatment of sexual dysfunction, and may have some value in treating sex offenders, who for various reasons may be devoid of respect for their own bodies as well as the bodies of others. Nudity may have a special place in treating the sexually abused, in whom acceptance of one's body is an important step to absolve perceived shame and restore a sense of worth and self-esteem.

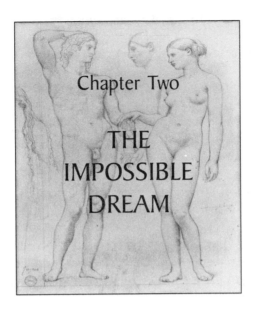

Chapter Two

THE IMPOSSIBLE DREAM

 The quest for the fountain of youth is eternal, a reflection of the unquenchable human urge to improve on nature—including ways to enhance the most pleasurable of all passions. The powerful urge to experience ever greater heights of sexual gratification developed at some stage in human evolution into a universal dream that captivated people of all times and places throughout history. The fact that hope and expectation almost always exceed accomplishment never stood in the way of people trying an amazing profusion of imaginative techniques, substances, and devices. The dream is as elusive as the proverbial pot of gold at the end of the rainbow, still there is more than a glimmer of hope that human ingenuity can bring the dream closer to reality as we begin a new millennium.

The modern word, *aphrodisiac*, is from the Greek *aphrodisia*, meaning sexual, and the corresponding *aphrodisiakos*, referring to something that excites sexual pleasure. In Greek mythology, Aphrodite was the goddess of love and beauty. Some people said she sprang from the foam of the sea, hence the origin of her name from the Greek *aphros*, meaning foam. It was claimed that she wore an embroidered girdle that had the power to inspire love in anyone who wore it.[1]

The number of items touted as aphrodisiacs at various times in history would probably fill a small encyclopedia. The ability to promote love or sexual desire was attributed to a wide variety of animal, plant, and mineral materials. Most of them were fake except possibly for their placebo effect, which, after all, is often the most important attribute of a drug.

Pliny (23–79 AD) in his *Natural History* described numerous aphrodisiac drugs, animal parts, and methods that would "mightily provoke fleshly lust," make the user "lusty and able to perform the act of generation youthfully."[2] Pliny said the Greeks had a herb they called *erythraicon*, the root of which if held in a man's hand "would cause the flesh to rise and incite him to the company of women." It was also given to goats and used as a drench on stallions when fatigue from overwork made them unwilling.

Pliny had the habit of repeating tidbits of information from various sources, apparently accepting most of them without question. He cited Theophrastus, a pupil of Plato and later a favorite disciple of Aristotle, as telling about a man who was able to "keep company" with women 70 times by touching or handling only one herb, although he made no mention of how much time he needed for the performance. Unfortunately, Theophrastus, who was the foremost student of botany in his time, failed to leave to posterity either the name of the plant or a description of it.

Pliny cites the ancient Greek poets Hesiod and Alcaeus in extolling the virtues of the common artichoke:

> when women are most desirous of men's company and hottest in lust, nature has provided a viand most powerful . . . to set their husbands to heat, and enable them to do that business. If taken in wine, it incites to wantonness and fleshly pleasure.

Artichoke even affects insects, for "when the herb flourishes, the grasshoppers chant loudest and sing most shrill."

Black beans, presumably because of their fabled ability to stir up action in the lower abdominal organs, were consumed as aphrodisiacs by the peasants. Garlic, a favorite seasoning of the Romans, is still touted as an aphrodisiac. Among herbs that kindle the heat of lust is one called orchis. There were two kinds of preparations, one to provoke and the other to repress the appetite for venery. If the root is given in ewe's milk, it "causes a man's member to rise and stand," but if taken in water, "it makes it go down again." Pliny named several herbs claimed by the Greeks to make one "very prone to the sports of Venus."

Animal parts that were hard to obtain were supposed to have magical properties. According to Pliny, if the hindmost end of the gut of a hyena, that is, its anus, were worn around a man's left arm as a bracelet, it would charm a woman so that if he but set his eyes upon her, she would leave everything and follow him at once. Pliny scoffed at the idea. He thought it was the most foolish idea he had ever heard. But he described numerous other treatments equally imaginative, for instance:

> If the frothy sperm that an ass exudes after covering a female is gathered up in a piece of red cloth, it has great power. For the contrary effect, nothing cools the lust of a man more than to anoint his private parts with the dung of mice and rats.

No doubt true. Among Pliny's innumerable remedies were the magical powers of frogs, especially to keep venery under control. If a husband would take a frog and impale it lengthwise on a reed, and touch the reed to his wife's menstrual blood, she would never after have any desire to entertain adulterers, but would "detest and loathe that naughty kind of life."

The Kama Sutra of Vatsyayana, an ancient Hindu treatise of uncertain vintage on love and social conduct, describes several bizarre "tonic medicines" for subjecting others to one's own will, and for increasing sexual vigor.[3] *The Kama Sutra* is of unknown date but is believed to have been written between the third century BC and the third century AD. An example: "If a man, after anointing his lingum [penis] with a mixture of the powder of white thorne apple, long pepper, black pepper, and honey, engages in sexual union with a woman, he makes her subject to his will." For increasing sexual vigor: "Drinking milk with sugar, and having the testicle of a ram or a goat boiled in it, is productive of vigor."

Some of the ancient drugs, like most of the modern ones, had effects that were derived from authentic physiological action. One such drug was "Spanish fly," the most spectacular aphrodisiac of ancient times.[4–7] The recklessly indulgent citizens of Rome often spiced their orgies with the drug, which acts as a powerful irritant, and stimulates the erectile tissue of the genital organs. A persistent erection goes by the medical term *priapism*, named after Priapus, the Greek god of fertility.

Spanish fly is neither strictly Spanish in origin nor a fly. It is derived from a beetle of the "blister beetle" group, so called because a "chemical warfare" secretion exuded from its body acts as a vesicant (causes blisters) when in contact with the skin. However, as an aphrodisiac it was taken internally. Commercial preparations of the beetles, *Cantharis vesicatoria*, are known as *cantharides*, from the Greek *kantharis*, meaning "beetle." The active ingredient is a chemical called cantharidin, a fairly simple organic chemical, but the only commercial source is from the beetles themselves. In Roman times, the cantharides came to be used to sustain sexual excitement, the practice was simply to swallow the powdered beetles to be absorbed into the system through the digestive tract. Unfortunately for the revelers, cantharidin is highly irritating to the kidneys and reproductive system, causing severe inflammation that may lead to serious illness or death. An Arabian toxicologist, Ibn Washiya, who practiced during the second half of the ninth century, described a preparation of blister beetles used for poisoning, only one of many evil potions used for murder, especially for political assassinations, throughout ancient and medieval times. Roughly a thousandth of an ounce (about 0.5 mg per kg body weight) is reportedly lethal to humans of average size.[8] Gladiators and others who used the drug regularly were supposedly able to reduce the toxic effects by taking hot baths to hasten removal of the poison from their systems. Cantharidin is so toxic that there must have been many cases of impaired health, and probably many deaths, from its use.

The magical properties of another natural product—the mandrake plant, *Mandragora ficinarum*—had a fascination that persisted into recent times. Belief in the plant's supposed aphrodisiac properties derived from its peculiar root growth that branches in a way resembling human legs, often with knobs suggesting the presence of male genitals. Surely, it was reasoned, this signified nature's purpose for the plant's roots and berries. The purpose included a wide variety of sexually related uses. The root was hung in the rafters to induce virility in flagging men and conception in barren women. The powdered roots and extracts were taken to promote passion, and were used to spice sexual orgies. The berrylike, yellow fruit of mandrake was called "devil's apple." The story is told in the book of Genesis that Jacob's wife, Rachel, who was barren—a calamity in biblical times—begged her sister, Leah, for some of her son's mandrake (Leah was also Jacob's wife but now barren and rejected). Leah, instead, took the mandrake to Jacob herself to sleep with him again, and became pregnant.[9]

The mandrake plant, a relative of the potato and tomato, contains several alkaloids including atropine and scopolamine. These are not aphrodisiacs, but nerve toxins that, instead, have strong sedative and sleep-producing properties. The plant was used extensively in medicines by the ancient physicians, and as an anesthetic in surgery. An extract of the plant is classified in modern medical terms as a hypnotic—obviously dangerous. Shakespeare immortalized the drug in Cleopatra's plea:[10]

> Give me to drink mandragora
> That I might sleep out this
> great gap of time.

The interest in aphrodisiacs in early times is seen in the writings of a Persian physician, ar-Razi, who lived about 860–930. Better known by his Latinized name, Rhazes, he devoted a chapter to aphrodisiacs in his *Book of Almansor*.[11] Among the remedies he listed were vinegar, other acids, and a number of foods, including lettuce. Another Persian physician, Avicenna (980–1037), gave thorough treatment in his writings to both love potions and contraceptives that were then thought to be effective.[12] Earlier, a Roman law known as the Cornelian Law, enacted under Sulla in 81 BC, provided for capital punishment for assassins and poisoners (*veneficii*). The law distinguished between different kinds of drugs. Some drugs, the act said, were used to kill people, and the law prohibited these evil drugs. Other drugs were used to cure, and still others were used to produce love, neither of which was prohibited by the statute.

Today in the Orient, as in centuries past, a variety of wild animal parts are deemed to be aphrodisiacs: horns, antlers, gall-bladders, and penises, for example, even crocodile semen. None of them have any physiological therapeutic value, but they are persuasive evidence of the power of suggestion. Bear bile is in such great demand that hundreds of so-called bear farms containing an estimated 10,000 caged bears have come into existence across China. The chained bears are fitted with catheters and milked of their bile weekly. Their bile contains ursodeoxycholic acid, which can be synthesized and is used by doctors to dissolve gallstones and to treat other liver ailments. But many customers demand natural bear bile. A bear gallbladder will sell for $2000 to $14,000, depending on its freshness and origin. A bowl of bear paw soup goes for $400 to $1000. Bear parts have been used for at least 2000 years in Asia to prevent and heal diseases, and to impart strength and prowess to the users. More powerful aphrodisiacs are the testicles of musk deer, now rare, and tiger bones. Eggs of the olive ridley sea turtle, threatened with extinction, sell for $1 to $5 each, an aphrodisiac bargain.[13]

A thriving trade in both animal and plant parts from Siberia goes through Vladivostok, yielding personal fortunes to poachers who plunder the countryside for tiger bones, reindeer antlers, gallbladders from Siberian brown bears, wild ginseng root, and sea cucumbers. A four-ounce ginseng root will bring as much as $1500 on the Asian market, and a small piece of reindeer antler will sell for $800 in Hong Kong.

The most highly prized animal-derived aphrodisiac is rhi-noceros horn, popular for at least 2000 years as a medicine and aphrodisiac. The ferocious animals that look like prehistoric monsters from a lost age are a lucrative source of illicit income for hunters and poachers. A pound of genuine rhinoceros horn will bring up to $2000 or more in the wholesale market of Bangkok. Rhinoceros meat was sometimes eaten, but today, the animals are hunted almost exclusively for their hide and horns. Usually the horns are sawed off, and the rest of the animal is left to rot. The horn is powdered and used like snuff, or in rare cases it is carved into a goblet and used for drinking. Rhinos are now rigorously protected in all areas of its habitat, but poachers still manage to hunt them down. The big white rhino and black rhino of Africa, the Sumatran rhino, and the little Java rhino are all badly threatened. The Indian rhinoceros has been hunted so relentlessly that it is on the endangered list, and is near extinction. It once roamed the entire Ganges basin, but now there are only a few hundred of the great beasts remaining, safeguarded in the Kaziranga National Park.[14] The rhinos of Africa have suffered a similar fate. *National Geographic* reported in 1993 that the continuing slaughter had sent the number of African rhinos plummeting from 20,000 to 8200.[15] According to Richard Emslie, an Africa-based rhino researcher, Zimbabwe's black rhinos numbered 430 in 1993, down from more than 1500.

Wildlife officials in Namibia and Zimbabwe devised a strat egy in 1989 to discourage poachers by sawing off the horns of as many rhinos as they could catch, then turning them loose. Several hundred dehorned rhinos now roam the savannah, and few of them have been shot by poachers.[16] The horns are not sensitive tissue, so cutting them, like trimming hair, is painless. The rhinos seem to get along well without their horns, which grow back at the rate of several inches a year.

The government of Namibia launched a campaign against the Cape fur seals, mostly by clubbing. They said the seals are competing with fishermen, and targeted 55,000 males and pups for culling in 1994. They hoped to reduce the colony to 500,000. The program enables Namibia to harvest the pelts and also sell the male genitals as aphrodisiacs at a large profit.[17]

Reindeer, related to the caribou of northern America, have been domesticated for centuries in the northern regions of Europe where they are used as a beast of burden and a source of milk, meat, and leather. In recent years a profitable business has developed in reindeer antlers for use in aphrodisiacs. Deer grow a new set of antlers each year. South Korean herbalists are reported to be willing to pay $50 a pound for select antlers, making reindeer ranching in Alaska and the Northwest Territories of Canada more profitable for antlers than for meat. Reindeer are not native to North America, but a few entrepreneurs found a way to make them thrive on Canada's far northwestern wastes and turn a profit by selling the antlers to herbalists and druggists, who dispense pulverized antler to Asians who are willing to spend big money for it.

Mary Walsh tells the story of reindeer coming to Alaska.[18] Missionaries, with government help, had brought the first reindeer to Alaska from Siberia in the 1890s. Clever promoters in Nome, taking a cue from Scandinavian deerpunchers, started stirring up an interest in reindeer meat in the cities on the west coast. The promotion was so successful that reindeer meat was being shipped to the United States in such volume during the 1920s and 1930s that cattlemen became alarmed and successfully lobbied protectionist legislation that blocked shipping the meat out of Alaska. Canadians saw this as an opportunity, so in 1929 the Canadian government bought 3000 reindeer from Alaskans in an effort to convert the Inuits from hunters of the dwindling caribou into reindeer herdsmen like the Lapps of Scandinavia. Reindeer have an advantage. They can be herded and milked, while wild caribou cannot be managed that way. But there was one hitch. The native Inuit would have to change their life-style, which they tried to do, but there were so many problems of ownership and grazing rights that they finally gave up in frustration. The government, licked in its effort to improve the lot of the Inuit, sold the entire herd along with grazing rights to a private investor. He, too, wearied of reindeer punching after a few years and decided to sell out.

Meanwhile, an Inuit, William Nasogaluak, had learned through a savvy business partner something that none of the other Alaskans knew, namely, the Asian appetite for the reindeer antler as an aphrodisiac. They bought the herd and soon became multimillion-aires. Nasogaluak is the only man in the remote Inuit village of Tuktoyaktuk ever to own a Cadillac, to say nothing of his pleasure boat, a pair of helicopters, and a collection of steel guitars—possessions acquired with the profits from Canada's largest reindeer herd. Nasogaluak began his operation of about 10,000 reindeer in 1978 on the shores of the Beaufort Sea. The reindeer are environmentally friendly, and their antlers grow back every year. The worst predators are the neighbors who admit to poaching on the herd with impunity, feasting regularly on reindeer steaks. But the owner's worst problem is a legal one. The Committee for Original Peoples' Entitlement (COPE) is maneuvering to "deprivatize" the reindeer once again. The latest word was that Nasogaluak had taken up ancient drumming to calm his nerves.

Asians are noted for the variety of natural products they favor as aphrodisiacs. Not surprisingly, serpents are still doing their biblical work of promoting human sexual activity. Xu Zhiwei, an entrepreneur in Jieshan Village, China, does a thriving business producing and selling snake products.[19] His Longlife Group turns 200 tons of snakes into handbags, wallets, belts, ties, meat, wine, medicines, and cosmetics. One of the products is a powder made from snake penises that is claimed to be a sexual restorative. "The sexual powers of snakes is well-known," says Xu, displaying a dried snake penis ready for pulverizing. "After one mating with a male, a female snake can become pregnant for the next six years." Xu says he exports penis powder to Japan, South Korea, Taiwan, and Hong Kong. "Shanghai consumers are very picky," he adds, "but they are buying 3,000 10-box cases of our new snake powder a month." Xu, coincidentally, was born in the year of the snake—1953.

A botanical aphrodisiac of perennial popularity is ginseng, an Asian plant used for centuries as a herbal remedy and tonic. Because of its popularity in China and other parts of the Orient, the plant generated sporadic interest in the West as a booster of virility. Surprisingly, much of the world ginseng supply now comes from Canada and the United States, where it grows wild from Quebec to the Gulf of Mexico (the North American ginseng is

Panax quinquefolium; the more well-known Chinese ginseng is *P. pseudoginseng*). Ginseng production in North America, scattered across two Canadian provinces and Wisconsin, is dominated by two publicly traded Vancouver corporations plus a handful of family growers and a hundred or so inexperienced entrepreneurs who have established "gardens" as they are called in the trade, on flatlands along the rivers. At the rate the business is growing in British Columbia, the acreage under harvest has been predicted to nearly triple in four years. The ginseng is said to be ten times more valuable than any other legal crop grown in Canada. Distribution is mainly controlled by a cartel of Hong Kong brokers who market it internationally. Most of it is sold to consumers as dry root, but some of it goes into capsules, tonics, lotions, shampoos, soft drinks, and even cigarettes and candy. Growers are trying independently to open up local markets for ginseng in health food stores, especially in California.[20]

The U.S. Food and Drug Administration agreed in 1982 to permit the importation of a tonic containing ginseng and royal jelly, claimed to be prepared according to an ancient pharmaceutical formula. Experiments with ginseng on animals showed some increase in sexual activity, but observations on humans have been haphazard partly because of uncertainties of dosage and side effects. Most herbalists refrain from claiming aphrodisiac properties for ginseng. They say that its reputation to overcome a sexual problem like impotence is related to its ability to strengthen the entire body, not just sexual organs.

A fermented extract harvested from the agave plant of Mexico is used to produce a brew called *pulque*, as well as the fiery distillate known as *tequila*, and another alcoholic beverage called *mescal*. Some of the mescal producers, mostly small distillers, still use *trapiches*, mule-driven grindstones, to crush the agave hearts called *pinas* to extract the sweet juice that is fermented and distilled. Mescal is lower in quality and rougher than tequila, but it has a reputation for having aphrodisiac as well as medicinal and tonic qualities. Women drink it to ease the pain of childbirth, and workers drink it for added strength. The powers of mescal are attributed to the grub, called a *gusano* (Spanish for "worm") that is dug out of the agave. Agave gusanos are either soaked in the beverage or eaten—by those who have acquired the taste.[21]

A practice in America during the 19th century was smoking cubeb, a powdered berry. Smoked as a cigarette, ostensibly for its purported medicinal value to relieve asthma and catarrh, cubeb was also presumed to be an aphrodisiac. The use of cubeb had an ancient origin. The famous Persian physician of the eleventh century, Avicenna, recommended eating cubeb as a sexual stimulant, and it is still used for that purpose and as a medicine in parts of Asia. The name *cubeb* comes from the Arabic *kubabah*. The product is obtained from *Piper cubeba*, a perennial vinelike bush of the pepper family, Piperaceae. The fruit encloses a peppery seed having an agreeable aromatic odor, but an acrid and slightly bitter taste that lingers in the mouth for several hours. The berries are picked fully grown but not yet ripe, and dried in the sun. It is the crushed berries that are smoked, but the first use by Europeans, in the 11th century, was as a spice. The berries were described as tasting like a combination of black pepper and allspice.[22]

A number of mineral and botanical derivations were at one time claimed to have aphrodisiac qualities. Strychnine, a highly poisonous alkaloid from the seeds and plants of *Strychnos nux vomica*, acts by indirectly stimulating the nervous system in a way that produces convulsions. Strychnine has no therapeutic value, so druggists won't sell it to you, but physicians used it during an era when some extremely dangerous poisons were routinely given to patients for imagined curative effects. No one knows how many people died from, or were made invalids by, the supposed cures. Salts of the alkaloid were used in minute quantities in tonics, especially to aid convalescence from illness, and to treat such diverse ailments as alcoholism, diminished vision, and sexual impotency. The Italian poet Gabriele D'Annunzio, who bragged that more than 1000 husbands hated him, was said to use strychnine as an aphrodisiac. Strychnine, like all poisons, has different effects at different dosage rates. Some chemicals, such as most medicines, if taken below the threshold for toxicity, may have presumed beneficial effects. But there are several reasons why strychine was an unwise choice. Its presumed effect as an aphrodisiac is highly doubtful, and strychnine is a dangerous poison, even in small amounts, causing convulsive illness and an agonizing death.

A former practice by women in Europe to enhance their attractiveness was to take a small dose of belladonna—an extract of the deadly nightshade, *Atropa belladonna*. The plant contains atropine and related alkaloids that have several physiological effects, one of which is to block the action of an important neurotransmitter, acetylcholine.[23] One manifestation is dilated pupils of the eyes, which conveys the impression that the lady is excited and vivacious. The Latin name *belladonna* means beautiful lady. It was a dangerous game because the drug increases the heart rate, and slightly greater doses adversely affect other organs. Belladonna preparations were known to the ancient Hindu physicians, and were used for centuries as medicinals. Because poisoners of the Middle Ages used the deadly nightshade to cause obscure and often prolonged poisoning, Carl von Linné, the indefatigable namer of plants and animals, gave it the genus name *Atropa*, after Atropos, in Greek and Roman mythology the oldest of the three fates, the one that cut the thread of life.

A widely used botanical substance having probable aphrodisiac properties is sarsaparilla, an extract from the roots of *Smilax aristolochiaefolia*, a plant of the lily family that grows throughout parts of Mexico and Central and South America. Sarsaparilla is used as a flavoring in some soft drinks and medicines.[24] The extract has been used and prescribed for centuries for the restoration of flagging male virility. There was little reason to think that the reputed medicinal effect was more than an old wive's tale until the folklore was supported by the finding that the extract of *Smilax* contains a sapogenin, specifically sarsasapogenin, a steroid related to testosterone.

The most interesting of the botanicals in use today is the alkaloid yohimbine, derived from the bark of a West African tree, *Corynanthe yohimbe*.[23,25] Yohimbine is used in Africa to treat impotence in humans, and to excite sexual activity in horses, cattle, and sheep. There was little convincing evidence that it actually worked until physiologists at Stanford University found experimentally that it made rats initiate sexual encounters twice as often as rats that were not given the drug. It remained to be seen how the drug would affect humans. When tests were proposed there was no lack of volunteers; 300 men were said to have applied for 40 places in a test group.

Yohimbine is an alkaloid chemically similar to reserpine, a drug obtained from the roots of *Rauwolfia serpentina*, used medicinally for treatment of hypertension. Yohimbine acts on the peripheral autonomic nervous system to stimulate the parasympathetic branch and decrease the action of the sympathetic branch. Activation of the parasympathetic branch of the nervous system dilates the blood vessels and theoretically facilitates penile erection. The supplier, Dayton Laboratories, cautions against the use of yohimbine in geriatric, psychiatric, or cardiorenal patients (it is a mild antidiuretic, which might tend to increase blood pressure, and it may increase anxiety). The liquid form, Dayton Himbin Liquid, also contains phenylalanine and phenylketonuric acid. For treatment of male sexual dysfunction, the pharmaceutical yohimbine is used at a dose of 18 mg per day. However, Goodman and Gilman say in their *Pharmacological Basis of Therapeutics*, "Yohimbine has been sporadically promoted as an aphrodisiac, but there is no convincing evidence for such an effect. It has no proven therapeutic use."[23]

The most prized botanical aphrodisiac to come out of the New World is the chocolate bean, said to be historically a more valuable find than all other loot taken by the conquistadores.[26] The Aztecs made a beverage called in their Nahuatl tongue *cacahuatl* or *xocoatl*, which the Spaniards translated as cacao and cocoa. Montezuma told his captors that he drank chocolate by the potful because it enhanced his sexual powers. He was said to have consumed 50 cups a day. Hernando Cortes forwarded a supply of the beans to Charles V along with a letter describing chocolate "as the divine drink that builds up resistance and fights fatigue." The Aztecs flavored their chocolate with spices, especially with extracts from the beans of an orchid the Spaniards called *vanilla*, which was also introduced to Europe by the conquistadores. Vanilla itself is said to be an aphrodisiac, but it's doubtful that the amount used in chocolate, ice cream, candy, and other confections is enough to have much effect. However, larger doses would probably be toxic. It never dawned on the Aztecs to sweeten chocolate with honey or to brew it in hot water (they did not have the common honeybee, imported from Europe later). Consequently, their chocolate beverage was a cold, thick, bitter concoction that would not pass muster in the cups of today's chocaholics.

At first the Spaniards didn't take to the bitter drink, but once they found that sweetening and heating improved the flavor, chocolate became a favorite beverage among the privileged throughout Europe. Word was passed around quickly that chocolate was an aphrodisiac. Casanova was said to have used it as well as his favorite, champagne, as an aid in his conquests. Carl von Linné, the famous Swedish naturalist, promptly named the cacao (chocolate) plant *Theobroma cacao*, or "god food," from the Greek *theos* (god) and *broma* (food).

In 1828, C. J. van Houten of The Netherlands found a way to produce powdered cocoa by removing some of the fat called cocoa butter. He also found a way to reduce the bitterness by treating the chocolate with alkali, a process that came to be known as "Dutching." Then in 1847, a British firm, Fry & Sons, learned how to make a solid "eating" chocolate. Today, Americans on average consume about 10 pounds of chocolate confection per year. Much of it is produced in Pennsylvania, the home of Hershey, M&M Mars, and Cadbury. But the Swiss are even bigger users of chocolate, consuming more than double that of Americans.

More than 300 chemical compounds have been identified in chocolate.[27] The principal active ingredient responsible for its stimulating effect is theobromine, an alkaloid closely related to caffeine, which is also present in chocolate, and methylxanthine, all mildly addictive. The effect of theobromine is similar to that of caffeine except that it is less active as a cerebral and central nervous system stimulant and is slightly more active as a heart stimulant and smooth muscle relaxer.[23] One theory for the presumed aphrodisiac effect of chocolate is based on the finding that when laboratory animals are fed sweet or fatty substances, the hypothalamus sends out pleasure signals. Chocolates are both sweet and fatty. The hypothalamus is a gland, technically part of the brain, lying just above and behind the pituitary, that has far-reaching control over glandular functions and behavior, including control of sexual activity. For instance, stimulation of the medial forebrain and neighboring hypothalamus areas causes penile erection in monkeys accompanied by emotional display.

Another theoretical explanation for the presumed aphrodisiac effect of chocolate is that it inhibits the production of serotonin, a powerful brain hormone responsible for the transmission of nerve impulses between neurons (nerve cells).[28] Serotonin itself has a stimulating and mood-enhancing effect, but in high concentration indirectly suppresses sexual activity because some of the serotonin in the brain is converted in the pineal to a derivative, melatonin, high concentrations of which reduce sexual drive.

A related theory for the aphrodisiac effect of chocolate is that phenylethylamine (PEA), a so-called "love drug," is thought to be present in high concentrations in the brains of people who are happy or in love, and is supposed to be why people disappointed in love eat a lot of chocolate. PEA is viewed as the parent compound of a group of neurotransmitters called *sympathomimetic amines*. Neurotransmitters are hormones that bring about the transmission of nerve impulses from one nerve fiber to another. Sympathomimetic neurotransmitters activate the sympathetic branch of the autonomic nervous system, a system of nerve fibers that stimulates excitatory reactions not generally under conscious control of a person, such as heart rate, blood sugar, and muscular strength. The overall effect of stimulating the sympathetic branch is to prepare the mind and body for action. Derivatives of PEA include epinephrine (adrenaline), norepinephrine, dopamine, amphetamine, and ephedrine.

A more important value of chocolate may be the direct effect of its odor and flavor on mood. The pleasure of eating chocolate, added to the mild physiological exhilaration from theobromine, is a combination likely to promote harmony and good feelings, even perhaps, intimacy.

People of the drug subculture have made claims from time to

time of enhanced sexual pleasure from most of the prescription and street drugs used for mood alteration. They include alcohol, LSD, marijuana, barbiturates, cocaine, amphetamines, MDMA (so-called "Ecstasy"), Quaaludes (methaqualone), and "poppers" (alkyl nitrite). It is well known that these drugs are addictive and may lead to severely impaired health. Death from a deliberate or accidental overdose is common.

The legendary film actor Errol Flynn, noted for his performances in swashbuckler roles, bragged that he slept with women 13,000 nights of his youthful career. It is said that he made a practice of treating the head of his penis with a bit of cocaine before having sex.[29] The local anesthetic effect of cocaine is well known. One of the systemic effects of cocaine at high concentrations is to stimulate the central nervous system; its local action as an anesthetic is to block nerve conduction. Presumably the effect on sexual performance, as per the Flynn method, is to prolong coitus. Addiction and health hazards of cocaine are well known, but the risk of using it according to the Flynn method are undocumented.

Another local anesthetic, procaine, introduced under the trade name Novocaine, was enthusiastically claimed in the late 1950s and early 1960s to have a variety of rejuvenating effects, including that of improving sexual activity. But laboratory experiments with animals failed to confirm the benefits, and its effect came to be thought of as psychological. A report by the Council on Drugs in 1963 was entitled *Procaine—Its Song is Ended*.

Alkyl nitrite, a generic term for butyl and isobutyl nitrites, is said to be a favorite with homosexual men.[30] The large number of users among those who contracted AIDS led to speculation that it might be a cofactor in causing the disease, but this idea was largely discounted when the AIDS virus was discovered. However, the drug may have made users careless, and many of the users were probably damaged physiologically by the toxic effects of the nitrites, making them more vulnerable to the virus. Nitrites are used as preservatives in foods, especially smoked meats, but the concentrations are so low that there is little toxic effect at those levels.

At higher concentrations it becomes toxic. The stimulant effect is obtained by inhaling the fumes, and to circumvent the FDA's restrictions on drugs, the alkyl nitrites were marketed as "room odorants" under such trade names as Rush, Bolt, Locker Room, Crypt Tonight, Aroma of Man, Bullet, and Heart On. Users reported that they received a temporary "high" as well as being sexually stimulated.

Room odorants do not come under the jurisdiction of the federal Food and Drug Administration, so several states banned "poppers" on their own. The medical use of alkyl nitrite dates back to the late 1800s when amyl nitrite came into use as a treatment for angina pain. The drug dilates blood vessels, making it easier for blood to get to the heart muscles. The volatile material comes in containers that make a popping sound when opened— thus the nickname, *poppers*.

In 1983, a Food and Drug Administration Panel on Miscellaneous Internal Drugs looked at a category (supposed aphrodisiacs) of over-the-counter (OTC) drugs that they hoped would be unlikely candidates for FDA review. They examined a number of exotic ingredients, including gotu kola, ginseng, licorice, sarsaparilla, cantharides, nux vomica, Pega Palo, strychnine, and yohimbine, along with the hormones testosterone and methyltestosterone. The panel said they found no evidence to support the claims of aphrodisiac action attributed to any of these materials. They stated that the claims were based largely on folklore and exploited by manufacturers who prey on the gullibility of people who most likely are in need of counseling or therapy. The panel said that all labeling claims for OTC aphrodisiacs are "false, misleading or unsupported by scientific evidence."[31] However, information available elsewhere suggests that the FDA panel's review was superficial.

Current medicinal drugs claimed by some users to have aphrodisiac qualities include: trazodone (an antidepressant), bromocriptine mesylate (a fertility drug), L-dopa (a treatment for Parkinson's disease), parachlorophenylalanine or PCPA (a migraine treatment), naloxone (a treatment for narcotic addiction), clomiphene citrate (a fertility drug), and papaverine hydrochloride (a treatment for coronary spasms and stroke). Forms of hormones that can be taken orally in capsule form as replacement therapy for patients deficient in male or female steroids are testosterone undecanoate and estradiol decanoate, developed in the Netherlands. Administration of the testosterone product in males was reported to cause a "marked increase in libido and sexual activity," and spontaneous erections for the first time in some patients.[38]

Most of the legal drugs that are reported to have aphrodisiac effects did not work well when tried on healthy people. One exception is naloxone hydrochloride, a product used to counteract the effects of narcotics. Naloxone, a chemical related to morphine, blocks the opiate receptor centers in the brain.[32] Its multiple effects may be partly explained by the way endorphins and enkephalins—natural opiates produced in the brain—have several roles including morphine-like action in controlling pain. They also affect behavior in several ways. According to one report of eight healthy men tested with naloxone, three had spontaneous erections, and three or four women claimed they had enhanced sexual pleasure. The effect of an intravenous injection of naloxone is apparent in two minutes. It takes an intramuscular injection slightly longer, but the effect lasts longer.

Another synthetic chemical claimed by some people to increase sexual libido is bromocriptine mesylate. Bromocriptine, a derivative of ergot and chemically related to LSD, acts as an antidepressant, prevents lactation, and is used in combination with L-dopa to treat Parkinson's disease. Its effect on depression is supposedly caused by its increasing the production or action of serotonin and dopamine, brain chemicals that are known to affect mood. But it probably stimulates sexual activity mainly by inhibiting the secretion of the hormone prolactin by the pituitary gland. Prolactin promotes milk production, probably depresses libido in women, and inhibits the synthesis of male hormones in men. Bromocriptine in clinical trials relieved depression and restored menstruation in women suffering from amenorrhea (lack of menstruation), and "in some women who never had an erotic feeling in their entire lives, bromocriptine restored sexual desire and led to normal sexual activity."[38] The drug increased sexual potency and restored sperm production in seven male patients in whom prolactin levels had been abnormally high.

The synthetic aphrodisiac most thoroughly tested in animals is p-chlorophenylalanine (PCPA), a medicine introduced for human use as a treatment for migraine. Alessandro Tagliamonte and co-workers at the National Heart Institute, Bethesda, Maryland, found in 1969 that PCPA increased the number of copulations and ejaculations in male rats exposed to receptive females. Rabbits injected with PCPA also showed compulsive sexual behavior that lasted up to three days.[33-35] PCPA has long been known to cause prolonged wakefulness in animals but not in humans. The action of PCPA is to block the formation of the brain hormone serotonin. It does this by inhibiting the action of an enzyme, tryptophan hydroxylase, that is responsible for converting the essential amino acid tryptophan to a precursor of serotonin. The result is a lower than normal concentration of serotonin, also called 5-HT, for 5-hydroxytryptamine. As described in a later chapter, serotonin suppresses sexual activity, probably indirectly by conversion of small amounts to another brain hormone, melatonin, high concentrations of which reduce sexual drive.

James Ferguson and co-workers at the Stanford University School of Medicine and Veterans Administration Hospital, who worked with cats, showed that PCPA caused dramatic changes in behavior within three to five days of the initial injection.[36] The cats became hypersexual, extremely aggressive, suffered perceptual disorientation, and insomnia. But in contrast to that work, Richard Whalen and William Luttge at the University of California, Irvine, declared that PCPA was not an aphrodisiac in the true sense because it did not prolong or intensify male–female sexual interactions, but only promoted homosexual mounting of the animals, probably by reducing the male's ability to distinguish appropriate sexual partners. However, their studies were questioned because they were conducted with animals that were already highly active sexually. PCPA was reported to be used as a street drug in San

Francisco, but its apparent decline in use may be because it wasn't as effective as anticipated or that side effects, possibly disorientation, insomnia, or other effects, were too severe.

Sexual excitement is sometimes increased when the action of an enzyme, monoamine oxidase (MAO), is inhibited. The function of MAO is to break down, and prevent an excess of, the excitatory hormones called catecholamines, an important member of which is epinephrine, commonly called adrenaline. Inhibition of the MAO allows an unnatural increase in concentration of the catecholamines and other hormones. Several medicinal drugs are MAO inhibitors (MAOIs) called psychic energizers. The effect of an MAOI is increased by some foods such as cheese and red wine, which contain high concentrations of the amino acid tyrosine, a precursor of catecholamine neurotransmitters, thus flooding the nerve junctions (synapses) of the brain with transmitter. This suggests one reason why the Bohemian custom of wine and cheese parties may promote romantic behavior. However, the effect, if any, may be transient because MAO inhibitors also increase the level of serotonin, which over time inhibits sexual functions. Besides, some people are so sensitive to MAO inhibitors that they suffer debilitating headaches.

Side effects of medicinal drugs are often unpredictable.[37] Anafranil (clomipramine), made by Ciba Pharmaceuticals and often prescribed to treat obsessive-compulsive disorder (OCD), caused ejaculatory failure in 42% of the men taking it in a clinical trial, and impotence in 20% of the men. But one woman in a Canadian study reported that the drug caused her to have an orgasm when she yawned. She was reported to have asked researchers how long she would be permitted to take the drug, and "sheepishly admitted that she hoped to take the medication on a long term basis."[39] The report of the "yawngasm" was published in August, 1983, in the *Canadian Journal of Psychiatry*. A possible explanation is that ACTH, a hormone produced by the pituitary, when injected into the cerebrospinal fluid of mammals induces stretching, yawning, spontaneous erections, and ejaculation. The normal function of ACTH is to stimulate the production of steroid hormones by the reproductive glands.

WHAT'S COMING

Western yearning for sexual stimulants is no less than that of Asians. The accelerating rate in the discovery of new chemical compounds, many of them by the pharmaceutical firms and others interested in biologically active compounds, will inevitably result in the discovery of new chemicals with aphrodisiac properties. Some of the uses will be side effects of drugs developed for entirely different uses. Many side effects of drugs are harmful or dangerous, but some drugs have side effects that result in their being used as multipurpose drugs. Although this "broad spectrum" effect is far from ideal, if the mechanism of action can be determined, chemists can use the knowledge to develop compounds that are more specific in their effect.

Another, even more powerful, tool for developing new drugs is the use of biotechnology, still in its infancy. Genes from plants or animals that code for specific enzymes, for instance, one that degrades melatonin, or other chemical compounds related to the catecholamine neurotransmitters, can be introduced into bacteria and other organisms that can then be cultured for mass production of the desired products. It would be remarkable if new aphrodisiacs were not discovered in this way.

Perfumes and colognes are presumed to be powerful aphrodisiacs. Although used at least since biblical, Greek, and Roman times, and developed to a high art by Arabian chemists during the Middle Ages, some of the secrets of odors and their aphrodisiac effects have been revealed scientifically only recently. Much has yet to be learned about naturally occurring aphrodisiacs, called *pheromones*, about their action, and how they can be mimicked. Determining the performance of pheromones on humans is difficult for a number of reasons. Their effect is partly on mood, which in turn is affected by any number of variables such as fatigue, stress, anticipation, memories, and past experiences. Also, the effect of pheromones may be partly or entirely subliminal, at the subconscious level. Moreover, cultural as well as individual responses to odors vary. And people differ greatly in their ability to detect odors. Women, generally, are better smellers than men, and studies indicate that women's sensitivity to odors is related to the sexual cycle, being highest when estrogen levels are high. The ability to detect odors declines with age in both women and men. Some people are unable to detect some or all odors. But there is increasing interest in odor studies at research institutions besides manufacturers of perfumes and animal pheromones for commercial use. The Monell Chemical Senses Center of Philadelphia is a leading institute of smell and taste. Aromatherapy is a way to relieve anxiety and induce relaxation with aromas that are associated with something pleasant, such as the woods, the seaside, or any of several aromas that evoke a familiar and pleasurable memory. The patient is encouraged to bring any problems to consciousness while relaxing in the soothing emotion aroused by the aroma. The pleasure of associated experiences, possibly some below the conscious level, is apt to prevail.

Aromatherapy is one of the least developed techniques for the use of pheromones. The olfactory system is a primitive part of the sensory mechanism, connected to a part of the brain that controls mood and emotion. Sexual experiences are associated with odors, whether we are conscious of it or not. Actually, some people are consciously aware of smelling "sex" during intercourse. When more becomes known about these erotic odors, the technique of sexual aromatherapy, especially when combined with sexually oriented massage, will be able to raise the delight of sex to a new level of ecstasy.

The worldwide demand for love potions, from historic times to the present, was and is met mostly by supplying animal and plant parts of purely imagined physiological effect. No matter how much we may view the practice as amusing, pathetic, immoral, or disgusting in regard to the destruction of endangered animals, the psychological effects on many people may be real. Luckily for endangered species, synthetic chemicals of precisely known physiological action, especially medicinals and related compounds, add a new dimension to the use of aphrodisiacs. As further knowledge of the effects of existing chemical and the development of new ones accumulates, commercially available aphrodisiacs are sure to follow. Some of them may be in production now but not generally known or available. No doubt, the future will see a number of such materials available by prescription, followed by some of the safer products being freed by the Food and Drug Administration for over-the-counter availability. They will open up a new market in the cosmetic areas as well as in drugstores. Ultimately, the sex manuals, or so-called "How to Make Love" books will have to be rewritten to take into account the effects of modern technology on making love.

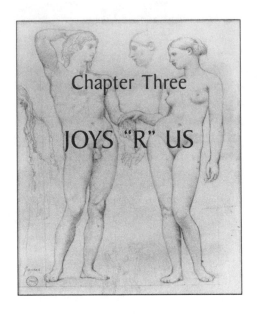

Chapter Three

JOYS "R" US

The joy store, with shelves of so-called sex toys, contains marvels of human ingenuity. Sex toys—devices to give or enhance sexual pleasure—have been in use since ancient times. A favorite in Persia was a wooden phallus said to be soaked in olive oil and smeared generously with pepper and powdered nettles. When inserted into either the male or female, this outrageous instrument was described as one that would convert the most unresponsive to a "demon of lust."[1] One must take into account the Persian penchant for imaginative exaggeration. Who can forget the flying carpet and other impossible feats of magic in *Arabian Nights* and the adventures of Aladdin, Ali Baba, and Sinbad? Another device was a rubber ring covered with fine bristles inserted between the prepuce and glans of the apparently uncircumcised male. They also used penis sheaths said to be made of corrugated or studded metal. In other cases, strips of bone or wood were inserted under the skin of the penis to increase its size and rigidity. The method is basically the same as that used in modern surgery to treat impotence.

The *Kama Sutra of Vatsyayana*, the ancient Indian treatise of uncertain date on love and social conduct, has a chapter "On the Way of Exciting Desire; and on Miscellaneous Experiments and Recipes," describes several sex devices, or *Apadravyas*, to enhance sensations of the lingum (male member) and the yoni (female external genitals, i.e., labia):

- An "armlet," called Valaya, should be the same size as the lingum, and its outer surface should be rough with globules.
- The "couple," called Sanghati, is formed of two armlets.
- The "bracelet," called Chudaka, is formed by joining three or more armlets to make them cover the full length of the lingum.
- A "single bracelet" is made by wrapping a single wire around the lingum to fit its dimension.
- A "Kantuka" or "Jalaka" is a tube open at both ends, rough on the outside and studded with soft globules. It is made to fit the size of the yoni, and tied to the waist. If this cannot be obtained, use may be made of a tube made of "wood apple" or a tubular stalk of the bottle gourd, or a reed made soft with oil and extracts of plants, or a row of soft pieces of wood tied together. These are used with or in place of the lingum.

People of the southern countries, according to Vatsyayana, think that for real sexual pleasure it is necessary to pierce the lingum, similar to the practice of piercing the ear lobes for rings. After piercing his lingum, it continues, a young man should stand in water until the blood stops flowing, and at night he should have vigorous intercourse to cleanse the hole, then he should wash it with ointments. He should increase the size of the hole by pushing in small pieces of cane, gradually enlarging the hole. He may wash the hole with a mixture of licorice and honey, increase the size of the hole further by inserting stalks of the simapatra plant, then anoint the hole with a small amount of oil.

Apadravyas of various shapes may be inserted in the hole, such as: the "round," the "round on one side," the "wooden mortar," the "flower," the "armlet," the "bone of the heron," the "goad of the elephant," the "collection of eight balls," the "lock of hair," the "place where four roads meet," and other things that have names describing their forms and uses. All of these Apadravyas should be rough on the outside depending on how they are used (clearly this was written before infection was understood).

The *Kama Sutra* gives detailed instructions for methods of enlarging the lingum. A procedure used by the Dravidians is for a man to rub his lingum with bristles obtained from certain insects that live in trees, then rub it with oil for ten nights, following which he should again rub it with bristles. By repeating this treatment, the lingum will gradually swell. He should lie on a cot with a hole in it to let his lingum hang down through it, and he should ease the pain by applying cooling concoctions. The swelling, called "Suka," is said to last for life.

A swelling lasting for a month can be produced by rubbing the lingum with the following: the plant *Physalis flexuosa*, the shavara-kandaka plant, the jalasuka plant, the fruit of eggplant, butter from a female buffalo, the hasta-charma plant, and the juice of the vajrarasna plant. If the above concoctions are boiled with oil, a swelling will be produced lasting for six months.

The lingum can also be enlarged by treating it with oil boiled over a moderate fire in mixture with the seeds of pomegranate and cucumber, and juices from the valuka plant, the hasta-charma plant, and eggplant.

Other methods of enlarging the lingum may be learned from experience or confidential sources, says the *Kama Sutra*.

Inserting objects into the penis to help excite women has long been a custom in many parts of the world. In Borneo, men pierce the end of the penis with a piece of bamboo or a brass wire if available. Men in Sumatra make slits in the skin of the penis into which they insert small stones. Skin grows over and heals the wound, leaving the penis with a knobby surface.

The Mongols of the Yüan dynasty of China used what they called the "goats eyelid," also known as the "happy ring," literally the eyelid of a dead goat with the eyelashes still attached. The severed eyelid was treated with quicklime, then steamed and dried to a leathery texture. When a man tied it to his erect penis, it was supposed to increase the woman's sensation by tickling the vagina.

An invention called *Ben-Wa* long used by Japanese women consists of a pair of hollow balls, one of which is filled with mercury.[2] They are inserted into the vagina, the empty one first. When the woman lies down or sits in a rocking chair, the mercury rocks back and forth in the outer ball, nudging the inner ball against the cervix. The gentle massage causes sensations that are transmitted inward to the uterus and outward to the labia and clitoris enabling the woman to bring on repeated orgasms. Some women are said to continue their movements for hours. A variation consisted of a narrow pouch made of soft, thin leather containing the balls. A modern gift for the American woman who has everything is a gift box containing two solid metal, gold-plated balls, each about ¾ inch in diameter.

Dildos—artificial penises—are ancient devices. The dildo, from the Italian *diletto*, meaning delight, is usually made of rubber, plastic, or similar material in the approximate shape of an erect

Ben-Wa balls. The original design contains small balls inside a larger 1-inch sphere.

penis. The dildo was actually of Greek origin.[3] The city of Miletus on the coast of Asia Minor was a manufacturing and exporting center for the devices, which they called *olisbos*. The Greek product was made of wood or padded leather, and was intended to be anointed with olive oil before use. According to Reay Tannahill in *Sex in History*, a short play of the 3rd century BC consisted of a dialogue between two young women, Metro and Coritto, during which Metro tries to borrow Coritto's dildo. But Coritto has lent it to someone else, who in turn lent it to still another friend.

A typical modern dildo measures 7 inches in length by 1¼ inches in diameter, and contains a multispeed vibrator powered by small batteries. Some dildos are curved upward at the end to massage the so-called G spot, in some women a sensitive area on the inside ventral surface of the vagina. Dildos come in various shapes and sizes; some are shaped in a design to massage the clitoris. Some are described as designed for anal penetration.[4]

Several devices are made to slip on the penis to enhance the sensation of the man or the woman or both. The simplest is a so-called "cock ring" made of rubber, available in several sizes, to fit at the base on the penis or about the penis and scrotum. The action is to restrict the return flow of venous blood, causing the penis to become larger and more rigid. A more elaborate device, called by the supplier a "love cage," is in the form of a sleeve, with a knoblike projection on top containing a vibrator, that fits snugly over the base of the penis. The tiny vibrator, which the supplier calls a "love buzzer," is powered by small batteries in a separate wired control box. Some vibrators come with various attachments to be used to provide different strokes for different folks. Whips of various designs are presumed to be used lightly or for tickling by most people. Restraints, some of them moderately expensive, are popular items. Most of them seem to be designed to enable the restrained person to easily free herself or himself.

For men with an erection problem, prosthetic penis aids (PPA) are available in different styles and sizes. The PPAs, designed to slip over the penis, are flexible but firm enough to permit penetration. The more elaborate PPAs contain a variable speed vibrator. Various designs of "penis pumps," actually small vacuum pumps, are designed to achieve an erection, an ejaculation, or both. The function of these is to pull blood into the penis, which causes an erection, after which a ring is usually slipped onto the base of the penis to hold it turgid. Some are battery powered, and some contain a vibrator.[5]

For really lonely people, life-size inflatable male or female dolls are made with movable arms and legs. The female has a multispeed vibrating vagina and anus, powered by a battery. The male doll has a detachable vibrating penis powered by two AA batteries. Kinds of devices for sexual stimulation and pleasure and their variations are almost endless. Information is available from mail order suppliers of such equipment, who readily furnish catalogs. Suppliers advertise in mainstream women's magazines, and retail stores that sell toys, erotic literature, and videos can be found in nearly all major cities.

Sex toy store managers say that most of their customers are women, and this is confirmed by others. *Good Vibes Gazette* made a survey of customers during 1995. Most of them (67%) are between the ages of 26 and 45, with 14% between 18 and 25, 14% between 46 and 55, and 5% being 56 and older. The survey found that about two-thirds of their customers are women (65%) and about one-third are men (34%), with 1% identifying themselves as "other." A tally of names on the company's list of survey respondents gave a breakdown of 57% women and 34% men, possibly indicating in part that women were more inclined to respond to the questionnaire. The majority of respondents identify themselves as heterosexual (63%). Of the women, 18% identify as lesbian, 14% as bisexual. Only 3% of the male respondents say they are either gay or bisexual.[6]

The level of education of customers is surprisingly high. All of the respondents graduated from high school, and nearly 50% have college degrees, 28% have postgraduate degrees, and 7% have Ph.D. degrees. *Good Vibes Gazette* comments, "If vibrators were allowed in the classroom, exams would be so much less stressful."

The survey asked customers to name their best and worst experiences with sex toys. High on the "most disappointing" list were Ben-Wa balls, "too large" dildos, and "too small" dildos. Repeatedly mentioned on the "most exceptional" list were the Hitachi Magic Wand (a nearly conventional vibrator), silicone dildos, jelly products, and harnesses. "We were pleased that 'my VCR' wound up on several folks' lists and intrigued by one person's tip of the hat to a 'wood darning egg'." Suggestions for making additional products available included "more amateur videos," "more audiotapes," "more gay porn," "more heterosexual porn," "more lesbian porn," and "more new ideas."

Good Vibes Gazette reports, "We'll continue to search for erotic computer games, remote-controlled vibrators, vibrators that plug into your car lighter, and 'items for backpackers.' " They say their survey showed that 75% of their customers shop exclusively by mail. For those with World Wide Web access, the supplier established a site in November, 1995, which included their Vibrator Museum and product information.

A reverse-purpose device intended to prevent women's indulgence in sex was the chastity belt, or chastity girdle, involuntarily worn by some unfortunate women in the Middle Ages. It was made in various forms and of various materials designed to cover the external genitalia in a way to prevent sexual intercourse or masturbation, and it required a great deal of ingenuity to design one that would permit elimination. A lock was usually placed on the part of the belt that encircled the hips. It is said that a German emperor before leaving on a crusade had an iron device made for his wife, the queen, and had it riveted by a blacksmith.

The origin of the chastity belt is obscure. Reference to the belts appears in the European literature as early as the 12th century, but samples of chastity belts in European museums date no earlier than the 16th century, and the authenticity of many of them is questionable.[7] The idea for the device, said to be popular with the Crusaders to keep their wives in line, is supposed to have come from the Oriental practice of jealous and suspicious husbands who wanted to prevent their wives and daughters from having illicit sex. Many of the men on the Crusades were gone for years, if they returned at all. It is suspected that many of the women found ways to circumvent their husbands' intentions, and that clever locksmiths did a thriving confidential business.

When women in Oriental harems were permitted to leave the grounds for visits, the usual practice was to have eunuchs accompany them as guards. But if no eunuch was available, one method to guarantee fidelity was to attach a belt around the woman's waist attached to a thong that passed through a hole in a round piece of wood four or five inches from the end. This was inserted into the vagina before securing the belt. As if she needed a further reminder of whose property she was, the other end of the wood extended to her knees.

Sex toys and erotic literature and videos were at one time a limited assortment of products available only in sleazy adult stores in areas that most people avoided. Most of today's stores are in unobstrusive but respectable locations that customers can visit without being conspicuous. Any of the products can be obtained by mail order catalog purchases from suppliers that ship in unmarked packages that give no hint of the contents, assuring customers of privacy. Sex toys are the least talked about of the techniques for enhancing sexual pleasure, but their use is becoming the subject of more open discussion. The relative merits of the various devices will, in the future, probably be a topic talked about with as much ease as today's talk of antiperspirants and condoms.

Erotic videos are increasingly seen as having value for instructional purposes as well as for stimulating and preparing viewers for sexual enjoyment. There's a great need for improvement in the quality of erotic videos, many of which are shabby, watered-down versions of porn movies. As the demand for quality videos increases, new producers will be able to afford more and better talent and a corresponding increase in quality.

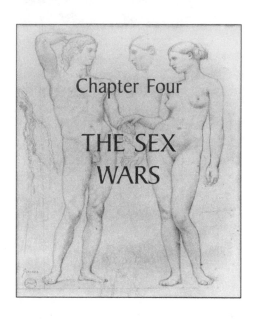

Chapter Four

THE SEX WARS

The first liberated woman was Lilith, Adam's first wife before Eve was created. Although hardly a role model for modern feminists, Lilith believed in sexual equality. She was tired of always being on the bottom, and maintained that she should have her turn on top. A Hebrew legend has Lilith so shrewish, or Adam so staid and unexciting, that they couldn't stand each other, so Lilith departed. Lilith is derived from a figure in Babylonian mythology named *Lilitu*, from the Semitic word meaning "night," and referred to in The Book of The Prophet Isaiah as "screech owl," and in the Revised Standard Version of the Bible as "nighthag." According to one story, Lilith connived with the serpent in a plot to bring about the fall of Adam and Eve. Lilith became "a demon of the night," and embittered by being childless, was a threat to children at night.[1]

Organized feminine activism is as old as ancient Greece, but it had a twist that was different from the modern sex war, at least as depicted in the art and literature of the day. Although Greek women of Athens had some freedom of action and expression compared to other societies of the time and most of those that came later, they were not always satisfied with their lot. In Aristophanes's bawdy comedy, *Lysistrata*, presented after the Sicilian campaign of 413 BC, the influential women of Athens became more than a little annoyed at their men spending so much time away from home fighting what seemed like stupid wars.[2] While their husbands were away, the wives plotted to go on a sex strike to bring the men to their senses. The actors on stage portraying the men indicated realistically that the holdout was distressing and provocative, if not torture. The immediate goal was to make peace with the Spartans—and the women made their point. Today's feminists have far different complaints. What they mostly want is equality of opportunity, something women have never had in all of previous history except in isolated societies.

The current gender war is being won or lost depending on which side you're on and what part of the world you're in. Historically, men have dominated in almost every culture despite the myth of the Amazons and the frequent ascendency of female monarchs. One view is that aggressiveness, typically more a male than a female characteristic, and one that is believed to be related to testosterone output, has given men power and allowed them to call the shots. Male dominance was clearly the rule when polygamy became popular, which was very early in history, if not prehistory, and flourishes today in many parts of the world where having multiple wives is a sign of rank and success. Male dominance reached a peak when harems became a mark of distinction; kings and potentates liked to keep their stable of women penned up and ready, exclusively for entertainment. Eastern harems have gone the way of slavery in the modern Western world where women often have their way in domestic, business, and political affairs, but as they repeatedly remind their male friends or combatants, not often enough.

Crusaders like Betty Friedan and Gloria Steinem were responsible for much of the momentum of the feminist advance. Friedan says of her book, *The Feminine Mystique*, that she wasn't even conscious of the woman problem until she started writing about it:

> I, like other women, thought there was something wrong with me because I didn't have an orgasm waxing the kitchen floor. I was a freak, writing that book—not that I waxed any floor, I must admit, in the throes of finishing it [the book] in 1963.

Friedan debunked the traditional definition of women, which she called the *feminine mystique*, "solely in terms of their sexual relation to men and their biological role as mothers," at a time when there were few career women to be found, and when, as Friedan says, "career" and "women's rights" were dirty words, and working women who had not married or had children were "freaks."[3]

Gloria Steinem, an attractive young journalist, made her debut in 1962 with a bitingly witty description of how out of curiosity she infiltrated the Playboy Club and, although over the club's age limit, landed a job as a "Bunny." The Playboy Club, popular in the 1960s, especially among traveling businessmen, was, for those too young to know, a chain of nightclubs established by Hugh Hefner, publisher of *Playboy* magazine. Steinem wrote with fiery passion about gender inequities, contributing articles to *Ms.*, a magazine that she cofounded, *New York* magazine, of which she was a founding editor, and other publications.[4]

Before blowing trumpets and hoisting the colors in preparation for joining the fray in the battle of the sexes, let's celebrate the natural condition that biologists call *sex dimorphism*, meaning that men and women are different in more ways than the shape and size of their genitalia. Sex dimorphism is a prominent feature of many animals besides humans, and most of the differences serve a biological purpose. Some of the sex differences are obvious; others are more obscure but no less fundamental. They are physical, physiological, psychological, and behavioral.

Girls mature physiologically about two years sooner than boys, and they apparently mature earlier intellectually as well. Girls are generally more skillful with words and intuitive thinking, while boys are generally better with numbers and spatial concepts. These differences are consistent in repeated tests over

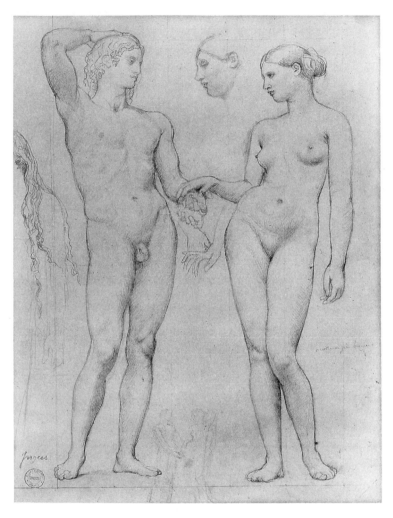

Two Nudes: Studies for the Golden Age, by Dominque Ingres. Courtesy of the Fogg Art Museum, Harvard University Art Museums.

the years, although some people may question whether they are from genetic wiring or learned behavior. Mature females are on average about 20% smaller than mature men, as a result of which men outperform them in most athletic sports. Also, boys generally have a higher metabolic rate and are more active than girls, partly accounting for the fact that boys are more apt to be truants, delinquents, inattentive, and rebellious, as well as accounting for a high proportion of the maladjusted and low achievers. But there are great differences among both women and men, and much overlapping between the sexes in size, strength, and physical performance. The differences are statistical, most easily expressed as averages. Intellectual performance probably differs between the sexes with respect to particular kinds of ability, but there is no evidence of any difference between males and females in overall intelligence even though women's brains, again on average, are smaller than men's (more on brains later). As with physical characteristics, physiology, and behavior, there is great variability in intellectual capability in both sexes.

In a 1972 interview, William H. Masters and Virginia Johnson, the famous sex authorities, discussed how much alike men and women are. They declared, "Aside from a few anatomic differences—let's concede they're fortunate differences—we think that male and female are incredibly alike, not only from a physiological but from a psychosocial standpoint." To be sure, men and women are much alike. After all, we're members of the same species. But it distorts the truth to force the two sexes into a Procrustean bed when the differences, whether perceived as large or small, account for much of the pleasures, passions, problems, and complexities of the sexes. Let's explore them here because they may explain some of the causes, and possibly point the way to resolution, of the sex wars.

Women's hormone systems differ throughout their lives from those of men, especially after puberty and before menopause. Men's hormone output also changes over time, but it continues to be qualitatively different from that of women. Men are, again on average, more aggressive than women and this is attributed to their higher output of testosterone and other androgens. Because of their aggressiveness, men are presumed to be more inclined to commit acts of violence and brutality. In fact, the preponderance of violent crimes are committed by men, including spouse-beating, murder, and, most notably, rape. Two-thirds of the 13 million alcoholics in the United States are males.

The basic difference between the sexes is in 1 pair of the 23 pairs of human chromosomes—the XY pair, called the *sex chromosomes*. The embryo will receive either two X chromosomes (XX) or one X and one Y chromosome (XY). The Y chromosome is much shorter than the X chromosome but it contains a crucial gene that is absent on the longer X chromosome, a gene called the *testis-determining factor* (TDF). The embryo that receives the Y chromosome and its TDF gene will become a male and will have male gonads. If an embryo does not have a Y chromosome, it will not have the TDF gene, so it will develop into a female and will have female gonads.[5]

Neither the chromosomes nor TDF necessarily have the final say in determining sexual behavior. The sex steroid hormones have the last word by turning important genes on or off. But the sex hormones do not act on the genes directly. They must bind with molecules called *receptors* in the brain and other tissues, enabling the receptors to make connections with the target genes. Adequate amounts of androgens (male hormones) produced by the testicles during fetal development determine whether the sex organs develop along male instead of female lines. A female fetus exposed to testosterone will, as an adult, behave similarly to a normal male. In contrast, depriving either a male or female fetus of androgen during a critical time of brain development will result in a female pattern of behavior.

The brains of men and women have physical differences. Simon LeVay, a neurophysiologist at the Salk Institute, in his book *The Sexual Brain*, describes several sexual dimorphic parts of the human brain.[5] For instance, the corpus callosum, a mass of neurons (nerve cells) that connects the right and left hemispheres of the brain, is larger in females. In most people, speech is controlled by the left hemisphere, while the right hemisphere is superior in spatial reasoning. A speculation based on preliminary research is that the larger corpus callosum enables women to engage more of their brains than men when thinking certain thoughts. This may explain why women generally have better language skills, because they are better able to tap into the right brain in a way that enriches their left brain vocabulary. It may also explain why men, who at times seem to be callously insensitive to emotions, differ so much from women, who find it easier to receive signals from the emotional limbic system.[6]

One reason the differences are important is that there is a crucial link between hormones produced by the gonads and the brain's hypothalamus–pituitary complex with connections to the cortex and the amygdala (cell groups in the amygdala are responsible for aggressive behavior). In some cases hormones have an overriding influence. Alan Fisher at the University of Wisconsin demonstrated in a classic experiment on laboratory animals that an area in the hypothalamus is responsible for male-typical sexual behavior, and another area a few millimeters away is responsible for female-typical sexual behavior. When Fisher injected a soluble form of testosterone into a specific part of the hypothalamus, it induced maternal behavior such as nest building, surprisingly whether the animal was male or female. But when he injected the testosterone into another area slightly to one side of the first, it induced the animal to engage in a male pattern of sexual activity, again regardless of whether the animal was male or female.[7]

The powerful effects of prenatal sex hormones in humans are seen in congenital adrenal hyperplasia (CAH), a genetic disorder transmitted by a recessive gene that prevents the adrenal cortex from producing cortisone, and instead, causes it to release an excess of androgens from fetal life on. If the fetus is a genetic female, the external genitalia are masculinized, and later in life, if not treated early, the female's body becomes masculinized. In a male fetus, the genitalia are normal. Boys with CAH show a high level of energy expenditure in play and sports, a male role characteristic.

The opposite condition comparable to masculinization by CAH is a syndrome misnamed *testicular feminization*, in which the genetic male has testicles with a normal output of testosterone, but the tissues of the body lack receptors for the hormone and are, therefore, insensitive to androgen. The result is that the external genitalia appear to be female but there is no uterus and only a short vagina. The usual treatment is surgery and hormone replacement. The child is usually reared as a female, but of course she cannot reproduce.

Testosterone and related androgens in the male fetus, and progesterone and estrogen in the female, affect not only sexual development, but later behavior as well. Anke Ehrhardt and Heino Mayer-Bahlburg of Columbia University reviewed and described behavioral sex differences that are related to the effect of sex hormones in the fetal stage of development.[8] They cite the following sex dimorphic characteristics as being influenced by sex steroid levels before birth:

Male characteristics:

- *Energy expenditure* in the form of outdoor play and athletic skills in humans, and in the form of rough-and-tumble play in nonhuman primates, is described as an essential part of psychosocial development of males.
- *Social aggression* in the form of physical and verbal fighting in childhood and adolescence of humans, and pursuit, threat behavior, and fighting in male nonhuman primates are predominantly male attributes.

Female characteristics:

- *Parenting rehearsal* as seen in child doll play (versus play with cars and trucks), playing house, mother, and father, participating in infant care, and fantasizing about having children of their own.
- *Grooming behavior and adornment* as indicated by clothes preference, jewelry, makeup, hairdo, and the like, may or may not be related to prenatal hormone levels, but may be interrelated with other temperamental characteristics that may be influenced by prenatal hormones.

Male or female tendencies:

- *Preference* of playmates by male or female sex in humans. Dominance behavior and sex segregation of play groups are seen in nonhuman primates.
- *Gender role* as indicated by being labeled "tomboy" or "sissy" is clearly influenced by prenatal hormones.

So we're different, but also the same. We have similar goals and ambitions, and men and women have learned how to cooperate in making a living and raising children. Contrary to the cartoon perception of the macho prehuman male dragging his mate by the hair with a club over his shoulder, the early male *Homo* must have had a subordinate role. It was the female who conceived, carried the unborn child, cared for and suckled the infant, fed and taught the adolescent, defended it from danger, and gathered and prepared herbaceous food for the family and tribe. By comparison, the male role was trivial. The male had fun—hunting game with loyal companions of the chase and enjoying the exhilaration of fighting enemies alongside brave compatriots with whom he forged lifelong bonds. He learned to trade meat and loot for female favors. As childhood became more prolonged during evolutionary development of the human primate, the females become increasingly dependent on the help of the stronger males. Though largely indifferent about family matters, the males, with ample testosterone flowing through their systems, assumed the dominant role. They became chiefs, witch doctors, and tribal leaders.

Some of this changed when people settled in permanent agricultural communities and became civilized. Men had to forego the pleasure of the hunt, except on special occasions, because tilling the soil kept them busy alongside their women from sunrise to sunset, too tired at night to take care of the kids but not too tired to breed. Woman's burden was at first the same as before, but as time went on, she became more domestic. Division of labor, trades, and professions tended to divide men's and women's responsibilities. This shift in roles is seen in what we know of life among so-called primitive people.

The !Kung of the Kalahari Desert in South Africa provide a window into the past with a panoramic view of the early and later status of women in a changing society. The !Kung have lived in the area as nomadic hunter-gatherers since the Pleistocene, at least 11,000 years. Recently, in the span of a decade, many of them have moved to live in agrarian villages in a life-style similar to that of their neighbors, the Bantu. Now, only a small percentage live by hunting and gathering. Patricia Draper of the University of New Mexico reported that !Kung women in the few remaining nomadic bands have a higher status, more autonomy, and more influence on group decisions than the sedentary !Kung women in agrarian villages.[9] Probably one reason for the higher status of the !Kung hunter-gatherer women is that they contribute by gathering at least 50% of the food. Both women and men who do not seek food on a given day remain in camp and share in taking care of the children. In the sedentary !Kung villages the women are less mobile and contribute less to the food supply. They remain at home to prepare food and take care of their shelters. The men leave to work the fields and work for the Bantu. They learn the Bantu language, and when the Bantu deal with the !Kung, they deal exclusively with the men. The Bantu herdsmen have a strongly male-dominated society. The nomadic !Kung live in such small groups that the children have little chance to engage in sex-oriented games and roles for boys and girls. They play no competitive games, and the adults quickly stop aggression. If a conflict develops among adults they simply leave to join another band. The village children, on the other hand, play in groups of the same sex and similar ages. The girls help the women with their chores while the boys leave to help herd cattle. Disputes among adults are settled by calling in the Bantu to mediate. Curiously, the sedentary !Kung, for reasons unknown, seem to have lost a natural check on the fertility rate experienced by their nomadic relatives. The village population is increasing rapidly.

Even in advanced societies, the role of women depends on circumstances. The Israeli kibbutz had equality for women as its founding principle, but as described by Lionel Tiger and Joseph Shepher in *Women in the Kibbutz*, it didn't quite work out that way.[10] Over time, men and women came to live as in two separate communities. Women, with their time freed by collective child care, are free to work anywhere in the kibbutz. In practice they devote most of their effort to service, food, clothing, and education, while activities of the men are concentrated in production, management, and kibbutz politics. Men hold most of the kibbutz offices, and although the women attend some of the meetings, they rarely talk in meetings. The women's complaint was not the reversion to traditional division of labor but that they did not have enough "femininity and familism." However, an explanation may be that during much of the existence of kibbutzim since their founding early in the century, they had a large majority of men.

In one sense, American society is reverting to that of the nomadic !Kung, in which the women bring in the wherewithal for half of the bacon and beans. What can happen in isolated communities belies the notion that male domination is inevitable. Juchitán is a town in southern Mexico's steamy Isthmus of Tehuantepec. The town market is a display of every conceivable commodity— from iguana stewed in a sauce of tomatoes and peppers to necklaces, bracelets, and earrings adorned with gold spangles. But the most remarkable thing about the market is the virtual absence of men. Women are in command. Vibrant, friendly, outgoing, joking, flirting, the women are in charge of sales. They are introduced to the art of customer relations as young girls by taking on the task of hawking their wares in the market. Where are the men? They're not idle; they're the producers, the artisans, the quiet workers who leave the economy to the women. Boys, by the time they are 9 or 10, separate themselves from the marketplace, embarrassed to do what they think is women's work. The women don't trust their men with money, because they fear the men are apt to blow everything on one night at the cantina. In short, Juchitán is a matriarchy. But the women make one concession. Men are allowed to run the political system, although some of the women complain that the men waste too much time talking. Women, busy running the economy, don't have time for that.[11]

In modern Western society, the sex roles are perceived as different from any before in history. Many women want to do the same work as men, plus have the freedom to take time out to conceive, bear children, and at least partly take care of the infants, still leaving a gap in equality that women have only partially closed by dint of effort and persistence. Colleges and universities that formerly devoted nearly all of their athletic funds to men's sports, now approach parity despite the fact that no women's sport event brings in the cash equal to big time men's sports. By contrast, equality between women and men in the workplace is not now a reality, but will improve dramatically through necessity. The United States is increasingly becoming a fatherless or two-income society, requiring mothers to bring in a breadwinner's income with enough surplus to provide child care. Women can demand and receive just compensation for their work.

Even so, it will be many years before women generally can achieve equality in income. Recent surveys show that there are slightly more women than men in the work force, but information is sketchy on how many of each sex are part-time workers. The percentages of males and females in the working age range is about equal, but an uncertain percentage of the female population will for the time being elect to pursue careers as homemakers, part-time workers, or hobbyists. Although many couples prefer to remain childless for economic or personal reasons, a high percentage of working women of childbearing age will want to have children, which in itself will temporarily keep them out of the workplace, even if on short-term paid leave. But in the future this situation will be at least partly countered by a trend toward many males electing to do the home work, child care, or part-time work if the income of a working partner permits it. Kathleen Gerson, in her book *No Man's Land*, gives the results of a survey of men, nearly all of whom were children in the 1960s and adolescents in the 1970s.[12] In young adulthood, only about a third of the men were primary breadwinners. Eighty-six percent of the breadwinners, or with a breadwinning outlook, were married. And of these, 21% had wives who were employed full-time and 35% had wives who were working part-time. Among the married breadwinners with children, 16% had wives employed full-time and 35% had wives employed part-time.

An update by a study announced on May 10, 1995, showed that 55% of the women who work provide half or more of their household's income. The study, "Women: The New Providers," was conducted by Louis Harris and Associates for the Families and Work Institute and the Whirlpool Foundation, a philanthropic organization.[13] Two-thirds of the 1502 women in the survey had jobs outside the home. In the study, 18% of the working women said they were the household's sole earner, while 26% of the working women said they provided about half of their family's income. However, according to the U.S. Bureau of Labor Statistics, women average only 73 cents for every dollar men make. Still, more women see employment as an option in caring for their families. Their main worries are about employers providing fewer benefits, especially withholding benefits from part-time workers, and the problems of balancing work and family responsibilities.

Presently more men than women pursue degrees in the professions, but that is changing rapidly. There are now more women than men in some grades of teaching, real estate offices, probably banking, and in some categories of retailing and other services. The number of women is increasing rapidly in the professions of law, medicine, science, college professorships, stock brokerage, and other enterprises, including entrepreneurships of various kinds. The American Council on Education reported that women heading up college and university campuses in the United States increased from 5% to 16% during the previous two decades. The biggest increase was in California where as of September, 1995, women accounted for 62 out of 269, or 23% of the chief administrators of regionally accredited, degree-granting institutions. The number increased 54% between April, 1992, and April, 1995. But even this is a slow increase in institutions where women have long outnumbered men as college students.

The health care field has a glaring disparity in compensation between males and females—physicians and nurses. Both numbers and compensation are due for a more equitable distribution. Some professions will probably end up with more women than men, and others with more men than women. Women, when given the opportunity, are as successful in managing businesses as men. The magazine *Working Women*, in its May, 1995, issue, gave its fourth annual list on the top female business owners. The list, which was compiled in conjunction with the National Foundation for Women Business Owners, included a wide range of business types, having a total sales of $17.9 billion in 1994. Revenue was not the only criterion for making the list of managers. In private companies the woman must have owned at least 20% of the stock, or in public companies at least 10%. She must also have been active in management with a title of chief operating officer or higher.

Women-owned businesses are a larger segment of the economy than most people realize. A study by the National Foundation for Women Business Owners in 1994, conducted in collaboration with Dun & Bradstreet Information Services, determined that there were 15.5 million people working in 7.7 million women-owned businesses nationwide, with more than double the increase in employment growth compared to all firms nationwide during the four-year period studied.

Most women-owned businesses are small, with less than 1% of them having more than 100 employees, but nationwide, women-owned businesses increased 43% from 1987 to 1992, far more than the 26% increase for small businesses as a whole. They make up more than a third of the country's 17.3 million small businesses.[14,15]

Affirmative action, which flourished during the 1960s, 1970s, and 1980s, and which accelerated opportunities for women, will wane along with affirmative action for minorities under the revived doctrine of equal opportunity for the equally qualified. The European Court of Justice, meeting in Brussels, issued a ruling on October 12, 1995, that European Union governments may not give women preference for jobs and promotions. The case referred to the Court of Justice by a German court, was brought by Eckhard Kalanke who was passed over for promotion in the Bremen Parks Department under a state law that required public agencies to give preference to equally qualified women. The Luxembourg-based court said that such programs violate an equal opportunities law within the European Union. But the momentum already created will continue to open opportunities for women by reason of the awareness of female capabilities and an increase in the availability of qualified women. In specific areas where most of the competition continues to come from men, most of the top jobs will continue to be occupied by men.

There are two places at the top where a big change is in the offing. Boards of directors of corporations have traditionally been occupied exclusively by men, many of them semiretired executives, while except for pension funds and mutual funds, the largest blocks of stock in some companies are held by women, many of them widows. Many corporations have begun to actively place women on their boards, usually far younger than retirement age. This trend will continue, ultimately resulting in women having a much greater say in the management of corporations. In a study conducted by Catalyst, a nonprofit research and consulting group, and released in April, 1995, 570 women were serving on the boards of America's largest companies. However, only 52% of the companies had female board members, and women made up less than 7% of total seats.[16]

A survey of chief executives showed that many corporate leaders have made the recruitment of women directors a priority. They said they could no longer ignore the fact that women compose about half the work force, more than half of college graduates, and about half of business school graduates. Typically, corporate boards have 12 members on average—3 directors from inside the company, and 9 outside directors—but there is great variation among companies. Cecily Cannan Selby was a pioneer executive in the almost exclusively male upper echelons of business. She was the first woman on the board of Avon Products Inc., recruited in 1972 from her job as national executive director of the Girl Scouts of America. By 1995, 4 of the 10 outside directors of Avon were women. Avon, however, is not typical because the company deals mainly in women's products.

A 1995 gathering in Raleigh, North Carolina, of about 250 members of the National Association of Women Business Owners (NAWBO) welcomed retired Congresswoman Lindy Boggs, who filled the seat of her husband, Louisiana Congressman Tom (Hale) Boggs, after he disappeared over Alaska in a small plane in 1972. Mrs. Boggs told of how in the mid-1940s she had been turned away from a congressional hearing because she wasn't dressed properly. She came back an hour later wearing white gloves and a veil, and was promptly seated.[17] Her experience emphasized the dramatic change in women's status that took place within half a century, and continues.

A mystery of the feminist movement is why women so readily acquiesce to the quaint practice of assuming the husband's name when they marry. This archaic convention is a carryover from the days when a woman, on marrying, became her husband's property, socially and legally. In the modern world it serves no purpose other than to identify the woman's husband, which is sometimes useful if he is an important person. Many women in business or professions find it an advantage to retain their maiden names, and especially in case of divorce, there is hardly any purpose served by retaining the name of someone with whom there is no longer any connection except possibly joint parentage of children.[18] Many women compromise by using their maiden names as a middle name, but in the future women will be retaining their maiden name as their last name in nearly all cases.

There are now many women in political offices at the city and county levels, but relatively few women in elected offices at the state and federal levels. Over time, there will be nearly as many women as men, possibly more, in the higher echelons of state and federal government in the United States, and there will be a similar trend in other countries, but more slowly. In some parts of the world, the trend will be barely detectable in the foreseeable future.

Some job categories are occupied mostly by women, in some cases because women are more competent in that particular field, but unfortunately, it is often the result of their being preferentially hired because they traditionally get lower pay. But comparable pay for comparable work will be the rule. It's clear that women will settle for nothing less. The so-called glass ceiling (a term coined by the *Wall Street Journal* in 1986) will be history.

The most urgent feminine problems in a society that increasingly consists of one-parent families, especially single-female-parent families, are the need for child care and paid leave for pregnancy, childbirth, and related contingencies. These needs call for understanding and compassion. When presiding judge Lance Ito of the notorious O. J. Simpson double murder trial in 1995 told the jury and participating lawyers on a Friday that it would be necessary to hold the court in session the following day, Saturday, to accommodate an important witness, the prosecuting attorney, Marcia Clark, recently divorced, informed the judge that as a single parent of young children she had child care responsibilities on Saturday. Judge Ito promptly reversed the instruction, and canceled the Saturday session.

Pregnancy-related problems of working women can be difficult, especially in the case of complications. Regardless, if sick leave can be granted for cosmetic surgery, as some companies do, it seems reasonable to grant needed time off to pregnant women. It is often just as important to have *paid* leave, and this will become the rule in the future with large corporate employers, as well as government allowances through tax deductions for women working for small employers. But these benefits most likely will be one-time only to conform to an enlightened public policy of encouraging limitations on population growth.

Two concurrent developments open new possibilities for women in the working world. Affordable computers, computer networks, business software, and fax modems enable both men and women to do some kinds of work at home that formerly had to be done in an office, saving on commuting time and expense. Also, as Susan Shuck, a networking and marketing executive for IBM, points out, the Clean Air Act, which requires businesses to reduce air pollution by reducing the number of people who drive to work, encourages employers to allow employees to work at home. According to Shuck, this has freed millions of employees to work at home. The development can greatly ease the burden of women who have small children, including nursing mothers.

An innovation is the establishment of telecommuting centers where people can go within easy commuting distance to use a computer, do paperwork, conduct correspondence, and make telephone calls on behalf of their employers. As streets and freeways become increasingly congested, causing workers to spend hours each day on exhausting commutes, telecommuting from nearby telecenters promises to be a wave of the future.[19]

A remarkable juxtaposition in sex roles is seen in the increasing number of single men who want to be fathers regardless of their marital status or sexual orientation. Adoption is the first choice of some men; others opt for contracting with a surrogate. Journalist Elizabeth Mehren, in an article "Going Solo," quotes social worker Andrea Troy, director of New York Singles Adopting Children, "Increasingly, single men are showing up at support groups for prospective parents."[20] Michigan lawyer Noel Keane, head of a chain of clinics called Infertility Centers of America, said he has acted as broker for dozens of unmarried men who contracted with surrogates to bear their children.[20] Mehren tells of Bill Tuttle of Fairbanks, Alaska, who became a father via surrogacy; how Ily Ash, a businessman in Miami, also turned to surrogacy. Another man adopted two boys as infants. The question of his being gay never came up because he didn't say anything about it to the adoption agency. One of the most successful adoption stories was of Don Viola who applied in Placer County, California, but was turned down because he was single. The adoption coordinator told him, "The only thing you've got going for you is that you're not gay." Viola turned to "California and Vietnam," an organization that specializes in adoptions of hard-to-place foreign children, those with physical anomalies or social and psychological disturbances. After a year's wait, Viola received word that a child (whom Viola had already named Jordan) was waiting for him. Jordan arrived, not quite 2 years old, "desperately ill, and tiny, with no hair, no teeth, and an assortment of revolting and unpronounceable parasites." Viola devoted his spare time trying to make Jordan healthy, and rushed him down to a new Vietnamese restaurant the minute it opened. True to storybook form, Viola fell in love with the small restaurant's only waitress. She became pregnant on their honeymoon.[20]

Bare-breast societies are rapidly losing their innocence under the influence of civilized behavior they see in visitors and pictures from the outside. Traditionally, bare-breasted people thought female mammary glands were primarily physiological adjuncts essential for nourishment of small children. When the female breast became glorified as the quintessential symbol of femininity and sexuality in sophisticated societies, modesty dictated a partial coverup, at least the nipples and surrounding areolae. The switch from breast to bottle, and from nipple to nozzle with the help of antilactating drugs posed no problem, and in fact made modesty easier. But the switch back to nature creates a dilemma for liberated women who prefer to nurse their babies. Small babies require frequent feeding, often at times and in places where privacy is limited. Many people think that feeding babies in the natural way should not be done in public view, and in fact, in some parts of the United States exposing the breasts in public is a criminal offense. However, six states have laws that establish the right of a woman to breast-feed in public. In California an identical bill was introduced in the legislature in 1995. Several women with babies testified that they had been asked to leave shopping mall stores and restaurants because they were breast-feeding. While a young woman quietly nursed her baby at the witness table, a committee considering the bill turned it down with 7 in favor to 2 against and several abstentions, but needing 8 votes for approval.[21] One of the objectors, an assemblyman, explained,

> I'm not a prude, and I'm not against breast-feeding. I've seen women breast feed . . . and I've not been offended because they have done so discreetly. However, under this bill . . . a woman could take her shirt off entirely.

"I don't know if I ever saw a mother take off her entire shirt to nurse," replied Assemblywoman Sheila Kuehl, "I don't know where he hangs out." A generation of grown-up bottle-fed babies are finding it hard to realize that humans are mammals, all of which breast-feed their babies in public. They are coming grudgingly to see the difference between the sexual and food supply services of the mammary glands.

SEXUAL HARASSMENT

Indignation against sexual harassment amounting to virtually a national uprising by women was an aftermath of the televised hearings in the U.S. Senate that subjected Anita Faye Hill to harsh verbal questioning and insinuations over alleged sexual molestation by Clarence Thomas, a Supreme Court justice nominee of President Bush. This extravaganza was followed by the sensational scandal of the 1991 Tailhook convention of Navy and Marine aviators in Las Vegas, where several women, mostly naval officers, complained of being groped and fondled by drunk pilots. Navy Lieutenant Paula Coughlin, a pilot herself, lifted the lid off the affair when she publicly complained of being manhandled. She sued the Las Vegas Hilton and the Hilton Hotel Corporation for not providing adequate security and the jury awarded her $1.7 million plus $5 million in punitive damages, reduced by the judge to a total of $5.2 million. Hilton appealed, and the case was still under litigation at this writing. Coughlin found it prudent to resign from the Navy. A rash of lawsuits by women in similar situations followed, some of them resulting in multimillion dollar awards.

Analyzing the Tailhook affair from a narrow biological view, the military pilots are among the most aggressive, usually law-abiding, members of society, and they are trained to give their aggressiveness full expression in their work as fighters. One commentator opined that the Navy will have to decide whether it wants its pilots to be fighters or socialites. But it won't come down to that. The Navy will constrain them to direct their aggression to fighting instead of fondling.

"Most people today know that sexual harassment, whomever the victim, involves power more than sex," says psychologist Dr. Joyce Brothers. "Sexual harassment is a way for a person to demonstrate control and authority; it becomes a weapon."[22] The exhilaration of being in command and the human drive to gain more power are not confined to men. As more women gain high positions, it can be expected that men will be harassed in one way or another. Both men and women subordinates have been known to complain about overbearing supervisors, female as well as male. Same-sex harassment, though it may not be sexual, is a well-known problem. There are many ways in which pressure can be brought to bear, and sex is one of them.

Sexual harassment is agonizingly hard for a woman to deal with because demotion or the job itself may be at stake, as well as the threat of an unfavorable recommendation if she quits in protest or disgust. And often the woman is blamed anyway. Openness by the victims and merciless exposure to public view, despite the risk, is the best defense. But how about the serious admirer who angles for a date or makes a casual remark that is misinterpreted as being personal and results in a multimillion dollar lawsuit? After all, meeting at places of work is a traditional path leading to many happy relationships and blissful marriages. Dr. Katherine Dowling, family physician at the University of Southern California School of Medicine, offers advice:

> Let's fight the battle that needs to be fought for equality of opportunity, but let's not get sidetracked in the process. If you're lucky enough to elicit admiration from the opposite sex but find this admiration unwelcome, well, you've got a tongue! Let's all treat each other with respect and common sense and cease this legal demonization. . . .[23]

However, some women think it's only the legal stick that works. As one woman put it: "Consider it this way: were the boss gay and the subordinate straight, how many straight men would want legal recourse to protect them from such unwanted advances?"

Rape is the ultimate molestation. A 1995 report by the U.S. Justice Department's Bureau of Justice Statistics estimated a half million sexual assaults on women annually, including 170,000 rapes plus 140,000 attempted rapes. The data come from the government's National Crime Victimization Survey, which interviews annually 100,000 Americans age 12 and older. The estimates are higher than the FBI figures, which show only 104,800 rapes and attempted rapes reported to police in 1993. But it's an open secret that many rapes go unreported because victims are embarrassed and, unfortunately, stigmatized. In a survey on college campuses, 15% of the women said they had been victims of forced sex. In a survey at Kent State University, 27% of the male students admitted to having used both physical and emotional force when a woman refused to have sex with them. No statistics are available on how many rapes go unreported, nor on how many women who are coerced into sex continue to have relations with the same men. When Lorena Bobbitt went into a rage over the behavior of her aggressively oversexed husband, John Bobbitt, she waited until he went to sleep, then cut off his penis with a butcher knife. A surgeon sewed it back on, but its performance compared to before the amputation was not disclosed.

Historically, rape was seen as a female hazard, with women given virtually no chance of recourse or bringing the aggressors to justice. But it is increasingly seen in modern society as a heinous crime with somewhat more consideration given to the victims than formerly, and more vigorous prosecution of rapists—who are often murderers as well. More stringent measures are needed to keep these criminals away from their potential victims. An answer proposed by some legislators is life in prison for first-time violent sex offenders. Even more stringent measures will eventually be taken to protect children from violent pedophiles, including longer jail terms, a requirement for frequent reporting following release, and stricter supervision of parolees.

One deterrent to sexual violence and rape would be for women to give support to each other against the mind-set of embarrassment and humiliation, and forthrightly report any rape or attempt of male sexual violence.

FIGHTING BACK

Some women attack with a verbal stiletto. When singer Sandra Gillette's single, "Short Dick Man," became a national dance club hit in the fall of 1994, it was plain that the title and lyrics were derogatory of small male genitalia. When disc jockeys at radio stations around the country resisted, the producer changed the title to "Short, Short Man," with no change in the lyrics. But then the singer had to answer complaints that the record was an attack on short people. "Believe me," said Gillette, a former University of Houston drama student, "the song has nothing to do with height. When people complain about that, I say, 'listen very carefully to the words.'"

"The point of the song," declared Gillette, "is to strike back at all the women-bashing songs in pop, especially in rap."[24]

When a teacher at Sacramento State University reportedly

told her class in general psychology (Psych 100) in December, 1994, that her life goal was to empower women to masturbate so they could overcome the "hardship" of sex with men, one of her students, Craig Rogers, said he had a visceral reaction. He threw up.[25] The teacher, according to a news item, went on to make remarks about genitalia and show slides. Craig Rogers fought back. He sued for damages related to sexual harassment. Aside from the lawsuit, the lecture stirred up debates about whether her comments were appropriate for a basic course in psychology, whether they were politically correct, and whether a man could get away with that kind of talk.

Fighting back sometimes seems amusing in retrospect. Early in the feminist crusade, a group of "chauvinists," calling themselves MS (Male Supremacy), and a sprinkling of female sympathizers picketed the Massachusetts General Hospital Sperm Bank as a protest against militant feminism.

"We think women's libbers are not satisfied with the dominion of man, that they would like the elimination of man," said Sandra Miano, whose husband, Richard, founded MS "If women ever get control of sperm banks, men have had it," Sandra declared. "There'd be no need to have men around at all. Therefore, we want to eliminate sperm banks."

"The Equal Rights Amendment has to be defeated because we're simply not interested in having a unisex society," said Richard. "We're not interested in having our daughters drafted and we're not interested in having the same washroom facilities as women."[26]

The Male Supremacy Movement didn't seem to have much influence in the long run. Sperm banks are flourishing more than ever, and some of them are run by women. Even lesbian couples have been recipients of sperm from sperm banks.

The gender war that began, according to legend, before the time of Eve, was for thousands of years a losing game for women. Male dominance, although today largely cultural, probably originated in early *Homo sapiens* as an evolutionary development of sexual dimorphism during which men became bigger and stronger, and developed or retained from more primitive ancestors a strong testosterone-driven aggressiveness. At first women used their men to help with the ever-present burden of bearing, feeding, and care of children, exchanging sexual favors for meat and other benefits, and feeding the male ego by allowing them to run tribal politics and settle intertribal disputes. But in recent times a revolutionary change in social conditions has brought about a revolution in women's view of their role in life. They realized sooner than men that the differences between the sexes are not as great as previously assumed, and that they are as smart. There are women who are better qualified for almost every role than many men. As highly educated as men, and with more time on their hands than even a few decades ago, women are increasingly vying for opportunity and control. The trend will culminate with almost as many women as men holding top positions in nearly all walks of life. Corporate leadership will increasingly go to women, and in politics, a field in which male dominance has left a dismal record, women may well become the major force for the betterment of mankind. And finally, tension between the sexes will diminish as women become more confident of their potential and men lose their fear of female competition and learn to appreciate their capabilities.

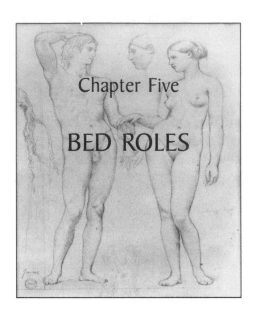

Chapter Five

BED ROLES

The latest skirmish in the Sex War changed everything. Before that, women wanted men to be men, and men were predictable. Women wanted dates to open doors for them, their chairs adjusted, their virginity respected, friendship before being propositioned, to be in love before having sex, and probably no sex before marriage, or at least a ring. In short, they wanted romance. At least that's what men thought women wanted. So men played the game of glorifying the feminine ideal, sometimes honorably, often dishonorably.

When women started winning the war for freedom, the male troops broke ranks in chaotic confusion, vacillating between yielding to the testosterone in their arteries and being politically correct. A common misunderstanding of men's and women's roles stems from the misconception of the typical male and the typical female. The myth ignores the existence of both masculine and feminine qualities in each sex, and the great variability of those qualities within both men and women. To be sure, some personality qualities are commonly recognized as distinctly masculine and other qualities as distinctly feminine, and the distinctions are borne out by scientific and statistical studies. But characteristics seen as male, for example, aggressiveness, high activity level, dominance, self-confidence, impulsiveness, and unquenchable curiosity, are also present in a high proportion of women. And characteristics seen as female that include verbal ability, intuitiveness, anxiety, compliance, closeness to friends, help-seeking, and social desirability, are qualities seen in a high proportion of men. Sandra Bem, in a study of sex role characteristics, devised what is called the Bem Sex Role Inventory.[1] By comparing masculine–feminine personalities in men and women, Bem concluded that about one-third of the women were distinctly feminine and one-third of the men were distinctly masculine, while about one-fourth of the women and one-third of the men were androgynous— neither strongly feminine nor strongly masculine. An androgynous person is described as a man or woman who has qualities about equal in degree of masculinity and femininity. The term *androgynous*, sometimes used in a pejorative way, is borrowed from the description of plants that have both staminate (male) and pistillate (female) flowers in the same inflorescence or cluster. The behavior of androgynous people is supposed to be less restricted to sex roles, and for that reason they are supposed to have greater freedom to act with an appropriate blend of masculine and feminine responses.

Bed roles, traditionally thought of as that of the aggressive, dominant man and the timid, submissive woman, are not always, for all couples, the most satisfying. The changing status of women, many of whom have as much authority and power as men, creates a state of confusion in some male lovers as well as a lingering uncertainty on the part of some liberated woman about how to act or what to expect in bed. In the current environment, if a man follows his natural impulse, he wonders and worries if he will turn his partner off by doing or saying something sexist. The drumbeat of women's liberation and criticism of the traditional macho male role may turn our potential male lover into a limp wimp or, conversely, prod him into a frantic display of superiority and dominance. Either way, he washes out between the sheets, leaving his frustrated partner in the embarrassing disillusionment of failure—or disgust. Betty Friedan, in her book *The Second Stage*, says that the problem is that men are not liberated enough to be themselves and to realize that women simply want to be treated as equals.[2]

Possibly bemused by the flood of attention to women's liberation and the inability of men to adjust to their new status, many women do not realize that most men like to have women make love to them, but with tact and delicacy, because if she comes on like a freight train, she'll lose him. On the other hand, the passive woman who signals, "Go ahead and use me" is neither liberated nor seductive. She is most seductive when she lets the man know what she wants without being dominant. And it is partly up to her to liberate her lover by being aggressive in the sense of showing that she can be an "equal" in making love.[3] This was and is the secret of famous courtesans, and why men have been known to lavish fortunes on them for their attentions.

The bed role of the man of the future is neither a wimp nor a dominator. And the bed role of the woman of the future is not the submissive sex object of a male on the make. She will want to be romanced, but she will just as readily romance her lover. She will occasionally have wine and candlelight with a carefully crafted meal. She will share the expense of meals and entertainment, and he'll accept the favor without embarrassment because she may be making as much or more money than he is.

Experts on lovemaking write recipe books containing an impressive list of techniques, overt and subtle, to enhance the pleasure of the male or female partner, all tried-and-true, guaranteed to leave the partner moaning and writhing in celestial ecstasy if expertly performed according to instructions. What the experts skip or treat lightly is that one person's needs, desires, and feelings are different from anyone else's. The cliché "different strokes for different folks" is nowhere more applicable than in sex. The secret to a satisfying sexual relationship is apt to depend on the partners telling each other what each finds most satisfying, what is pointless, and what is disagreeable. Most people are reticent about asking their partner what they want, never learning his or her preferences, so for years or for life never giving satisfaction. If she is passive and lifeless, ask questions and find out why. If he is a lousy lover and seemingly unimaginative or inhibited, offer to teach him some things. You'll find him to be a good understudy (pun intended). Read all the how-to books, study the illustrations, and brush up on the positions and myriad techniques. But the talisman is closer at hand, though hard for many people to grasp. Letting your partner know what you want and don't want by easygoing talk, and asking the same, is the magic key to pleasurable sex.

Experts in the art of love describe erogenous zones, and in truth, most people have areas of the body that are especially sensitive to sexual stimulation. But the untrumpeted fact is that the entire body is an erogenous zone. Touch has been called "the forgotten sense." Northern Europeans are averse to personal contact compared to people in some other parts of the world. British and Anglo-Americans, for example, prize their privacy and independence. By tradition and upbringing, they generally recoil from touching one another, except to shake hands, as an invasion of privacy and an affront to their dignity. In short, they're apt to be touchy. They have to learn, if they learn at all, to touch and hug as expressions of affection. Unfortunately, the aversion to touching is not always confined to daytime activity; it can be an impediment to affection in bed.

Massage has long been used in sports to treat sore muscles and sprains of athletes, and is increasingly used as therapy for a variety of afflictions related to muscles, joints, nerves, and the circulatory system. The 15,000 or so professionally trained massage therapists in the United States have tried to dissociate their public image from the "masseurs" and "masseuses" in so-called massage parlors that are covers for prostitution. But even the authors of *Hands-On Healing* acknowledge that "massage does have its sensual aspects." They quote Paul Davenport, director of the Florida School of Massage in Gainesville:

> Sexuality is often associated with performance and self-concept, which can cause a lot of anxiety. Learning to touch and be touched in a way that's not oriented toward a goal can help people stop worrying.[4]

Tensions of the day—anger on the job, failure to make a sale, rejection of a recommendation, missing a deadline—tend to carry over into bed, causing worry and insomnia. If not relieved, they also blunt the performance and pleasure of lovemaking. Nothing is more effective in relaxing the nerves, or removing the awkwardness of initial contact, as massage. It releases emotions and opens the gates to a burst of energy. It will give your sex life an added touch.

When both men and women become more fully liberated, they will discover that despite the proliferation of books, articles, movies, and talk shows on the mechanics and acrobatics of sex, the most enjoyable and most satisfying sex is simply sex of whatever kind they both find pleasurable, accompanied by an uninhibited exchange of love and affection between caring and sharing equals.

MANHOOD AND WOMANHOOD

A man has to contend with social pressures to prove his manhood from before the time he becomes capable of reproducing. Much of the same applies to a woman. Boys lag on average two years behind girls in physical and sexual development, causing embarrassment and timidity in mixing with girls who they are closely associated with—their classmates. However, there is great variation depending on environmental and cultural influences, and there are great differences between individuals of the same age, with a spread of about three years in either direction from the average in both boys and girls. Jewish tradition honors a young man's coming of age at 13 by the ceremony of Bar Mitzvah, at which time he assumes adult religious duties. But in other respects and in other cultures, society generally gives him no such recognition of maturity. He does not legally become an adult in most states until he reaches 18, long after he is capable of reproducing, and for some privileges he must be 21.

Girls are viewed in a similar way, although they are usually permitted to do a number of things at a younger age than boys. In some states they can even order and drink beer sooner than boys. A girl can usually marry without parental approval three years sooner than a boy, commonly at 18 and 21, respectively. She can voluntarily engage in sexual intercourse at an age ranging from 14 to 18, depending on the state in which she does it, without her partner committing the felony of statutory rape.

Our young man or woman is apt to be hampered in starting to produce a family by subtle pressures that keep them away from the competitive marketplace. Education sometimes keeps a young man or woman out of competition in the work force with older adults several times longer than is needed to give them the learning they require to do the work they are eventually engaged in. This is done by requiring studies that satisfy the professional growth of teachers whose interests lie in highly compartmentalized specialties that have little relationship to the needs of the young people. Even though they may be leading an active sexual life, they do not achieve full manhood and womanhood in the workaday world until they can compete on equal terms with older people.

For a man, the guillotine falls again when our erstwhile youth reaches the age of 55 to 65 and up. Once again he is no longer qualified to compete with the young and middle-aged, and he is apt to succumb, mentally, physically, and sexually, in hypnotic fashion to the stereotype of his age. He is usually conditioned by then to keep both his pants and his economic fly zippered and settle down to a life of retirement and celibacy. When he romanced women as a young man, he was called, and thought of himself as, a stud. Now, if he displays a casual interest in sex, especially with younger women, he's a "dirty old man." The powerful suggestion of the image of an impotent old man is apt to be a self-fulfilling prophecy.

THE SEARCHERS

In the recent past when most people knew their neighbors, a girl was apt to fall in love with a boy she grew up with. Often he lived within a few blocks of her; they went to the same school and often walked partway home together; their parents knew each other and probably went to the same church. But the old-fashioned way of finding a mate has mostly gone the way of the buggy, the Model T flivver, and clanging streetcars. Commuting to fewer and bigger schools, big corporate employers, highrises, fast cars, and superhighways do not favor being friendly with the boy next door because mobility makes for fleeting friends. While young people come in contact with more people than ever before during their peripatetic, often frantically active, lives, their chances of forming solid, lasting friendships are minimal. Their isolation may become acute after leaving school for work in a city. Apartment life with people tightly packed together causes neighbors to erect barriers against strangers to preserve privacy and sanity. Paradoxically, the more people, the more isolation and loneliness, and the harder it is to make friends.

What can a woman do to meet an interesting man? Singles bars are apt to lead to disillusionment. Work may or may not offer friendship with men who are single, the right age, and attractive. Sometimes friendship can develop with a married man or woman, leading to disaster. Church clubs may lead to friendship and romance, but they're not for everyone.

One can advertise. It has become increasingly respectable for men and women of all ages over 18 to publicize their availability, qualifications, and desires. Most metropolitan newspapers carry ads in their classified sections under such headings as "Dateline" or "Personal." Some magazines and publications of private special interest organizations run dating ads. Here's a typical, though hypothetical, ad under *Women Seeking Men*:

FOR ALL SEASONS
Attractive blonde DWF, 32, 5'7", affectionate, intel, UCLA grad, loves sports, outdoors, sailing, hiking, ISO good-looking, fun-loving SWM to be soulmate for lasting relationship.

Abbreviated translation: Divorced white female is in search of a single white male (classified sections list abbreviation codes).

A typical dateline section will list ads under the headings: *Women Seeking Men, Men Seeking Women, Men Seeking Men, Mutual Interests*, and *50+ Seeking 50+*. Some papers run so many ads, filling two or three pages or more, that editors might be helpful to readers by adding headings that indicate areas of interest such as golfers, sailors, hikers, sports buffs, theater fans, or travel lovers.

Some people feel uncomfortable about answering ads or placing ads, fearing the motives of some respondents. There is an alternative. Most communities have organizations that make a business of matchmaking. One organization has franchises in more than 50 cities throughout the United States. Clients provide detailed profiles that enable the company to identify potential matings. The cost will usually run several hundred dollars, probably a bargain when compared to the cost of a typical trial-and-error search for a mate. But there have been accusations that some of them are not reliable. In one case, the proprietor ran off to Europe, leaving clients holding an empty money bag.[5] It would be heartrending to be stiffed by a service purporting to provide heartthrobs.

With the rapidly increasing use of telecommunications in both business and personal dealings, and its replacement of old-fashioned face-to-face meetings, there will be more isolation and greater need than ever for innovative ways for boy to meet girl and man to meet woman. Ads, mating services, and especially the Internet will increasingly become the substitute for falling in love with the boy or girl next door. And there will be increasing need for precautions against fraud and exploitation. There's no formula. Meet, at least initially, in the presence of friends.

Sometime in the future, ways will be found to match partners for compatibility by using genetic profiles. This will come about gradually as knowledge of the human genome comes closer to completion. Computerized records will make it possible to obtain comparisons of chemical and brain pathways, personality traits, sexual drive and preferences, physiological and physical characteristics, talents, and health prospects with a compatibility rating of 0 to 100 percent.

David Buss, a psychologist at the University of Michigan, asks, "What do men and women want in a mate?" The question has puzzled behaviorists since Charles Darwin related sexual selection to evolution in his 1871 book, *The Descent of Man and*

Selection in Relation to Sex. Darwin looked for qualities that gave males a competitive advantage in fending off other males, or for the preference of females for males with particular characteristics such as attractive plumage. Buss answers the question of human mate preference based on a worldwide survey in collaboration with 50 other scientists who surveyed the mating preferences of more than 10,000 men and women in 37 countries on six continents and five islands.[6–8] The study was conducted over a six-year period from 1984 to 1989. They found that the choice of a mate is species-typical as in other animals instead of varying from culture to culture. Buss points out that for the most part, we are completely unaware of why we find certain qualities attractive in a mate, but that because men versus women have always had different mating problems, they have evolved different mating strategies. They relate to each other differently depending on whether the other person is a short-term or long-term mating prospect. He describes nine strategies used in different situations, each having an evolutionary advantage. For example:

- *Short-term mating (casual sex) is more important for men than women.* The man's parental investment is, at a maximum, no more than sperm.
- *Men seeking a long-term mate will identify with reproductively valuable women.* Men tend to prefer younger women, and standards of attractiveness for all women evolve accordingly.
- *Men seeking a long-term mate need assurance of paternity.* A mother knows that a baby is hers, but a man cannot be sure that a child is his own. Accordingly, his demand for fidelity is stronger than women's.
- *Women seeking a long-term mate will prefer men who can provide resources for their offspring.* In 36 of the 37 countries surveyed, women placed high value on this trait.

Among other differences between men and women, when 148 college students (75 men and 73 women) were asked how many sex partners they would like to have in the course of a lifetime, the men on average said 18, and the women, no more than 4 or 5.

When sexologist June Reinisch was asked what people are most anxious about when it comes to sex, she said, "Impotence is a big problem," and she mentioned sexually transmitted diseases, sexual orientation, and worries about orgasm, especially how to achieve it, and, among men, penis size. But for women, penis size is of far less concern than cleanliness. "Clean hair," says Reinisch, "is very high on the list." Reinisch is director emeritus of the Kinsey Institute for Research in Sex, Gender and Reproduction, in Bloomington, Indiana, formerly the Kinsey Institute for Sex Research. Reinisch has a habit of exploding myths. One of them is the idea that the market for erotic videotapes consists of lonely weirdos and perverts. She finds that one-third of them are checked out by married couples. She sees that as a perfectly healthy sign. She's convinced that sex education does not make people more promiscuous. "Couples with the most information have the best marriages," she declared.[9] Many people view the so-called skin-flicks as pornographic trash, but if well done, they can be informative, stimulating, and contribute to the pleasure of viewers.

A comprehensive 1990s survey shows that American sexual activity among adults is not as rampant as many people suppose. A study completed in 1994, called the National Health and Social Life Survey, was conducted by the National Opinion Research Center, a widely respected scientific research organization. Their report, initially entitled *Sex in America, A Definitive Survey*, said that Americans on average have sex once a week, and only about a third of the Americans in the age range 18 to 59 have sex twice a week or more. About 14% of men and 10% of women in that age range don't have sex at all, although about a third have sex more than once a week, and 7% of the women and 8% of the men indulged four or more times a week.[10,11]

The study consisted of 90-minute face-to-face interviews with 3432 randomly selected Americans ages 18 to 59, who remained anonymous. The study was first proposed in 1988 by the National Institutes of Health to gain information that might help stop the spread of AIDS. But the study was delayed because conservatives in the federal government vigorously objected, fearing that the findings might be used as justification for the sexual practices studied. Funding was finally obtained from private sources, including the Robert Wood Johnson Foundation, Henry J. Kaiser Family Foundation, Rockefeller Foundation, Andrew Mellon Foundation, MacArthur Foundation, New York Community Trust, AmFAR, and Ford Foundation. The study was the most comprehensive since the prototype sexual studies nearly half a century earlier by pioneer sexologist Alfred C. Kinsey, and far better because it looked at a cross section of Americans instead of Kinsey's narrowly selected subjects.

According to the study, about 75% of married men and 85% of married women say they have remained faithful. These values for fidelity are much higher than those obtained in other surveys, an indication of the unreliability of answers to questions on sensitive sexual topics, or maybe fear of AIDS has changed our behavior. The median number of sexual partners for American men over a lifetime is six, and for women, two. The sexual practice preferred by most Americans is vaginal intercourse, which has nearly universal appeal. Distantly following in appeal were watching a partner undress and oral sex.

In answer to a question about masturbation, about 60% of men and 40% of women masturbate occasionally or frequently, and the practice increases with education and salary. Surprisingly, the highest rates are among middle-aged married people who also have active sex lives with their marriage partners. The question on frequency of masturbation was placed on a card, so the participant could hide the answer from the questioner by sealing it in an envelope. The idea of masturbation was expressed by W. C. Fields when asked by a movie mogul to join him in a game of golf. "If I want to play with a prick," said Fields, "I'll play with my own."[12] Contrary to most earlier estimates, but closely confirming European studies, only 2.8% of men and 1.5% of women said they were homosexual or bisexual. However, 4.9% of the men and 4.1% of the women reported having sex with a same-gender partner since age 18.

Sociologist Edward O. Laumann, coleader of the study, along with Robert Michael, thought the results were good news for people who are trying to find ways to block the spread of AIDS among heterosexuals. He pointed out that, in general, people tend to mate only with people who have sexual practices like their own, so there is relatively little opportunity for sexually transmitted diseases to pass from one group to another. The authors of the study concluded, "We are convinced that there is not and very unlikely ever will be a heterosexual AIDS epidemic in this country."[11] Time will tell whether that optimism is valid.

THE FEMALE FORM

Known technically as mammary glands, female breasts are the quintessential symbols of femininity and sexuality. The story is told that Louis XIV, in a gesture to appease his petulant mistress, ordered his artisans to cast a mold from one of her breasts and produce glasses in its shape so he could always sip champagne from her bosom.[13] We still drink champagne from glasses the shape of her breast. And there was the medical student taking an exam that called for giving four reasons why mother's milk is better than cow's milk. Stumped for the fourth reason, he had to rely on personal observation, "It comes in better looking containers."

Unfortunately for glands that serve such a useful purpose in motherhood as giving milk—if the mother will permit it—the breasts are vulnerable to serious problems, chief of which is breast cancer, the second most common form of cancer in women next to lung cancer, and the second most common cause of death after cardiovascular disease. But a major cause of anxiety in younger women is the size and shape of their breasts. Cosmetic surgery to enhance the beauty of breasts expanded into a large industry. But unexpected failures caused by leaking or ruptured silicone implants, causing severe reactions, became a source of agony. The number of failures is so great and the effects are so serious that many lawsuits were filed.

Women's anxiety about the size of their breasts is diminishing. June Reinisch says that women generally are not obsessed about it because there is a current mania for the 15-year-old look.

They want to look thin and muscular. Most men, she says, would rather have a rounded woman, but preference goes in cycles. In the 1950s we assumed that all men like enormous breasts. "There are many men," she says, "who prefer small-breasted women."[14]

The typical female physique is partly the result of an accumulation of fat in the upper arms, hips, breasts, buttocks, and thighs. About 23% of an average woman's weight is in her thighs alone, and some women fear it detracts from the appearance of youthfulness. Cosmetic companies devised thigh creams of which there are said to be 50 different brands with sales of $90 million a year. The therapeutic effectiveness of thigh creams is doubtful, but a known effective treatment is to remove the fat by liposuction. The operation is costly, the results are apt to be painful and possibly dangerous, and the fat can return in time.[15]

Cosmetic surgery will increasingly enable people to improve their appearance. For instance, studies and experience indicate that saline solution in breast implants will be much safer than silicone. Genes that cause breast cancer have been identified, and further studies may lead to a cure or prevention. Life-style, including food habits such as a high-fat diet, may be found to be more closely related to breast cancer than previously realized, in which case reduction in breast cancers would be simple, though difficult for some women, comparable to preventing lung cancer by quitting smoking.

PENIS PROBLEMS

The male counterpart of breast cancer is prostate cancer, the number one cancer in men and the number two cause of cancer deaths in men. Prostate enlargement and cancer, especially when the prostate is removed by surgery, may adversely affect or destroy penile performance. Prostate cancer accounts for 92% of male cancers. Each year, more than 244,000 men will be diagnosed with prostate cancer, and 40,000 of them will die, as against 183,000 women who will develop breast cancer, and 46,240 of whom will succumb. Ironically, funding for research on male reproductive cancers is less than a fourth of the money spent for research on breast cancer.

After age 45, the prostate, which surrounds the urethra, starts to enlarge, interfering with urination, and by age 80, 60–70% of men have evidence of carcinoma at autopsy. Cases of testicular cancer, the most common malignant disease of young men, have doubled in the last 50 years. There is speculation that the causes may be environmental, related to the ominous, though controversial, reports of a worldwide fall in sperm counts. One study of sperm counts over the past 50 years reported a decline from an average of 113 million per milliliter in 1940 to 65 million per milliliter in 1990.

Several theories have been proposed to account for the increase in male reproductive maladies. One theory is that an increase in dietary animal fat consumption increases the production of testosterone and its more powerful by-product dihydrotestosterone (DHT) produced in the prostate, which are supposed to spur cancerous cell proliferation. Another theory is that frequent sexual activity is a risk factor by increasing testosterone and DHT.

The wide spectrum of sexual capability among men leaves them open to a variety of problems. Impotence is the closet malady of the human male, affecting, according to estimates, about 10% of the adult male population. Sigmund Freud, at the age of 37, wrote to a friend about his troubles with impotence.[16] Even the ancient Roman paragon of lovemaking, Ovid, wrote of his episode of impotence. King David, according to the *First Book of the Kings*, when in his old age "gat no heat." So the servants searched the kingdom for a beautiful young woman who "ministered to him, but the king knew her not."[17]

Irwin Goldstein, professor of urology at the Boston University School of Medicine, was quoted as saying that about 30 million American men suffer from impotence. Others put the figure at 10 or 20 million. Most physicians maintain that every man probably experiences impotence at one time or another. Thus, the problem is almost universal among men at some stage in their lives. As British feminist Rosalind Miles says, "It goes with the territory."

When *Homo* is no longer *erectus* the causes are many: fatigue, worry, anxiety, stress, drugs, or organic disorders such as diabetes, vascular disease, trauma from paraplegia, quadriplegia, pelvic damage, prostate surgery, and cancer of the prostate, rectum, and colon. Alcohol, though still mostly underrated as a cause of impotence, was acknowledged to be a problem long ago by Shakespeare in *Macbeth*:

> MACDUFF: What three things does drink especially provoke?
> PORTER: . . . nose-painting, sleep, and urine. Lechery, sir, it provokes and unprovokes. It provokes the desire, but takes away the performance.

Masters and Johnson refer to some forms of sexual inadequacy as secondary impotence. Among the "phallic fallacies" described by Masters and Johnson, the top of the list was "fear of performance." The burden of the cultural demand for partner satisfaction falls heavily on the man, in whom fear of failure is a breeding ground for dysfunctions ranging from clumsiness to premature ejaculation and impotence.[18]

The effect of medicinal drugs is variable depending on the individual. Several, probably most, of the drugs used to treat high blood pressure take away the joy of sex in some males; nearly all of the phenothiazine drugs used as antipsychotics are reported to inhibit ejaculation; some of the monoamine oxidase (MAO) inhibitors used as antidepressants can cause impotence or sexual disturbances; and weight control drugs including both amphetamines and nonamphetamines can cause impotence or a decrease in libido. The Association for Male Sexual Dysfunction (AMSD) in New York City identified over 200 medicines that cause sexual dysfunction as a side effect.[19]

Methods of treating impotence depend on whether the cause is psychological, physiological, or physical. Psychological impotence often appears abruptly following a traumatic experience such as the death of a spouse. Impotence from other causes is more apt to come on gradually. Hormone abnormalities are rarely the cause of impotence, but some diseases may cause impotence by interrupting the nerve supply to the penis. Radical prostatectomy is a common cause of impotence. However, drugs are the most common cause of erection problems, which doctors can often correct by changing prescriptions.

The physiology of an erection is complex. Simply stated, nerve impulses signal certain muscles to relax and others to contract. When muscles controlling the arteries entering the penis relax, they permit up to a sevenfold increase in blood flow into the spongy tissue. At the same time, contraction of the veins carrying blood away from the penis restrict its flow, causing tumescence— an erection. Men will ordinarily have an erection sometime during the dream phase of sleep. If this does not occur or occurs infrequently, as can be monitored electronically by instruments, it is a sign that the cause of impotence may be a physical one, often caused by blood flow abnormalities associated with hardening of the arteries, high blood pressure, diabetes, or scar tissue in the penis.

If there is an artery obstruction restricting the flow of blood into the penis, a surgeon can sometimes correct it by constructing a bypass, similar in principle to bypass heart surgery. If veins are at fault (veins return blood to the heart), they will drain the blood away from the penis too fast to permit an erection, a condition common in older men. Surgeons are reported to be experimenting with tieing off or removing certain veins to reduce the flow.[20]

A highly publicized surgical procedure is to implant inflatable plastic tubes in the penis, a method both praised and condemned as a last resort. Another type of implant consists of semi-rigid rods, rendering the penis always ready, but this leaves a problem of concealment. A more highly recommended implant consists of malleable rods that can be bent for concealment. Rods can be implanted with an inexpensive operation using a local anesthetic. A physical device not requiring surgery is a ring or small tube to fit around the penis together with a vacuum pump to pull blood into the vascular tissue. One such device is supplied with either a hand-operated or battery-powered pump. Some of the manufacturers make their devices available only by prescription.

According to one report, men can learn to achieve an erection through biofeedback training. A device called a plethysmograph attached to the penis makes a continuous measurement of the blood volume. The subject, listening through earphones, hears the voice of a female therapist who is in another room monitoring the equipment. When there is an increase in blood volume, she lets him know and encourages him to maintain his mental state or whatever he feels at the time. The clinic that used biofeedback therapy reported a success rate of nearly 100%. It is well known that biofeedback can be used as a learning procedure, so presumably the men in the study learned to produce an erection without the help of laboratory biofeedback.

A widely used treatment is injection of a medication into the penis before intercourse. A commonly used material for injection is papaverine hydrochloride. After being demonstrated by a physician, this can be done at home with the use of a small-needle hypodermic. Papavarine, which is either obtained from the opium poppy or made synthetically, is a smooth muscle relaxer, having the effect of expanding the arteries and allowing an increase in blood flow. The Food and Drug Administration has not approved this use of papaverine, although there is no restriction against physicians using it. But in the absence of FDA approval, pharmaceutical suppliers refrain from recommending the procedure, citing instances in which prolonged erection, called *priapism*, required medical intervention to avoid permanent injury. It is reported that papaverine causes priapism in 5% of the patients, but a reduction in dose usually prevents a recurrence. The drug is recommended medicinally for the approved use as a relaxant for spasms of smooth muscle, for which purpose it is supplied in ampules for injection or as capsules to be taken by mouth.

Some physicians prescribe another drug, phentolamine (regitine), often in combination with papaverine to enhance the vascular muscle relaxant effect. Phentolamine is approved by the FDA as an antihypertensive agent. It blocks the so-called alpha-adrenergic receptors located in smooth muscle, and prevents constriction in such areas as blood vessels, sphincters, uterus, and penis, especially when injected directly.

A newer drug for treatment of impotence, Alprostadil, commonly known as prostaglandin E_1, had been used for several years to treat penile dysfunction when finally approved for the purpose by the FDA in July 1995 and given the name Caverject. The drug had been in use for at least 20 years, under the trade name Prostin VR Pediatric, for treating infants with restricted lung blood flow, causing them to be "blue babies." The drug dilates the blood vessels and reduces blood pressure, accompanied by a reflex increase in heart rate and output.

A product developed in Norway, called "Libido," is made from fertilized chicken eggs. A three-week supply, available by prescription, costs $150. The active ingredient and mode of action, if known, have not been revealed.

An intriguing lead for development of a new chemical treatment for impotence came with the discovery that a gas, nitric oxide (NO), present in the blood in minute amounts in all parts of the body, is a neurohormone precursor responsible for a number of physiological functions, and is essential for an erection. Could nitric oxide be administered where it is needed and in the proper concentration? Unfortunately, there is no simple answer because the action of NO is indirect, through a reaction with an amino acid neurotransmitter, glutamate. Finding the answer, if there is one, would be an attractive research project for pharmaceutical companies with visions of outrageous profits. But the difficulties and enormous costs inherent in testing drugs specifically for treatment of impotence, and obtaining FDA approval, favor confining the research effort to being alert for potency side effects of drugs intended for other purposes. Almost certainly new therapeutics will be discovered, eventually available over-the-counter without a prescription.

An embarrassing male condition suffered by many men is premature ejaculation. Fear of performance in the younger men of Masters and Johnson's study group was primarily about the ability to delay ejaculation long enough to satisfy their partners. This concern was confined to members of the group who had attained college or postgraduate levels of formal education. Only 7 of 51 of those whose education did not include college matriculation expressed the slightest concern about the man's responsibility for the woman's satisfaction. But fears of erectile inadequacy were expressed by every member of the group over 40 years of age regardless of the level of education.

It was discovered inadvertently that drugs used for other purposes, and having the normally undesirable side effect of suppressing the sex drive, slow down the action enough to prevent premature ejaculation. Prozac (fluoxetine hydrochloride), an antidepressant and treatment for obsessive-compulsive disorder (OCD), turns out to be effective. The action of Prozac and the tricyclic antidepressants (TCAs) is to increase the action of serotonin at the synapses (nerve junctions).[21] Serotonin acts as a neurotransmitter when it is released at the synapse, and after performing its function is reabsorbed for reuse or breakdown. Prozac and similarly acting drugs prevent the "reuptake" as it is called, thus increasing the available concentration of the neurotransmitter at the synapse. A high level of serotonin, although stimulating for some people, tends indirectly to reduce sexual desire and performance, a desirable or undesirable side effect of Prozac depending on the individual. Prozac is reported to have severe negative side effects in some users.

The full story on serotonin is not clear. Part of the action is a closely related nerve hormone, melatonin, which suppresses sexual development, desire, and activity. Melatonin is formed in the pineal of the brain by an enzyme that converts one of the breakdown products of serotonin to melatonin. Both serotonin and melatonin have circadian rhythms. Serotonin peaks in the daytime, and by nightfall the formation of melatonin begins to climb, peaking around midnight. Melatonin is sold as a natural product in health food stores as a sleeping pill, and is also touted as a cure for jet lag.

Another of Masters and Johnson's phallic fallacies is the fear of dire consequences from excessive ejaculation, a fear that is surprisingly common. The most concern is about harm from masturbation. Masters and Johnson's conclusions were derived from a study group of 312 men among whom the frequency of masturbation ranged from once a month to two or three times a day. Tales of horror from the past, purveyed largely by religious zealots warning that blindness, insanity, or other mental derangements would result from masturbation, established a persistent phobia in the public mind despite physicians' repeated assurances that frequent ejaculation from either sexual intercourse or masturbation has no harmful effects mentally or physiologically. Physical and physiological harm is prevented by the fact that the frequency of ejaculation is self-limiting through sheer exhaustion or failure to respond to stimulation.

Several years ago there was a search on for antiandrogens, with one aim being to find a treatment for prostate cancer. The female hormone progesterone has weak antiandrogen effect, so a search was made for potent orally active progestins. A synthetic derivative of progesterone called Depo-Provera, produced by the Upjohn Company, was introduced as a treatment of endometrial and renal carcinoma.[22] When it was found that one of the many side effects was to cause changes in libido, the drug came to be used, under a physician's supervision, to reduce sex drive and erotic fantasies of men with a record of sexual molestation of minors. In some cases of convicted or confessed offenders, the court dispensed lenient sentences in return for an agreement to receive Depo-Provera treatment. In the Roman Catholic Church scandal in the 1990s during which some priests were accused of molesting boys and girls, it was reported that some of the alleged offenders were given injections of Depo-Provera as part of their treatment.

The future may see a choice of several drugs to reduce libido, which may be useful in treatment of some sex offenders, but unfortunately, there is little chance of finding a drug that will be effective as a preventive or cure. The motivation of sexual molesters, especially rapists, is generally believed to be more than sexual desire, often a compulsion to exert power or even release of anger.

Penile Proportions

Women are not the only ones who worry about the size and shape of their sexual attributes. When June Reinisch, then director of the Kinsey Institute, was asked what problems people were most anxious about when it comes to sex, she said, "Penis size is a real American male concern . . . [they] are suicidal about it." When women are asked about it, they don't think it's that important. "It's way low on their list," says Reinisch.[23] The trouble is, women don't tell that to men, so all but a few ponderously endowed men with egos to match go through life imagining the worst. If women could realize that men's worry about the adequacy of their apparatus is a common closet anxiety, they would reassure their partners instead of unknowingly fuel their anxiety with deadly silence.

Sydney Biddle Barrows, the "Mayflower Madam," tells how her New York escort service kept notes on clients:

> . . . if a man was very well endowed, we would note this fact with the code LP. (The original designation was BD, but we changed it when I realized that if we were ever raided by the police, those letters might be interpreted as a reference to bondage and discipline, which was definitely not a service we provided.)[38]

What difference did it make to the escort girls?

> . . . when a client was more generously endowed than most, some of the smaller girls would refuse to see him. As for the age-old debate as to whether size makes any difference to a woman's sexual fulfillment, most of our girls agreed with Ginny that "it's the singer, not the song. "[38]

Ernest Hemingway, in *A Moveable Feast*, relates how F. Scott Fitzgerald told people that his neurotic wife, Zelda, said he had a small penis.[24] "Zelda said that the way I was built I would never make any woman happy. . . ." Hemingway claims that he took Fitzgerald into the toilet for a comparative inspection, and reassured him: " 'You're perfectly fine,' I said, 'You are O.K. There's nothing wrong with you.'

'But why would she say it?'

'To put you out of business. Zelda just wants to destroy you.' " Hemingway explained to Fitzgerald that it only seemed that way because he was looking down at it from above. Hemingway tried to further reassure Fitzgerald by taking him on a tour of the Louvre to view the Greek statues. "[I]t's not basically the question of the size in repose. It's the size it becomes. . . ," Hemingway told him.[25]

Zelda also questioned Hemingway's virility. "No one is as masculine as you pretend to be," she told him. In fact, Hemingway was strong, handsome, and tough, but in view of his calculated macho performances, he may have been tormented with the demon of inadequacy. Says biographer Jeffrey Meyers, "Hemingway always made the adolescent association between heavy drinking and masculinity. . . ."[26]

Cosmetic surgery to enlarge the penis is an expanding business. Surgeons can make the penis larger in diameter or longer. A newspaper advertisement carrying the headline MEN ONLY says, "Most patients achieve 2" in additional length. Surgery requires about one hour, with immediate results." The ad further says, "*Us Magazine* reports that [this doctor] has completed surgery on over 20 major entertainers, movie stars and recording artists." There you have it. If it's good enough for celebrities, there's no need to be squeamish about you (or your boyfriend) going for it, too, if size is a real problem. In the April 1, 1996, issue of a large metropolitan newspaper there were eight advertisements by doctors and clinics that specialized in treatment of male problems. Appropriately, such ads are usually in the sports section of a newspaper.

The cost of a penile lengthening operation will range up to $5000 to $6000, including the operating room, anesthesiologist fee, and all postoperative care. But there have been numerous complaints. In 1996, a physician who had used a high-profile marketing campaign with offices in several major cities was suspended by his state's medical board. The physician, a urologist, was quoted in 1994 as saying that he did 150 penis enlargement operations a month. At least 37 malpractice suits had been filed against the physician. Penile enlargement operations consist of injections of fat to increase the diameter, and the cutting of a ligament to lengthen the penis. Some of the patients complained about intense pain, noticeable scars, and loss of feeling. Dr. Mark Litwin, a professor of urology and public health at UCLA, was quoted as saying that penile enlargement surgeries are still considered experimental. "Most everyone at any major medical institution has seen at least a handful of disastrous complications from this procedure," he said. "Patients should approach it with the greatest of caution."[27]

DOING SIXTY

Nobody wants to get old, but everyone agrees that it's better than the alternative. So barring a catastrophe, it's part of your future. Psychologists, sociologists, sexologists, writers, researchers, survey specialists, film directors, and talk show entertainers produce a running sideshow of every sexual life-style and problem conceivable among young and middle-aged men and women. But from the time of pioneering studies by Alfred C. Kinsey beginning in 1938, very few sex specialists have given any attention to sex after 60. Kinsey recorded data on over 5000 men of whom only 126 were men past 60. Why? Masters and Johnson put it this way: "Victorian influence upon our society has decreed for years that the aging male possesses little or no socially accepted sexuality."[28] They neglected to say that society's view of older women is much the same. Sex is for kids, young studs and fillies, sexual acrobats, and oversexed middle-aged wanna-bes. In 1920, Walter Pitkin wrote a book, *Life Begins at Forty*, trying to console 40-year-olds who felt they were over-the-hill. In 1987, Saul Rosenthal wrote *Sex Over Forty* giving specific instructions for making love for those who thought they were past the age of virility and had lost it.

The experts recoil from even thinking that there are a lot of old men and women out there doing it, what it's like, how they can do it better, what their problems are, and what they can do about them. But that is changing, if for no other reason than the growing number of older people in the population. Sexagenarians are in their 60s, and their numbers are increasing. So are the septuagenarians (70s), the octogenarians (80s), the nonagenarians (90s), and everyone else beyond the so-called prime of life. People in the United States and some of the European countries are having fewer babies and growing older, leading inevitably to an increasingly higher proportion of older people in the population. In the United States there are roughly 19 persons over 65 for every 100 persons between 18 and 64, and the ratio of older people is expected to increase sharply when the crop of postwar baby boomers reaches 65 in about 2030.[29]

Women lead the pack because they generally live longer than men. In 1975, there were only 69 men for every 100 women over the age of 65, and the ratio was expected to decline in 25 years to 65 per 100, at which time there will be 6.5 million more women than men. The ratio may not change much beyond that, but as the population increases, the numerical surplus of women will increase. Women are more apt to be widowed, to live alone, and to have a decreased income. However, older women tend to become more engaged in social activities such as churches, clubs, and community groups than men. Often a widowed woman must take financial responsibility for the affairs her husband formerly handled. Half of all millionaires are women, many of them managing the estates left by their husbands. Older women also tend to have more friends than older men, and to be more involved in family relationships. Men are more apt to desire and rely on a single intimate relationship. Older men and women tend to retain the same social status that they achieved in middle age except for variables such as income. The men, although not as active socially as women, are more likely to retain much of their former social status and to have more opportunities for sexual relationships than women.

A too-obvious feature of life is that the physiological, physical, and sexual abilities of men and women change throughout their lives. In men, the changes are usually gradual. The peak in vigor is reached in early manhood, then there is a gradual deterioration beginning to be noticeable in midlife along with a decline in testosterone output, followed by accelerating decline as age progresses. In women the sequence is much the same but with a dramatic change in physiology at menopause, marked by a sharp drop in estrogen output which, however, is often medically corrected by hormone replacement.

These changes over time in men and women are accompanied by important, but often unrecognized and largely unappreciated, changes in personality in the later years that have a significant effect on their sex lives.[30] Several studies made of sex roles of older people are summarized in a review by Douglas Kimmel in *Adulthood and Aging*. The studies consistently showed a shift in sex-role behavior with aging, men becoming increasingly submissive, and women becoming increasingly authoritative. Men tend to "mellow," to become less contentious, more submissive, accommodative, and less aggressive. Women tend to become more domineering, sharper, resolute, impatient, assertive, and sometimes a bit "bossy." These changes do not occur in all men and women to an appreciable extent, and when they do, they may be slight and in only one or a few characteristics. There are feisty old men, and charming old women. However, the shifts in sex roles, when they occur, are apt to be accentuated by the man's declining general vigor in the face of the woman's continued high level of vitality at the same age bracket. The unfortunate confluence of these personality characteristics, at a time in life when one or the other partner may need the reassurance of earlier expectations, can have a devastating effect on sexual life, and accounts in part for the occasional surprising and apparently unaccountable separations and divorces in later life. The woman may have developed independent interests, and the man may yearn for the attractions, vanished intimacy, and feminine tenderness of former years, and he may be attracted to younger women. There is a theory that a man's desire for younger women is an evolutionary heritage derived from the urge to maximize his genetic progeny. In any case, the increasingly divergent differences between men and women call for a high degree of mutual understanding and flexibility.

As a man gets older, the particular age depending on the age and perspective of the observer, he is generally thought of as having entered the stage of life in which he no longer has any interest in or capability for sex. In the words of Masters and Johnson, "The fallacy that secondary impotence is to be expected as the male ages is probably more firmly entrenched in our culture than any other misapprehension."[31] One of the best-known exam-ples in vindication of Masters and Johnson's assertion is the venerable senator Strom Thurmond of South Carolina. At the age of 66, Thurmond, a physical fitness fanatic, married a 22-year-old beauty queen with whom he had four children. At the age of 93, he boasts a combination of vigor and virility that is legendary on Capitol Hill.[32] His stamina is commemorated by a Sears Roebuck Thumper baseball bat that sits atop the mantel in the Senate Republican cloakroom. The display memorializes the late Texas Senator John Tower's earthy remark when Thurmond was in his 70s and siring children with his wife, still in her 20s: "When he dies, they'll have to beat his pecker down with a baseball bat to close the coffin lid."[39]

Another classic vindication of Masters and Johnson's observation is the 72-year-old grandfather, Bill Goodwin, of Costa Mesa, California, who transformed his home into a meeting place, known as the Panther Palace, for about 200 couples who gather regularly for partner-swapping and potluck suppers. "I can go four, five, or six girls in one night," boasts Goodwin. A retired truck driver and carpenter, Goodwin keeps physically fit with exercises, and did much of the work on the Panther Palace himself, including a 40-person Jacuzzi heated to 100 degrees. Goodwin says his guests come from all professions and are mostly from southern California, but some are visitors from other states. They range in age, he says, from "generation X-ers" to octogenarians. The oldest lady was 84. "She wasn't too bad, you know," says Goodwin, "helluva nice little party gal."[33]

Still, on average, it would be unrealistic to try to fit an older man into the Procrustean bed of a young stud. At the age of 20, the average angle of erection is 10% above the horizontal, and by age 70 declines to as much as 25% below the horizontal. At 70, the average sperm count is only half what it was at 35.[34] Masters and Johnson made a study of the effect of age. In a young man, full erection develops within 3 to 5 seconds after any form of sexual stimulation. The reaction time increases with increasing age; generally, the older a man is, the longer it takes, and he may lose it before penetration. But a partial compensation is that after penetration an older man can usually last longer than a younger man before ejaculation. If there is an interruption that causes a man's penis to go flaccid, a young man can normally regain a full erection quickly, several times if necessary. If a man over 60 attains a full erection, and loses it before ejaculation, he may have trouble returning to full erection at all. During ejaculation, a young man will expel his seminal fluid with a force sufficient to propel it 12 to 24 inches. By age 50, the force is reduced to propelling the semen an average of 6 to 12 inches, and as he gets older, the expelled seminal fluid may become merely a flow or seepage. After ejaculation, the penis of a young man usually remains rigid for considerable time; after he reaches 60 or 70, detumescence is almost immediate, and his penis returns to its original flaccid, unstimulated state within seconds.[18]

Because a man is increasingly prone to impotence with increasing age, and a woman ordinarily remains fully capable, although she usually secretes less vaginal fluid, a special responsibility falls on the woman to stimulate him into reasonably normal action. And it's the responsibility of both to talk with each other to determine each other's needs. If they have lived a life of sexual inhibition, embarrassment, and reticence, or if a man has been a lousy lover all of his life, they may find it hard to adjust to their new roles. It will usually be easier for the woman than the man to take the initiative.

The great first century Roman authority on the art of love, Publius Ovidius Naso, usually called simply Ovid, was married three times and had many affairs. He wrote from experience to women of all ages in what some people refer to as a "seducer's manual" or a "guide to infidelity," in his book of poetry, *The Art of Love*:[35]

> What you blush to tell is the most important part. Let every woman know herself, and enter into love's engagement in the position most suited to her charms. If a woman has a lovely face, let her lie on her back. If she prides herself upon her hips, let her display them to the best advantage. Melanion placed Atalanta's legs on his shoulders; if your legs are as beautiful as hers, put them in the same position. If you are short, let your lover be the stallion. . . . If your thighs are still

lovely with the charm of youth, if your breasts are flawless, lie aslant across your couch, and don't be ashamed to let your hair drift unbraided around your shoulders. If the labors of Lucina [goddess of childbirth] have left their mark, then like the swift Parthian, turn your back to the encounter. Love has a thousand postures; the simplest and the least tiring is to lie on your right side. . . . So then, my dear ones, feel the pleasure in the very marrow of your bones; share it fairly with your lover, while saying pleasant, naughty things. . . .

Emperor Augustus, who became a "family values" crusader, took a dim view of Ovid, and used his morality movement as an excuse to ban the popular rogue from Rome. Ovid was exiled for the rest of his life to an isolated military post on the Black Sea at the outlet of the Danube. Apparently the real reason for the Emperor's action was a mysterious high-level scandal during which Ovid was given a choice between silence or death. Writer Diane Ackerman speculates that Augustus's wife took a fancy to him, in which case Ovid would have been at risk to say either yes or no.[36] But historian Kiefer said that Ovid's fate was linked to Augustus's daughter, Julia.[37]

The Kama Sutra of Vatsyayana describes numerous common, uncommon, and seemingly difficult positions, as well as various other forms of sexual practices.

Love did not become a lost art through the centuries, and the writers of countless volumes of sex manuals from Ovid to the present have provided increasingly explicit instructions for eager lovers. But in the end, men and women must find their own way through the intricate maze of making love. Exchange of thoughts, questions, ideas, experimentation, and consideration of mutual needs and desires are keys to soaring the elysian heights of sexual pleasure. Increasingly, openness about sexual matters is replacing the reticence and embarrassment that inhibited former generations. Unfettered exchange of ideas and information will free people from their inhibitions. It will lead to better relationships and better sex.

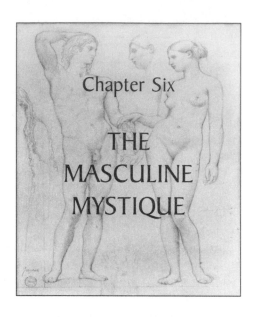

Chapter Six

THE
MASCULINE
MYSTIQUE

When Betty Friedan wrote about the yearnings, frustrations, and buried anger of millions of women in her book *The Feminine Mystique*, which appeared in 1963, a throng of inspired women took bold steps over the threshold into a world that seemingly deified thousands of years of male dominance and subjugation of women.[1] An angry Gloria Steinem lashed out at men for dominating the world, hoping with the sting of her words to embolden women to whip their tormenters into docility and equality.[2] Indeed, women upset the macho applecart to a remarkable degree in the span of a few decades.

Unfortunately, the answer to "empowerment" gained momentum so quickly and slickly that it left a crucial element largely out of the equation, namely, sex and mating. Half of all people who marry get divorced, some several times. Based on estimates ranging from 20% to 40% for extramarital affairs, all is not devoted love and affection in the wonderful world of opportunity, position, and power.[3] Friedan, in *The Second Stage*, 20 years after her earlier book, *The Feminine Mystique*, writes of unsolved problems. The biological clock is turned backwards, she reminds us, requiring women to have children—if they are going to have them at all—while still in the upward mobility phase of their careers. Friedan quotes a medical student, "I work thirty-six hours in the hospital, twelve off. How am I going to have a relationship, much less kids, with hours like that?"[3a]

The masculine mystique is the counterpart of the feminine mystique at the beginning of the women's movement, a stereotype patterned after society's image. Friedan says that in the first stage of the women's movement, the feminine mystique "defined women solely in terms of their relation to men as wives, mothers and homemakers." But she continues, "we sometimes seemed to fall into a *feminist* mystique, which denied that core of women's personhood that is fulfilled through love, nurture, home." Similarly, the masculine mystique can be described as the domineering, abusive, insensitive, woman-hating oppressor of women, caricatured by Germaine Greer, who says in *The Female Eunuch*, "Women have very little idea of how much men hate them."[4]

Men view with mostly unexpressed bewilderment the changes they see taking place in their relationships with women and the workaday world. They see with double vision through the murky chaos of shifting values and demands on their psyche. The rites of passage from boy to manhood have been constant for generations beyond counting. Sam Keen, in *Fire in the Belly: On Being a Man*, boils the traditional rites of passage down to war, work, and sex. "A Martian anthropologist," says Keen, "would find men encouraged to fight, drink, brawl, defend their honor, strive without ceasing, and risk life and limb in order to prove their manhood."[5]

The ascendency of women from subservience to equality, or in some cases dominance, may cause panic in the soul of a man who envisioned from boyhood the time when he would be called on to learn how to face the enemy and kill him without flinching—to kill or be killed—often the inevitable outcome of combat (we've often seen in politics the value of earning and the price for failing that rite of passage). Our young man is confused about how he can demonstrate his manhood by his dream of striving competitively

The Romans erected numerous sculptures of phalluses in honor of the god Priapus, who personified male procreative power. Modern phallic symbols represent creative power in more varied and subtle ways, commonly as campus clock towers or campaniles, which symbolize the power of the mind or knowledge, or as church steeples, spires, or towers in celebration of the power of the Almighty.

with every fiber of nerve and every molecule of testosterone to climb the peak of accomplishment to total dominance. He is vainly trying to read the shifting compass of women's desires for sex and work, desperately trying to decide between gonads and gut how to fulfill his rite of passage in relationship to women. The subliminal questions spin in his mind, should he fuck or fight? Or neither? Is work a goal or a refuge?

Says Betty Friedan in 1993, thirty years after her seminal book, *The Feminine Mystique*:

> Much is being said among American women today about the strange dearth of vital men. I go into a town to lecture, and I hear about all the wonderful, dynamic women who have emerged in every field in that town. But frequently, whatever the age of the woman, she says, "There don't seem to be any men. The men seem so dull and gray now. They're dreary, they're flat, they complain, they're tired."

"And," Friedan added, "if they're my age, they're dead."[6]

"I want a girl like the girl who married dear old dad," is a lost refrain. But the cavernous vacuum it left in the brain echoes questions asked by anthropologist Margaret Mead almost half a century ago in *Male and Female: A Study of the Sexes in a Changing World*.[7]

> Have we overdomesticated men, denied their natural adventurousness, tied them down to machines that are after all only glorified spindles and looms, mortars and pestles and digging sticks, all of which were once women's work? Have we cut women off from their natural closeness to their children, taught them to look for a job instead of the touch of a child's hand, for status in a competitive world rather than a unique place by a glowing hearth?

To our man in a quandary, women often seem to give mixed signals that he can, and often does, misinterpret. When ravishingly beautiful young women display their breasts and cleavages barely short of the nipples, and shout "exploitation," can it be Orwellian doublethink? It's widely believed that men generally have a stronger sex drive than women, although the future will tell whether this is an artifact of our culture. In any case, cockteasing

Angeline, a billboard personality. A caricature of what is supposed to be the male view of women as sex objects. Photo by Lawrence Lombardis, courtesy of Angeline, Inc.

can be more honestly called exploitation of men, the more so that men demonstrably like being titillated.

The business of titillating has thrived for years in topless bars, honky-tonks, and swanky nightclubs. It reached a new pinnacle of popularity and profitability in tony watering holes like Rick's Cabaret in Houston, which became the first publicly traded strip-tease club in the history of the stock market with an initial offering of 1.6 million shares on NASDAQ.[8] On a busy midweek night, as many as 300 women, each an independent contractor, may show up to bare their breasts. Depending on the number of $20 bills customers tuck under their G-strings, the women can earn as much as $300 a day in tips. Says Paulita Romero, a 26-year-old performer at Rick's. "I'm here to tease 'em, not to please 'em." Her work paid for her education at Christian University, where she earned a degree in psychology.

The kind of sexual relationship men and women have, whether in a society dominated by men or in a milieu of equality, is the product, in large degree, of their ancestral heritage. Not that all relationships are a stereotype fixed in evolutionary time. Psychologist David Buss, in his book *The Evolution of Desire*, makes it clear that the human species has a repertoire of mating strategies, the choice depending on goals and circumstances.[9] Male strategies differ from female strategies, and the tactics of each differ depending on whether they are looking for long-term or short-term sexual relationships. There are differences in psychology between men and women, one of the most pronounced of which, Buss finds, is their view of prospective mates. Men want fidelity in their women but crave variety for themselves. Women want men with resources who can provide for them and their offspring. Again, these are generalities, not specific for any man or woman.

Love and mating are as apt to be on a bed of thorns as a bed of roses. Despite the romantic allure of the poet's rhapsodizing refrain, conflict is the norm, and most of the causes have their roots in the remote prehuman past, for each of us is a living encyclopedia of our ancestral evolutionary journey. The most mischievous mating tactics of men and women are those that have the strongest emotional impact, located in the most primitive parts of the brain.

The rage of a man whose wife cheats on him is the fury of males throughout the animal kingdom, who expend enormous energy in strategies, and engage in violence when they must, to protect their paternity. The male damselfly inserts a plug of glue into the genital opening of his mate to foil rivals, and the male spiny-headed worm not only plugs the female's genital opening with cement after mating, but will render rival males impotent by plugging their genital openings during homosexual rape. The iguanid lizard holds off rivals by remaining coupled with his mate, with the aid of a barbed penis, for hours, and the sea lion, which guards his harem night and day, attacks bold bachelors with a viciousness that may be fatal to the intruders.

An enormous amount of energy must be expended to raise a hominid child to puberty. If his mate is impregnated by another male, he will have to devote his energy and resources to raising a child that has another male's genes. In humans, the emotional drive for defense against adultery is called jealousy, often leading to the most violent behavior known to mankind, including torture and murder. Customs and laws in many societies traditionally have little concern for the legal and human rights of an adulteress and her lover. Cheated husbands are generally granted leniency and wide latitude, even toleration for killing or maiming the offenders and torturing or killing their unfaithful wives. In some countries a man is legally within his rights to kill an unfaithful wife and her lover if he catches them in bed together. In the United States where murder may be punished by death or life imprisonment, killing for infidelity is often referred to as a "crime of passion," which juries are often persuaded to see as justifiable, and to vote for relatively light penalties.

If jealousy were the only obstacle to sexual adventure there would be more forgiveness, fewer divorces, and less marital violence. More devastating than jealousy is the ego-shattering shame, ridicule, and loss of status of the husband. His humiliation is aggravated by his anger at being deceived and the knowledge or suspicion that he was the last to find out about it. According to Buss, a woman who engages in casual sex typically beds down with a man of higher status than her mate, but even if of lower status, it is the final put-down that erodes any remaining shred of the betrayed husband's self-esteem. The cumulative emotional blow is greater and more devastating than the intense but less permanent fury of a man being refused sex after being led to expect it, and is probably comparable to a woman's psychological trauma from date rape. Women underrate the ferocity of a mate's mental and emotional turmoil from infidelity, probably because women traditionally are more tolerant of infidelity by men (some women say that today, because they are more economically independent, they are now less likely to be tolerant of infidelity). Men underrate the fear, anger, and shame of women who are raped, probably because men are less apt to be resentful, and are certainly less fearful, of aggressive sex by women.

In the fabled harems of the Middle East and the Orient, some of the eunuchs who guarded the wives or concubines were capable of getting an erection, depending on the method of emasculation and the age of the victim.[10] They were not thought of as a threat and in some cases were valued for being able to keep the women contented without threatening the owner's paternity. But any virile man caught messing around would face instant death, as would any suspected wife or concubine.

Men are notorious risk takers. They are willing to take great risks for casual sex. All men know this, so married men engage in precautionary strategies to guard against cheating. They are always on the alert for mischievous flirting, they check on their mate's whereabouts and activities, and they become jealous and suspicious of unusual friendliness between their mate and another man. In the present as in the past, the ancestral urge to spread his seed around compels a man to seek casual sex as well as sex with a committed mate. More men than women seek casual sex. The fact that there are more men looking for sex than there are attractive, willing women accounts at least in part for the prevalence of prostitution, especially in societies where polygamy is practiced and keeping mistresses as well as wives by affluent men keeps some of the most attractive women out of circulation. The Emir of Kuwait is reported to marry a virgin every Thursday night and divorce her on Friday morning.[11]

Stories abound of philandering cocksmen. Frank Sinatra is said to have dubbed John F. Kennedy "cocksman emeritus," a title Sinatra himself might be proud to have.[12] The conventional view is that philandering cocksmen are largely responsible for the high rate of extramarital sex. But it takes two to tango. For every adulterer there is an adulteress. Why so much infidelity? When protohuman apes branched off from the line that led to us instead of chimpanzees, our closest relatives, our humanlike ancestors developed far different mating strategies than those of our cousins, the chimps. Both female and male chimps are openly promiscuous. A female in heat has no compunction against receiving sperm from innumerable males among her acquaintances. The more circumspect behavior of protohuman females was not for lack of sexual desire, but for the need of a committed mate to help with the responsibilities of rearing her children. Why, then, do some women stray from the marital bed? Does this behavior also have origins in the dim and distant past?

There are several reasons why females may have sought or accepted the advances of men other than their regular sexual partners. Resources were always in variable supply, depending on the season, vagaries of weather, availability of game, and the success of the female's regular provider. According to anthropologist Helen Fisher, exchange of sex for food or other favors became a time-honored custom.[13] Upward mobility may have been another reason. She may have found that her mate was, after all, an inadequate provider. Ever since females learned this strategy, women have had a strong preference for mating with, or marrying, men with status and resources. David Buss showed that, today, this is a universal quality desired by women throughout the world regardless of ethnicity.[14]

If a woman cheats on a mate to satisfy her material needs, she does so at some risk, so she is careful to do it surreptitiously unless she is ready to break with her mate for a new one under the belief that her co-cuckolder is looking for a permanent mate instead of casual sex—a risky assumption. However, it would be naive to assume that most women who commit adultery are simply looking for a permanent mate. Casual sex with men who have an extravagant life-style, physical attractiveness, or both, reflects a mating strategy unrelated to the desire for a permanent partner. If it's true, as some psychologists claim, that women who engage in casual sex typically choose men who are higher in status than their mates, the choice makes it probable that a young woman of reproductive age will get better genes for her progeny, a tactic made respectable by the ancient Spartans who urged husbands voluntarily to lend their wives to physically superior men. A similar practice was made legal in Rome where Julius Caesar was given the right to enjoy any wife in the realm.

Casual sex may have been a strategy among female ancestors to ensure a secondary source of support. Women must have known instinctively that a man is more apt to help provide for a woman and her child if he thinks the child is his progeny. Under trying circumstances, promiscuity would be good strategy to foster the belief among several men that each is the child's father. The idea that women are the passive victims of male sexual exploitation becomes mythical when women are seen to engage in fierce competition with each other for both casual and committed sex if qualified men are in short supply.

An emotion in women comparable to the fury of a betrayed man is her anger at sexual aggression, also a heritage of her ancient need to maximize her reproductive potential. In contrast to her male counterpart, who had nothing to lose by multiple mating except part of his abundant supply of sperm, the female when she became pregnant was committed, each time, to months extending into years of nourishing the growth and development of the child both before and after birth. It was to her advantage to be impregnated by a male selected as one who could help with resources or had promise of being a good provider. Many female animals other than humans show pronounced mate preferences, and will sharply, sometimes savagely, rebuff unwanted males. In humans, the need for a male mate who could be a provider became a biological imperative. As David Buss says, "Those in our evolutionary past who failed to mate successfully failed to become our ancestors."[9] The environment of our remote ancestors was mostly harsh and cruel. Women, if they were to become our ancestors, had to find men who showed signs that they would be willing to make a commitment to a long-term relationship. Most animals have comparatively little responsibility for the young after they are born, and in most species the young are able to fare for themselves immediately after birth. All mammals must suckle their young, but human babies require intensive care.

The existence of a preponderance of domineering men in positions of power, and their seeming reluctance to yield to women, apparently also has its roots in the evolutionary past. David Buss, in the most extensive survey ever conducted of men's and women's mating behavior, found that men of all cultures prefer beautiful, youthful women, and that women of all cultures prefer men with status and resources, or the potential for them, as long-term mates. Men know that being seen with beautiful, youthful women adds greatly to their status, and indirectly to their resources and power. Male protohumans having status and resources were apt to have power and dominance among their fellow protohuman apes, and their male human descendants with status are apt to possess power and dominance among their fellow humans. Humanoid males with those qualities were more apt to mate and have children than males who were seen by females as less qualified. In short, they were more apt to be our ancestors.

WHAT'S COMING

Now that women are gaining in position and power, will their success nullify the value of men's status and resources as a mating gambit? Again, Buss shows that women who achieve high position and power still prefer men of status and resources as marital partners. In the historical past, men have been seen as more aggressive then women, and this is attributed largely to their high testosterone output. In the present milieu of feminine upward mobility, men have become resigned to competition with women, and with benign good nature, sometimes for political reasons, help place them in positions of power. In the future, as women come closer to gaining equality, men will learn to compete with women as fiercely as they have traditionally competed with men. Many women have, and will continue to have, the ambition and drive to outdo many men in climbing to the pinnacle of success, power, and dominance. Women are not completely devoid of androgens. Tests show that when an individual, male or female, gains a position of power, their testosterone output increases. But the evolutionary heritage of men—testosterone-powered aggressiveness and drive for dominance—will continue to give men a competitive edge.

A prominent feature of the masculine mystique throughout all of known human history is the practice of men forming alliances with other men as in "all for one and one for all" in Alexandre Dumas's *The Three Musketeers*. The result is a proclivity for clubbiness, often with the formation of strong bonds. The purpose is to gain success in overcoming big game, dominance over other groups of men in warfare or business, or as often in the past, dominance and subjugation of women. Women also typically join together in organizations or clubs in which they form strong bonds, and it is rare for a man to seek entrance. But many men's clubs and organizations have been compelled to accept women, and the members have usually taken them reluctantly, kicking and screaming. When Shannon Faulkner applied for admission to the Citadel, an all-male military academy in South Carolina, she had to take her fight through the courts. After 2½ years of legal wrangling, the Supreme Court ruled that the Citadel, a tax-supported institution, could not deny her admission. In August, 1995, 20-year-old Shannon Faulkner became the first female cadet in the Citadel's 153-year history. But six days later, in the hospital, suffering from heat exhaustion and stress, she dropped out. She was said to be 20 pounds over the army's weight standard for cadets of her age and height. Four male cadets were also treated in the hospital, and 30 cadets were reported to have dropped out during or after hell week, a rugged ordeal intended, as the saying goes, to "separate the men from the boys." Several prominent feminists pronounced it a victory that a woman had gained her fight for admittance to the Citadel, but none of the male cadets expressed any regret at Faulkner's leaving.

The Citadel is one of two public all-male military colleges in the country. The other is the Virginia Military Institute (VMI). Both were sued for allegedly discriminating against women, and both are said to be working on alternative programs to keep women out. If the ruling against all-male public schools is upheld, the next female assault will have a better chance of success if several applicants join forces, instead of a lone female trying to hold her own against 2000 men. If they are successful, the walls of VMI will also crumble—to the dismay of the masculine horde steeped in tradition, a tradition that probably dates back to protohuman times, of troops emboldened by the unspoken loyalty and cohesion of male bonding, going forth to kill beasts or to battle the enemy in defense of the clan, rob neighbors for loot, or steal wives. Military academies will never be the same. Shaving the heads of male recruits may be prohibited as discriminatory, the ordeal of hell week with pushups and physical exercises to the limit of human endurance will be gauged by female standards, and separate women's restrooms will be installed in each dormitory. Some cadets will be more fascinated with females than fighting, spit and polish will succumb to antiperspirants, swearing will be according to the book under penalty of court martial, and dirty jokes will be more private.

But all this may not happen. The court said that states could keep tax-supported all-male schools if they have comparable schools for females. Virginia established a military program for women at Mary Baldwin College, and South Carolina started to plan a similar program. But U.S. government lawyers said that "separate but equal" is not acceptable, and that they would take the issue to the Supreme Court.

Not all women think that separate but equal is bad. Some urged the court to tread cautiously. Among them are Susan Estrich, a USC law professor; Diane Ravitch, former Assistant Education Secretary; and Lynne V. Cheney, former chairwoman of the National Endowment for the Humanities, who filed briefs on VMI's side. They ask, what about men's and women's prisons, and high school and college sports where "separate but equal" are taken for granted as acceptable and desirable? Closer to the dispute is the question of separate men's and women's colleges, an idea that finds support from many women. About 64,000 women and about 11,000 men are enrolled in single-sex colleges.[15]

According to a 1992 survey, one-third of the female board members of Fortune 1000 companies were graduates of women's colleges, although they account for only 4% of all college graduates. About 24% of the women serving in Congress graduated from women's colleges. First Lady Hillary Rodham Clinton attended Wellesley College in Massachusetts.

A gender problem that seemed to have been settled when nearly all states, over a period of time, abolished separate boy's and girl's high schools, leaves a nagging question: Is there uncompromising virtue in unisex education, or is there some obscure value in separate schools for boys and girls? Some scholars say that sexless learning, so-called coeducation, may not be fair to either boys or girls. Nearly half a century ago, Margaret Mead put the question this way, "In educating women like men, have we done something disastrous to both men and women . . .?"[7] According to some astute observers, when schoolmasters became obsolete, and "schoolmarms" took over, boys especially were the losers. Patricia Sexton is emphatic. In an article, "Schools Are Emasculating Our Boys," she suggests that we make the early education of our boys, "active, exploratory, problem solving, adventurous, and aggressive."[15a] Failure to recognize the differences in physiology, rates of development, mentality, behavior, and needs of boys and girls, may actually contribute to gross inefficiency and inequality in the educational system. Says Vance Packard in *The Sexual Wilderness*: "human fulfillment of our potentialities would seem to lie in the direction of working for a world in which males and females are equal as people and complementary as sexual beings."[16]

If the masculine mystique is a reflection of the past, is there in the present mating maelstrom a prediction of the future? Nothing is more constant than the increasing frequency of sex, but mating and reproductive habits are among the most culturally diverse features of human behavior. In much of the Eastern world mating behavior in the next century will not change at all, in gridlock with religious and cultural tradition. In much of the Western world mating behavior is changing at a pace that is knocking the pins from under mores, morals, and values of centuries. Until recently, virginity was highly prized by both men and women, and an essential requirement for marriage in the minds of many men. For one thing, virginity was a promising indication of future fidelity. Surveys on campuses today show virginity low on the list of what men seek in a future mate. In Sweden, other Scandinavian countries, and parts of northern Europe, virginity is irrelevant, and this is rapidly becoming the norm in the United States. Premarital sex is no longer under a blanket of secrecy. It's more commonly without a blanket, and is probably already as socially acceptable as kissing and petting were when these quaint practices were indulged in privately after sundown. Sexual practices in Sweden have long been a harbinger of acceptable behavior in other parts of the Western world. Many Swedish children are born out of wedlock, and divorce is increasingly common. Indications are that the trend will continue in other parts of the Western world for a combination of reasons, chief of which is the changing life-style.

A persistent problem for which society may find only a partial solution is the prevalence of male violence against women. British feminist Rosalind Miles maintains that it is not testosterone but masculinity that drives men to violence. She calls it "the terrible tyranny of the penis." She maintains that "the truth of male violence is that maleness itself provides the key." But not all men are violent. The dual effects of testosterone-driven aggressiveness are the yin and yang of human sexuality. The same irresistible force drives a man to create or destroy, to reform or corrupt, to build empires or tear them down, to be generous or a thief, to be magnanimous or greedy, to be compassionate or violent, to save lives or kill, to make love or rape. Some of the dichotomy is innate, but much of the direction it takes is determined by cultural and environmental circumstances. They are starkly evident in the Pleistocene lyrics of rapper Ice Cube's *Gangsta Gangsta*:[17]

I'm the motherfucker that you read about,
Taking a life or two,
That's what the hell I do,
If you don't like the way I'm living,
Fuck you!

A civilized man with the same testosterone drive might be a physician:

I'm the othermucker you read about,
Saving a life or two,
That's what on earth I do,
If you're in pain the way you're living,
I'll pray for you!

It's well known that in both men and monkeys testostcrone rises to high levels during combat and after victory, and recedes to low levels after a defeat. This is true whether the conflict is in battle or purely mental, for example, on the chessboard or in the boardroom. Surprisingly, testosterone levels rise and fall in spectators as well as in the participants, depending on which side they favor. Psychologist James Dabbs at Georgia State University sent graduate students into sports bars in Atlanta to take saliva samples from rabid soccer fans of the finalists, Brazil and Italy, during the televised 1994 championship match of the World Cup tournament. The students took saliva samples just before the game started, and again after Brazil trounced Italy. Testosterone rose in 11 of the 12 Brazilian fans by 28%, and fell by 27% in 9 Italian fans who remained from those who were so depressed that they left before samples could be taken.[18] Clearly, testosterone is more closely related to competition and the feeling of competitiveness than to violence. Dabbs had shown earlier that trial lawyers have higher testosterone levels than other lawyers.

Dominance is not necessarily associated with physical violence. The duality of masculinity is puzzling to men and misunderstood by many women. Writer Paul Liben quotes a feminist, "What's happening to men today? They're either wimps or barbarians." Liben referred to C. S. Lewis's *The Necessity of Chivalry* in which he argued that males tend to fall into "two sections, those who can deal with blood and iron (in war) but cannot be 'meek in hall' (around women and children) and those who are 'meek in hall' but useless in battle." In other words, men are shelved into categories: either barbarians or wimps. Liben contrasts O. J. Simpson, a tough, hard-hitting football hero, accused wife-beater, and suspected but acquitted murderer, with Jimmy Carter, who builds houses for the poor and is a gentle, compassionate negotiator who even persuaded the government to give a criminal dictator freedom to avoid violence and bloodshed. Liben declares, "In short, our culture has succumbed to a pernicious lie—that society must choose between meekness and sternness as suitable ideals for young males to follow."[19]

One scenario for the future is that the macho man of classical image is on the verge of extinction. Innovative technologies have so altered the work requirements of both men and women and so influenced the aspirations of all people that life-styles are fast changing and will dramatically change in the future. Two-provider families and single-parent families will be the norm, and they will require vast changes in life-style. the one-upmanship game of keeping up with the neighbors will become relatively less important, and devoting time and attention to children will become relatively more important. Breast feeding may be greatly desired, but for a husband at home alone with the baby, a bottle is better. However, a breast pump may be even better, enabling a woman to produce and leave a supply of milk for the baby while she is away.

According to this hypothetical scenario, both men and women will compete as ferociously in the marketplace as ever, but there will be more cooperation and more sharing in their married lives. More husbands and wives will each work part-time. Men will share more in both housekeeping and caring for children, and together they will engage in a resurgence of nurturance that, paradoxically, will be increasingly vital in an era of cyberspace with its overwhelmingly kaleidoscopic messages and alluring attractions. The single-parent family will find life more difficult, hopefully alleviated by a public policy of nurturing its children at least as tenderly as it nurtures its so-called senior citizens.

However, the idyllic scenario of the sharing sexes ignores the reality of the goals and aspirations of men and women. Men are torn between the lust for intimacy and the compulsive need for freedom. The toddler, pulled one way and the other by the irresistible force of his nature, demands both mother love and escape from restraint. The grown man wants sex and female companionship, but he also wants freedom (as do women). He wants to explore in search of beckoning unfulfilled dreams. In short, he wants to escape. There are many ways to escape. Golf is a good way to escape because it can be stretched into a full day if you count the 19th hole. Hunting, fishing, the ball game, poker, hiking, biking, and rock climbing are escapes, not only from work, because work is also an escape. A day at the park with the kids can be a way to get out of washing the dishes or vacuuming. Couch potatoes take the easy route.

Men and women want to pursue goals, to accomplish, to achieve success and recognition. Many of the more responsible positions are incompatible with part-time work. They demand full-time focus, energy, and effort. The worker who diverts his or her attention from the tasks at hand is apt to be eclipsed by men or women who are on the job when they are needed. In the competitive race to the top, the guy on the ball will have the edge over the guy at the ball park. Demands at times will be excessive. There are many domineering, power-hungry bosses like the Hollywood movie mogul, Harry Cohn, president of Columbia Pictures, who was supposed to have said, "I don't get ulcers, I give 'em."[20]

Partners in a relationship featuring the "new father," when there is one, will be limited in the degree and nature of their sharing by the realities of the business of living.

The masculine mystique, molded eons ago by the genes of ghostly ancestors, is in transition but not in revolution. Modern man still embodies a legacy of the past, but it's not on a single track into the future. Masculinity takes various forms and options. Men will continue to seek multiple partners more eagerly than women. Some of them will seek casual sex with wives of other men, and some wives will be unfaithful, maybe more so than in the past. Men will strive for success, power, control, and dominance. Eventually, men will grant women equal opportunity because women seize it, but in the heat of competition when a state of sexual equilibrium is achieved, men will not grant women unequal advantage. The sexes will compete on equal terms. The yin and yang of masculinity will throw many men—and their feminine critics—off stride with misunderstanding. Men will be aggressively kind, considerate, compassionate, and creative, or aggressively cruel, vicious, violent, and destructive depending largely on how their families and society rear them and on genes that are unrelated to masculinity. The greater sensitivity and compassion of women will change the way society treats its children and the mentally, morally, and spiritually handicapped. However, the greater influence of women in public affairs will not eliminate the violence of wars because wars are not started by the troops, but by those who control political life—domineering men and women.

The masculine mystique of the historic past—still alive and thriving in much of the world—when men thought of their women as property and breeding stock, has disappeared in the Western world, gone the way of polygyny and slavery. The new masculine mystique, dating from the beginning of the modern feminist movement, retains the evolutionary legacy of testosterone, high level of activity, and aggressiveness. It will be easily recognized in the future because it will have changed very little—but bent by the feminist windstorm to enforce social and economic equality between the sexes.

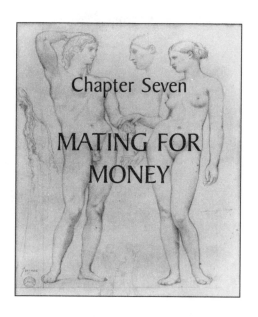

Chapter Seven

MATING FOR MONEY

The cliché that prostitution is the oldest profession may or may not be true, but it is almost certainly true that mating for food or favors, not just for fun, is one of the oldest play-for-pay sports. Anthropologist Helen Fisher in *The Sex Contract* tells us something of its origin. By 10 million years ago our protohuman ancestors experienced revolutionary changes in life-style. The female, like other primates, was sexually available at infrequent intervals, but at such times was highly promiscuous like our close primate relatives. But feeding and carrying the helpless human young caused motherhood to become a grind, so females increasingly needed males to help them raise the children. But how to get the males to help? The human female evolved into what Fisher says was a "female sex athlete" that brought gifts of food and favors. This development inevitably led to male–female bonding, a help-mate, sharing, and family—what Fisher calls the "sex contract"— more than 4 million years ago.[1]

We have it on good authority—the Bible and other early

documents—that prostitution was a thriving occupation in ancient times. Stories of hookers, courtesans, mistresses, and concubines, some of whom became wealthy, influential, or famous, enrich human history. In the Tigris–Euphrates Valley, where writing was invented, the Sumerians and their ancestors left a record of their cultural life and theology. Although the principal gods were all males, a powerful female god was the god of fertility, Inanna, later called Ishtar. She came to be identified with the planet Venus, and when she descended to earth, she was accompanied by amorous females and prostitutes. She had many lovers, and was noted for her power to arouse erotic impulses in men.

In the epic of Gilgamesh, one of the earliest pieces of literature—written on tablets by Sumerians and in final form in Akkadian, the main language of ancient Babylonia and Assyria, in about 2000 BC—the heroine is a prostitute.[2-4] Gilgamesh, the king of the city of Erech in the Tigris–Euphrates valley, is an undisciplined tyrant who ravages the city with his enormous sexual appetite. He demands to have sex with every bride before her husband can have her. The Erechites cry out in anguish to the gods and appeal to the mother-goddess Aruru for relief. She answers their entreaties by creating a man from mud, Enkidu, to rid them of the menace. Enkidu is a powerful man, naked and long haired, who lives among the wild beasts of the plain, devoid of all human relations. Before this brute of a man can be suitable to clash with Gilgamesh, he must be civilized, a task that falls to the lot of a woman. A temple prostitute takes off her clothing, and uses her attractions to seduce Enkidu. After six days and seven nights of intercourse, Enkidu is so weak that his knees buckle when he tries to chase game. Although he loses stature and physical strength he gains mentally and spiritually. The prostitute teaches him the social niceties of eating, drinking, and dressing. Now humanized, Enkidu is ready to engage Gilgamesh in his mission to subdue the tyrant and rid the city of his arrogant reign. They engage in a bitter fight, but after prolonged combat they suddenly quit, embrace, and become lifelong friends destined to join in heroic achievements.

We get insight into ancient prostitution in the Middle East

from a description in the Book of Genesis in which the story is told of Tamar, a daughter-in-law of Judah. Tamar had been given in marriage to Judah's first son, Er, but they had no children because Er was a wicked man, so God killed him. Whereupon Judah, in accordance with custom, ordered his second son, Onan, to marry Tamar to perpetuate the patriarch's seed. Onan was a rebellious young man who resented substituting for his deceased brother. When he "went in unto her," a euphemism for having sex with her, he "spilled it on the ground," the earliest record of *coitus interruptus* as a method of birth control. This so infuriated God that he took Onan's life too.[5]

Judah, by this time disenchanged with his daughter-in-law, sent her back to her family. Twice-widowed Tamar was humiliated and distraught at being left childless in a culture that mandated fertility, so she concocted a scheme to perpetuate the patriarch's seed. Upon learning that Judah had gone up to his flock of sheep to shear them, Tamar removed the widow's garb, donned her street robes, veiled her face, and sat in an open place along the road that Judah would take on his way home. Judah, taking Tamar to be a hooker, offered to send a kid from his flock if she would let him have her. Tamar agreed but cannily demanded his signet, bracelets, and staff as security.

When Judah was told three months later that his daughter-in-law was pregnant from whoring, he ordered her to be burned, but rescinded the judgment when Tamar presented him with the signet, bracelets, and staff. He blamed himself for not giving his third son to her in marriage as custom required. Tamar gave birth to twins as Judah's heirs.

It is evident from the story of Tamar that in those early days, hookers plied their trade along the byways, and that it was apparently the custom to hide their identity with subtly revealing veils. It's also evident that the family patriarch had the power of life and death over the conduct of family members, even widows, and that engaging in prostitution by family members justified the death penalty.

Some prostitutes had their own houses as described in the story of Rahab, a whore who had her place at the city wall of

Canaanite Jericho. Joshua, Moses's military aide who became commander in chief of the Israelites after Moses died, sent two spies to Jericho to get information on the city's defenses. The spies entered the city through Rahab's brothel, which was apparently allowed to receive outsiders. Rahab turned out to be a traitor and turncoat. She told the spies that her people, the inhabitants of Jericho, were frightened and dispirited, and she hid the spies from the Canaanite authorities in return for a promise that the Israelites would protect her and her relatives from harm when they took the city. Thus encouraged, Joshua ordered an attack. The walls of Jericho fell as if by a miracle, and the city was destroyed.[6]

Hosea was a prophet who preached in Israel, probably during 750 to 720 BC. God ordered him to marry an unfaithful woman to show by comparative example how much God loved the children of Israel despite their whoredom in taking other gods and drinking flagons of wine.[7] The woman given to Hosea was described as an adulteress, interpreted by some to mean that she was a harlot. But the most famous prostitute of ancient times was a woman, presumed by some to be Mary Magdalene, who washed Jesus's feet with her tears, dried them with her hair, kissed his feet, and anointed them with an ointment. Jesus used her as an example to his disciples of forgiveness.[8]

It would be hard to find any part of the world where prostitution was not a thriving industry. Marco Polo wrote of his 13th century visit to Kinsay (The City of Heaven), later Hang-chou:

> Certain of the streets have women of the town in such numbers that I dare not say how many, not only near the markets which are usually designated for their residence, but in every part of the city. They exhibit themselves splendidly attired and perfumed, in finely furnished houses with lines of waiting women. They are accomplished in all the arts of allurement, and are adept in the art of conversation with all sorts of people. Strangers who have once tasted their charms seem to become bewitched, and are so taken with their fascinating ways that they can never get them out of their minds. When they return home they tell people they have been to the City of Heaven, and their one desire is to get back there as soon as possible.[9]

The Greeks were the earliest of the ancients to leave a voluminous record of how they lived, loved, fought, and thought. Imaginative and creative with an unquenchable zest for life, even their gods were endowed with common as well as uncommon human foibles and lives spiced with innumerable erotic adventures. Prostitution was simply part of daily, or nightly, life. Brothels were virtually everywhere in Athens and other cities, and though they varied from unkempt and smelly hovels to those of higher quality, in general the price was right, being affordable to nearly everyone. The brothel whores were in the lowest stratum of society, but they contributed directly to the state through a brothel tax. Slightly higher in public esteem were the many streetwalkers, who would bargain with passersby, sometimes through an agent or maid.[10,11]

Some of the hetaerae, comparable to modern courtesans, were received in the highest circles and a few of them were indirectly influential in public affairs. Probably the most famous was Aspasia, who, through her beauty, intelligence, and social talents, managed to attract most of the important men of her time. Socrates saw her frequently. Pericles, a powerful statesman, became infatuated with her and divorced his wife to marry her. Her influence became so great that Plutarch credited her with instigating a war between Athens and Samos.

Demosthenes summed up the role of women of Greece: "Man has the hetairae for erotic enjoyment, concubines for daily use, and wives of equal rank to bring up children and to be faithful housewives." The great orator himself was said to have had children by a hetaera.

In Greece, as almost everywhere in ancient times, religion had a strong infusion of sexuality. In some regions of the ancient world, temples were built in honor of Aphrodite, the goddess of love and beauty. Temple prostitutes, called priestesses, performed sacred rites as a service to male worshipers. It was thought of as an act of communion with the gods, comparable in purpose to the Christian ritual of communion.[12] The idea was widely believed that women, at sometime in their lives, should offer themselves to the deity by presenting themselves at the temple. Priests, serving as the deity's emissary, would come to them in the darkness. The

Greek historian Herodotus, who lived in the 5th century BC, wrote of a custom among the Babylonians that he decried as wholly shameful. Every native woman of the country was required once in her lifetime to visit the temple of Aphrodite for the purpose of giving herself to a strange man. Once a woman took her seat, she was not allowed to leave until a man threw a silver coin into her lap and took her away. She was forbidden by law to refuse the first man to throw a coin, no matter what its value. According to Herodotus, ugly women, unfortunately, had to wait a long time, often for as long as three or four years.[13]

The sexual life of ancient Rome was even cruder and more extravagant than in Greece. The brothels, called *lupanaria*, were both within and outside the city walls. Many of them were near the Circus Maximus where the sadistic excitement of the games stimulated the passions of the customers. The brothels of Pompeii, a resort city, are well preserved, with lewd paintings on the walls still intact. The brothel prostitutes were virtually all slaves, bought and sold like slaves everywhere, many of them kidnapped. They were all registered with the state, a practice that began in early times. Some of the lupinaria were privately owned; others were public utilities owned by the state, in which the slave girls were offered for a small fee. During the persecution of Christians, girls and women considered attractive were sent to the lupinaria as slaves instead of being killed in the arenas.

According to Otto Augustus Wall in *Sex and Sex Worship*, the authorities encouraged the use of women, even if promiscuous, in order to check the popular vice of homosexuality, called "Greek love."[14] Prostitution was thought of as necessary and indulged in generally. The use of prostitutes was not considered adultery, which could only be committed with a married woman. Prostitutes of every conceivable rank were available: The *Quadrantariae*, whose fee was the smallest copper coin made; the *Gallinae*, who were professional thieves as well as prostitutes; the *Forariae*, country girls who displayed themselves at roadsides in hope of earning a little money; the *Diabolares*, whose fee was a diabolon (about two cents); the *Blitidae*, so called because they were usually drunk on Blitum, a cheap wine; the *Noctiliae*, or hookers who

The area surrounding the Colosseum in Rome was a favorite for brothels and prostitutes, who profited from the passions of the customers incited by the bloody games.

walked the streets at night; the *Copae* were the slave servant girls in taverns and inns, who could be hired by the guests as bedmates; the *Bustuariae*, who lived in cemeteries where they worked as professional mourners with prostitution as a sideline; the *Elicariae*, who were bakers' slave girls, were sent out on the streets to sell little cakes made in the shapes of male and female genitals that were used as sacrifices in the temples of Priapus and Venus, and moonlighted as prostitutes; the *Lupae*, or she-wolves, plied their trade in alleys or back-streets and lived in dilapidated shelters in the woods, under the arches (fornices) of the colosseum or temples, or in the ruins of buildings. The *Famosae* were daughters of families who engaged in prostitution to make extra money or simply because they enjoyed it. The highest rank were the *Delicatae*, courtesans or mistresses of wealthy patrons.

Slave girls were kept by taverns and shops, including bakers, bathhouses, barbers, and perfumers, for the entertainment of their customers and supplementary sources of income. The price could be as little as one-half cent. Unregistered freelanders of a higher quality—flute players and dancers who engaged in free love—did not count as prostitutes, so they did not have to register. A tax on prostitutes was levied during Caligula's reign, and later it was extended to brothels as well. As in all societies, before and since, prostitutes were not allowed to socialize with respectable girls and matrons.

Harems were a fixture in the Middle East and the Orient where potentates had legendary wealth and power and men were allowed to take as many wives as they could support. Romanticized versions depict women of the harem living a life of luxury, but in fact many of them were little more than slaves. In Egypt, according to Bullough and Bullough, the word for harem was synonymous with prison.[15] Some of the pharaohs had several harems in different parts of the kingdom. One can only speculate about the living conditions of Solomon's 300 concubines (in addition to his 700 wives) but a look at the gloomy harem cubicles at the Alhambra, the 13th to 14th century citadel of Moorish kings near Granada, Spain, belie the storybook life of comfort that harem wives were supposed to enjoy.[16]

In an earlier era of the United States the whorehouse was a prominent, and in many cases an accepted, part of the American scene. In small towns, the cathouse, if there was one, was in an unobtrusive location apart from the business and main residential parts of town. In cities of moderate size, there were sometimes several houses clustered along a street in an older, sometimes dilapidated, residential part of town comprising the "red-light" district. A red porch light served to identify and advertise the establishment as well as to prevent the embarrassment of a mistaken intrusion. Memories of these are reminiscent of districts in some of the modern European cities, for instance, Amsterdam. In larger cities in the United States, the houses were more apt to be converted downtown small hotels, apartments, or rooming houses, the locations of which could be learned by asking bartenders or taxi drivers.

Romanticized movie versions of frontier saloon madams and their friendly shady ladies were but a small facet of the largely vanished professional bordello business. A whorehouse in Texas known locally as the Chicken Ranch was more or less typical of the better establishments. Jan Hutson, in *The Chicken Ranch: The True Story of the Best Little Whorehouse in Texas*, gives an entertaining history of the place. It came to be called "the chicken ranch" after it converted to a poultry standard of barter exchange during the depression—a chicken for a screw.[17]

The Chicken Ranch was not the only whorehouse in Texas, nor in the rest of the country, although it lasted longer than most. San Antonio was said to have the largest red-light district in Texas, and there were many others. The Mustang Ranch still thrives in Nevada, where prostitution is legal. But the old-fashioned bordello has gone the way of the horse and buggy. The few remaining are nostalgic reminders of a time when lawmen were tough on the toughs but tolerant, even protective, of unlawful activity that was seen by the citizenry as criminally benign at worst and socially beneficial at best.

It should not be assumed, however, that the romanticized saloon bordellos and public-spirited cathouses on the outskirts of prairie towns represented the average prostitution business. There was plenty of sex for sale by streetwalkers, dance hall harlots, barroom hustlers, and in seedy back alley joints frequented by criminals of all kinds where customers were apt to get more of a screwing than they bargained for from the hoodlums and hangers-on. In the better-run towns it kept lawmen busy closing the joints or running the chippies out of town, often with a one-way ticket on the train or a bus with the advice, "Don't look back!"

In the more untamed parts of the country, treatment of unsuspecting clients was often vicious and violent. The largest and most boisterous red-light district in the country was along the Barbary Coast of San Francisco where saloons, gambling joints, deadfalls, dives, and brothels of every description thrived from the time of the discovery of gold at Sutter's Mill on the American River in 1848 until its gradual demise between 1914 and 1917 when a reasonably honest new mayor got the help of William Randolph Hearst's *Examiner*, and several crusading preachers. During the heyday of the Barbary Coast, unwary customers were regularly shanghaied by being given Mickey Finns (drinks spiked with knockout drops, typically tobacco juice, or chloral hydrate in the more sophisticated joints), leaving the victims to wake up with a headache and a job on the crew of a freighter on its way to China or other distant ports (crew members were hard to come by because many arriving sailors jumped ship on arrival to rush to the gold country in the Sierras, hoping to strike it rich).[18]

Prostitution was the big moneymaker of the Barbary Coast saloons, of which there were hundreds. Some of the establishments were multistory structures lined with dozens of curtained cubicles where the girls could entertain their customers in semiprivacy. The quality of service in San Francisco ranged from that of the streetwalkers, the so-called cribs, or stalls, waiter girls, decoys in the deadfalls, and the supposedly higher-class women in the parlor houses of the uptown tenderloin, besides the harlots in tents and slab shanties on Telegraph Hill and the Chinese indentured slave girls, brought over and held under duress, supposedly until their passage was paid for.

The Alaskan gold rush of 1896–1899 spawned an equally lascivious industry. The most visually evil of the tenderfoot traps were saloons and other businesses owned by Jefferson Randolph (Soapy) Smith in Skagway. Soapy and his loose confederation of thieves, swindlers, and murderers seldom overlooked an opportunity to gull miners and visitors. One of these numerous scams was a telegraph office, although there was no telegraph line in Alaska. His clients even received replies, invariably collect.[19] But Soapy's most innovative and vilest business was a saloon and whorehouse in which a new arrival or tipsy miner would be directed to a beckoning doorway with a landing 20 feet below on a rocky bank of the river. After being relieved of his wallet or poke by one of Soapy's men, the victim, usually semiconscious, was rolled into the icy water to be carried away by the current.

In other parts of the world, notably far east Asia, women caught up in unfortunate circumstances traditionally have been exploited as slaves in the prostitution trade. The Japanese government recently issued an apology, after a long period of reluctance, to women who were forced into prostitution to serve Japan's armed forces before and during World War II. The sex slaves, called "comfort women," were from Korea, the Philippines, Indonesia, and China. Of an estimated 200,000 women forced into prostitution, about 1000 are believed to still be alive. In July, 1995, Prime Minister Tomiichi Murayama announced, "I wish to deeply apologize to all those who suffered emotional and physical wounds that can never be healed." The Japanese government rejected appeals for compensation, but hoped instead to raise about $20 million from private sources to pay each sex slave 2 million yen, equal to $22,700, about the amount the United States and Canada paid their citizens for Japanese descent sent to internment camps during World War II. Despite the small compensation for the infliction of irreparable harm, only $1.16 million had been raised four months after the appeal.[20–24]

Former madams have capitalized on the mystique of the whorehouse by writing their memoirs and stories from their selective memories. Polly Adler, Xavier Hollander, Pauline Tabor, and others have given their titillating accounts of the goings-on in a working whorehouse. A flamboyant madam known professionally as Sally Stanford set a high standard for the parlor house crowd in San Francisco from about 1930 to the time of her retirement across the Golden Gate in Sausalito, where she opened an upscale restaurant, the Valhalla. She became one of the directors of the Sausalito Chamber of Commerce and a member of its Ways and Means committee. She even ran for a seat on the city council against stubborn opposition from gentry on the hill but with strong support of the laidback downtown community on the Sausalito waterfront.[25]

Romantic fiction depicts the prostitute as a lady of low social status by circumstance, but of noble spirit and a heart of gold. Stories like John Steinbeck's *Cannery Row* and Robert Mason's *The World of Suzie Wong* portray their beautiful heroines with warmth and sensitivity. But the harsh reality is that the run-of-the-mill prostitute is not apt to be especially attractive; many of them have one or more venereal diseases, are hooked on drugs, are of less than average intelligence, or have other problems that keep them from getting work in the normal job market. Some of them, of course, are just down on their luck when they get into the business through desperation or out of the need to make money to pay for a drug addiction. Part of the sordid side of prostitution is the hassling of hookers by the criminal justice system that puts them outside the protection of society. This makes them defenseless against abuse and health hazards, and victimizes society itself by the spread of uncontrolled venereal diseases, including AIDS.

The present-day sexual scene is in a chaotic state more reminiscent of ancient Rome than one would expect in the modern age of enlightenment. Hookers roam downtown streets in shorts and miniskirts, often to support their expensive pimps, drug appetites, or both, in a race to see who will find them first, customers or vice cops, both of whom are numerous, eager, and superficially indistinguishable. The main difference from earlier times is that most of the hookers carry condoms in their purses. Male prostitutes have also taken to the streets, and their business seems to thrive despite the danger of AIDS.

Gloria Steinem, in her book *Outrageous Acts and Everyday Rebellions*, writing about Linda Lovelace, the star of *Deep Throat*, describes the uglier side of the sexual scene:

There are other, nameless victims of sexual servitude: the young blonds from the Minnesota Pipeline, runaways from the Scandinavian farming towns of Minnesota, who are given drugs and 'seasoned' by pimps and set up in Times Square; the welfare mothers who are pressured to get off welfare and into prostitution; the exotic dancers imported from poorer countries for porn films and topless bars; the body of a prostitute found headless and handless in a Times Square hotel, a lesson to sisters.[26]

The elite of the prostitutes are the call girls and escort service girls, who are apart from the bordello scene. Some of them may work part time and have other jobs. They have a wide range of pay scale and often more than earn their money. The call girl business run by Hollywood madam Heidi Fleiss was probably typical, although its reputed clientele of celebrities was probably more exclusive and star-studded than most.[27] Fleiss was the protégé and eventually the unwelcome competitor and successor of the legendary Beverly Hills madam, Elizabeth Adams, known in the trade and to her clients as Madam Alex. She became a millionaire from an international prostitution network that dispatched charming young women to pricey Beverly Hills hotel suites, European cities, and Caribbean cruises for fees ranging from $300 for two hours to $2000 a day, before inflation. Fleiss's business became public knowledge when she was busted by a sting operation in June, 1993. The 28-year-old high school dropout, the daughter of a prominent pediatrician, was widely known in Hollywood circles, and was said to have many of the movie stars and prominent entertainment executives among her clients. It took a phony wealthy Hawaiian businessman, actually Sammy Lee, a Beverly Hills undercover detective, and a phalanx of more than 20 eavesdropping cops to get the evidence on her at taped meetings. Sammy Lee arranged with Heidi for four girls to entertain him and three supposedly wealthy colleagues at a luxurious Beverly Hills hotel suite. The girls were given $1500 each but were arrested when partly undressed before they could deliver. Fleiss was also accused of selling and delivering cocaine for the party at Sammy Lee's request, but she was acquitted of that charge. The names of

Fleiss's customers were never made public, and none of them was ever indicted. She did not surrender her "black book," and the police apparently did not ask for it. However, anxiety among men of the Hollywood glitterati was reported to be at an unusually high level.

Three of the jurors in the Heidi Fleiss case were conscience-stricken when they learned that the pandering charge of which she was found guilty carried a mandatory jail sentence of at least 3 years, while the cocaine charge of which she was acquitted called for no more than a fine. They appealed to the court, protesting that they had broken the rules by discussing what they thought were the probable penalties among themselves before the finding, but the judge held that the original decision was valid. She was sentenced to three years in prison but remained temporarily free pending an appeal.

Some cities make what they call prostitution sweeps to entrap male customers, using female cops posing as hookers. On one night in November, 1994, the city of Anaheim arrested 38 men "suspected" of soliciting undercover cops. Sting operations are a favorite of the vice squads. Many people think it smacks of dirty pool to trick someone into committing a crime, but lawyer-legislators have stacked the deck. To prove entrapment, the defendant must show that police tactics would induce a normal, law-abiding citizen to break the law. So sting operations will probably continue to be the most effective way the police have of making prostitution arrests.

The Los Angeles Police Department is said to have nearly three dozen vice officers assigned to the prostitution war along a stretch of Hollywood that has come to be known as the sex capital of the West Coast. During 1994, the squad made 2462 arrests, including 1100 for prostitution. Journalist John Glionna quotes Dino Caldera, a vice officer with the LAPD, "Whatever it is, the place draws them—pimps, prostitutes, and johns come in a never-ending supply. Believe me, business is good in Hollywood vice."[28]

Some people ask, "Why bother? Why is selling sex a crime?" A study published by the *University of California Hastings Law Journal* in April, 1987, said that police officers arrested 74,550 people for prostitution (probably a few of them were johns) in America's 16 largest cities in 1985. The study was conducted by Julie Pearl, a 1987 graduate of the Hastings College of Law. She found that law enforcement agencies in America's largest cities spent an average of about $2000 for each arrest of a prostitute. That came to more than $120 million a year in enforcement costs. Figuring an inflation rate of 5% per year, the average cost is now more than $3000 for each arrest. Pearl was quoted as saying, "We can't afford to keep prostitution illegal anymore."[29]

Gloria Allred and Lisa Bloom, prominent feminist lawyers, ask, "Why is it immoral to be paid for an act that is perfectly legal if done for free?" They go on to say,

> The problems with prostitution are a direct result of its illegality. Sexually transmitted diseases would be decreased if sex workers were licensed, screened, tested and treated rather than being driven underground.[30]

Attorney Alan Dershowitz, commenting in his column on the Heidi Fleiss affair, says

> In those countries in which prostitution is regulated, there is less sexually transmitted disease, less exploitation and fewer other evils associated with a profession that will always be needed to satisfy the urges of people who cannot achieve sexual satisfaction in the traditional manner. (The "traditional" manner has, of course, always included prostitution).[30a]

Peggy Miller, founder of the Canadian Organization for the Rights of Prostitutes (CORP), at a meeting in Toronto to promote understanding between feminists and "sex trade workers" asked, "What's so terrible about fucking for a living? I like it, I can live out my fantasies." But an unidentified participant had a different perspective:

> I was a prostitute for eight years, from the time I was fifteen up until I was twenty-three, and I don't know how you can possibly say, as busy as you are as a lady of the evening, that you like every sexual act, that you work out your fantasies. Come on, get serious! How can you work out your fantasies with a trick that you're putting on an act for? . . . Do you know what it's like when you have nothing to eat so you have

to go turn a trick to feed yourself at fifteen? Have you ever known what it's like to be without a roof over your head, and you have to pretend to some dude that you like him for the night? . . . prostitution to me was degrading. I grew to hate it. If I had had to fuck one more of them—boy. I would have killed him.[31]

Margo St. James, founder of Call Off Your Old Tired Ethics (COYOTE), probably expressed the viewpoint of many prostitutes and other people:

I really think that women are put in jail for asking for money. It's not sex because in most states in the U.S. consensual sex between adults is perfectly legal unless you do it on the doorstep. Then, of course, you'll scare the horses.[32]

District judge John Covington of Baton Rouge, Louisiana, stated the case for decriminalization of sex clearly and succinctly in a ruling made in 1974 concerning a woman, Charlotte Devall, who was charged with prostitution.[33] Judge Covington said that Louisiana's prostitution laws are unconstitutional because they discriminate against women. He said in his ruling that state prostitution laws punish only women and provide for no penalties for men involved in such activities.

We then see the problem as one of the exploitation of the female. Since Louisiana law does not punish extramarital relations between men and women and women of age unless money is involved, it must be the money which makes the otherwise lawful act criminal.

Which handler of money does the law single out? The buyer or the seller of the services? Neither the giver nor the recipient in the female–male transaction is condemned, nor is the giver in the male–female transaction condemned.

The state is unable to demonstrate any rationality to the sequence. In applying principles of logic to the case, we are met with a horrifying conclusion.

Since sex is not criminal, and female–male monied sex is not criminal, but male–female monied sex is criminal, the law is irrational.

However, some states have made both selling and buying sex illegal.

The gist of Judge Covington's ruling is that sex is not criminal. Then why is paying for or getting paid for sex criminal? There are several reasons. The religious tradition of original sin makes sex for the sake of sex forbidden fruit. Sex for hire in which there is no intention or desire to procreate circumvents the biblical command to "be fruitful and multiply." Besides, prostitutes have always been low on the social totem pole, and those at the bottom are both the most vulnerable and the easiest of all criminals to prosecute. Finally, there is a vast constituency that benefits from the criminality of sex, not the least of which are members of organized crime who profit from prostitution rings they control. Their adversary, the criminal justice system, is a vast industry in itself, comprising vice squads, informers, ordinary cops, defense lawyers, judges, and prosecuting attorneys. And, of course, preachers are against it. The only rational reason for penalizing sex—to prevent the spread of venereal diseases—is made worse by putting prostitutes beyond society's protection, control, and even collection of taxes that would go far toward paying for health costs.

A commission appointed by the governor of Pennsylvania recommended that the state should abolish its laws prohibiting prostitution.[34,35] The 251-member Pennsylvania Joint Council on the Criminal Justice System issued its resolution in 1975 after two years of study and hearings. Charlotte Ginsburg, Pittsburgh director of the Pennsylvania Program for Women and Girl Offenders, said,

> The whole prostitution situation in Pennsylvania is unfair. High priced call girls or prostitutes protected by organized crime almost never spend time in jail while poorer street prostitutes are generally the main target of law enforcement.

There are several ways to decriminalize sex. One way is the method adopted by the state of Nevada where prostitution is legal but regulated. The state leaves it up to the counties to decide whether to allow prostitution in areas they designate. There is a tradition in Nevada dating from the days of the early miners when prostitution was a thriving industry in the mining towns. Prostitution was openly tolerated almost everywhere in Nevada until recently. In *Harlots, Whores & Hookers*, writer Hilary Evans tells a story that has become part of American frontier folklore. There was a Nevada law that prohibited prostitution within 300 feet of a school. When the residents of Beatty, Nevada, were told that they had a whorehouse too close to the school, they complied with the law immediately by moving the schoolhouse.[36]

The best-known brothel in the country today is the Mustang Ranch, eight miles south of Reno on Route 80, established many years ago by Joe and Sally Conforte and operated under unofficial traditional tolerance until 1970 when Storey County officially licensed the establishment. The Mustang is a far cry from the old-fashioned whorehouse of an earlier time. It is clean, starkly furnished with a decor more like a motel, and with few fancy trimmings. The girls receive regular medical examinations and are allowed time off like any other worker. Some of them have residences in Reno where prostitution is not legal. About half the girls' pay goes to management. The Mustang was purchased in 1986 for a reported price of $18 million by Strong Point Inc., whose stock was to be sold over-the-counter. The 108-room Mustang property included 510 acres of surrounding land. Strong Point already owned and operated Sue's Bordello, a 12-room establishment in Elko, Nevada, that they had purchased in 1985 for "less than $1 million." At the time of the Mustang purchase, John D. Davis, president of Strong Point, reported that the company had about 4000 stockholders with about 5 million common shares outstanding and that they expected to file for listing with the National Association of Securities Dealers.[37]

Prostitution in Storey County, Nevada, is in sharp contrast to that elsewhere in the United States where every conceivable form of whoredom proliferates on the fringes of criminality, from street-walking prostitutes, pimps, and pushers to barroom pickups, massage parlors, dating services, part-time chippies, and call girl establishments to accommodate every level of appetite and affluence, all without medical supervision or services, and with little, if any, of their collective multibillion dollar income known to the Internal Revenue Service. Indentured women imported in the so-called white slave market and the vilest of all prostitution rackets, the use of children, both girls and boys, are a dismal reality in the underworld of sex.

Janice Raymond, professor of women's studies at the University of Massachusetts, Amherst, and executive director of the Coalition Against Trafficking in Women, claims that much of the prostitution throughout the world is the result of the military's traditional tolerance and encouragement of it as recreation for the troops. She refers to the Council for Prostitution Alternatives, which calls prostitution "bought and sold rape." She calls prostitution "a human rights violation," and says, "Surely the question is not why women are in prostitution, but why so many men buy women and children in prostitution."[38]

WHAT'S COMING

When people start toting up the cost in money and health of criminalized sex, the Nevada scheme or a reasonable facsimile may become the ripple of the future. Sex scholar Vern Bullough says in his 1994 book, *Science in the Bedroom*[39]

> Increasingly, prostitution in the United States has been decriminalized, the double standard has been weakening, and the nature of the customer has changed. . . . Many of the recent generation of feminists who have been concerned with prostitution have concentrated on eliminating the stigma associated with prostitution and have argued that it represents a female response to the larger social forces that have fostered and maintained the practice of sexual inequality and oppression of women.

It is unlikely that a wave of reform will sweep the country in the near future. But unfortunate circumstances may bring change. A frighteningly high percentage of prostitutes with the HIV virus in many parts of the world may be a preview of the predicted heterosexual epidemic worldwide. Licensing, examinations, and control may become a practical necessity. Although they will not eliminate the AIDS epidemic, such measures, by removing diseased prostitutes from legal practice early, will reduce the incidence of all venereal diseases, including AIDS.

Sex therapy to treat impotent men is thought of as a modern innovation, but Bullough and Bullough point out in *Women and Prostitution* that Sumerian documents tell of sex therapy in Babylonian times, probably by prostitutes. The method described was to rub the penis with an ointment containing a massage oil mixed with pulverized magnetic iron ore, which probably increased the friction.[40] Modern methods are more sophisticated, and since intercourse by surrogate partners is sometimes part of the treatment, there is the question of whether surrogate sex therapy is prostitution. A Berkeley, California, group called the Berkeley Group for Sexual and Social Development, formed in 1971, said they used women surrogates, all of them volunteers on a part-time basis. One of the psychologists admitted to having employed prostitutes for the purpose. A spokesman for the Berkeley group said, "We used a call girl in the early days, but she found it difficult to be self critical." At first, therapists were worried about the legal problems of using surrogate partners, who have to be paid for their services. But the role of the surrogate is to teach how to achieve intimacy as a means of overcoming sexual dysfunction; the sex act is only a small part of it. Besides, surrogates perform under the supervision of licensed therapists, psychologists, or psychiatrists. The client does not pay the surrogate, but instead, pays the professional therapist for appropriate services. An article by attorney David LeRoy in the *St. Louis University Law Journal* set forth the logic that there is no relation between the use of sex surrogates and prostitution, and his view seems to prevail among law authorities.[41]

Sex therapy is expensive, beyond the reach of many who could benefit from it. Health insurance coverage for sex therapy is at least as hard to get as for mental illness, but it is a needed service that would be widely used if the cost were affordable to the average person. Could prostitutes provide the service? Probably not many. Even women of the general population who can qualify by personality, temperament, attitude, and interest are a rarity. But an exceptional few, after a course of training, could no doubt provide useful service, comparable to that of a paralegal or paramedical professional. In earlier times, it was not uncommon for a father to take his teenage son to the local whorehouse where the madam would instruct a sympathetic associate to initiate the lad into the mysteries of sex.

A prostitute of exceptional qualities of personality and view of humanity might be a relatively unrecognized, unappreciated, and untapped therapeutic resource. Can anyone say that it is not possible for prostitutes to better themselves in the hierarchy from hookers to courtesans and serial husband collectors? It's conceivable that some segments of the profession could be elevated to a higher level. Surgeons at one time ran barber shops. With their razor-sharp instrument, bloodletting—the state of the art at the time—was their stock-in-trade. The surgeon's sign, the blood-red line of the barber pole on a white background, can still be seen in front of some old-fashioned barber shops.

Media attention to society's hedonistic pursuit of perfection in pelvic pleasure obscures the universal role of prostitution as a part of human sexuality that has thrived from at least the beginning of recorded history. Most parts of the world are tolerant of prostitution, though in varying degrees, reflecting the views of St. Augustine, the most antisex leader of the early church, who argued that prostitution was a necessary evil. The United States is at or near the restrictive end of the spectrum of suppression, so it has a long way to go to even approach St. Augustine's view. But if Vern Bullough's observation is correct, there is a strong trend under way toward increasing tolerance of prostitution, and if it continues, it will lead to decriminalizing the selling of sex during the 21st century, at least in some parts of the country in addition to Nevada, followed by licensing and mandatory examinations for the purpose of disease control.

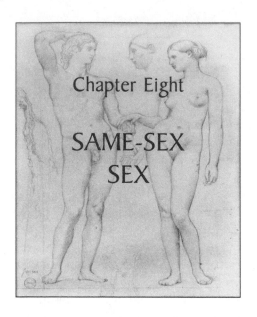

Chapter Eight

SAME-SEX SEX

Homosexual relations are an ancient practice, mostly condemned or prohibited, but with variable degrees of acceptance and condemnation depending on the culture and customs of the time. The Greeks and their immediate predecessors may have set an unchallenged world record for uninhibited sexual activity. We see a reflection of the Greeks' attitude in their panoply of gods. The Greek gods indulged in all the fun and folly typical of people on earth, and because they were omnipotent, added heroic touches beyond the realm of human experience.

The top god, Zeus, was a cannibal, incestuous, philanderer, repetitive fornicator, adulterer, bisexual, kidnapper, and rapist. His father was Kronos, a son of the male Uranus (Heaven) and the female Gaea (Earth). Zeus took his sister, Hera, as his wife, and swallowed his own father, Kronos, thereby taking charge of all creation. He created a new world, the present one, and put a son, Dionysus, born of Persephone, in command. But before Dionysus could take over, he was killed, cooked, and eaten by the Titans, who were some of the offspring of Uranus and Gaea. Zeus vented his anger on the Titans by burning them to ashes with thunderbolts, but the goddess Athena rescued Dionysus's heart from the ashes and gave it to Zeus. This inspired Zeus to father another Dionysus, born of another mother, Semele. In this way, the new world was imbued with a duality, a mixture of the divine and the mundane.

Zeus, in one of his innumerable erotic adventures, kidnapped Ganymede, a beautiful boy of the Trojan royalty, and took him to Olympus to share his bed. Thus, love for another of the same sex became established in Greek tradition as a pastime of the gods.[1]

Greek men were obsessed with the beauty of boys. The ideal of beauty in boys and youths is depicted lavishly in Greek art. The Greek word meaning "beautiful boy" is inscribed on an enormous number of vases. By contrast, the inscription meaning "beautiful girl" is relatively rare. The lyric poets raptured over the beauty of boys endlessly, and many other writers commented on the attractions of boys. Extolling the beauty of a boy's hair or his eyes was a typical theme. Aristotle noted, "A lover looks at none of the bodily charms of his favorite more than at his eyes wherein dwells the secret of boyish virtues." The poet Ibycus compares the eyes of a boy with "the stars that sparkle in the sky when dark with night." The names of favorite boys were written on graves, columns, basins, footstools, and a large number of other objects, even including discus rims.[2]

"Boys" in Greek terminology meant youths who had reached puberty or beyond. Sexual relations with boys who were sexually immature was improper and was punished. But men had a special fondness for youths in early puberty judging from references such as "a youth with the first down on his chin," and as Hans Licht points out in *Sexual Life in Ancient Greece*, Aristophanes in *Clouds* praises boys, except "the down he speaks of is not the down of their cheeks and lips." Licht quotes the Greek writer Straton on age preferences:

> The youthful bloom of the twelve-year-old boy gives me joy, but much more desirable is the boy of thirteen. He whose years are fourteen, is a still sweeter flower of the Loves, and

even more charming is he who is beginning his fifteenth year. The sixteenth year is that of the gods, and to desire the seventeenth does not fall to my lot, but only to Zeus.[3]

When Socrates was a boy, he had been a favorite of his teacher Archelaus, according to Diogenes Laërtius. And Porphyrius claimed that Socrates, when a youth of 17, was much given to sensuality that was later supplanted by zealous intellectual interests. In fact, Socrates was known for his disdain of sensual love for boys. In a warning to Xenophon, Socrates says:

> Beautiful boys with their kisses inspire something fearful. Do you not known that the animal called Beautiful and Blooming is more dangerous than poisonous spiders? . . . Therefore, my dear Xenophon, I advise you, when you see a beautiful boy, to take flight as quickly as possible.

It is unclear to what extent or in how many cases the love of youth was erotic, platonic, or both. As part of Greek intellectual life, men attracted to themselves a boy or youth and acted as his friend, guardian, and counselor, and encouraged his physical and educational development as a matter of civic responsibility. The opinions of scholars differ. According to Hans Licht in *Sexual Life in Ancient Greece*, "Pedophilia was to the Greeks at first the most important way of bringing up the male youth." But G. Rattray Taylor in *Sex in History* says, "It seems quite clear that, while a relationship of love existed between them, the performance of sexual acts was strictly forbidden. Lycurgus made it a felony punishable by death to lust after a boy." The Greeks called sex relations with a boy *paedomania* as distinct from *paederasty*.[4] In short, the Greeks made a distinction between love and lust. Plato put it this way: "The one love is made for pleasure, the other loves beauty. The one tends to the good of the beloved, the other to the ruin of both."

To the Greeks, beauty had something of the divine quality that was justice in itself, as demonstrated by the story of the hetaera Phryne, chronicled by Athenaeus. Phryne was brought to court on charges of profaning the Eleusinian mysteries and corrupting illustrious citizens of Rome, accusations that could lead to the death penalty. She engaged a renowned orator, Hyperides, in return for becoming his mistress. Despite her lawyer's impassioned plea, she was on the verge of being found guilty when Hyperides, in a moment of inspiration, opened Phryne's garment at the shoulders and pulled it down to her waist, revealing the superlative charm of her torso and breasts. It seemed clear to the judges that such beauty must have been under the benevolence of Aphrodite, so they let her go. Phryne was held in such awe that Praxiteles, a famous sculptor, was commissioned to make a statue of her honoring Eros.[5]

But Hellenic society was thoroughly male, with women coming into their lives for two purposes: as the "ideal girl" for the purpose of having their children and running the household, or as slaves and hetaerae for pleasure outside the home. The ideal boy had a far different standing and purpose in life than the ideal girl, who received less attention to development and less education than boys.

Female homosexual activity was said to be common on the island of Lesbos, hence the reference to lesbian love and lesbianism. Lesbos was the birthplace of Sappho, the lyric poetess, described as the queen of the lesbians, born about 612 BC. Sappho's life and poetry were imbued with love of her own sex. But it's not clear that Sappho's love of girls was erotic. She was married and had a girl child of her own. She was certainly a feminist, for she ran a boarding school for aristocratic young ladies, and her attachment to her pupils may have been comparable to the relation between teacher and pupils at the school of Socrates and Plato's Academy. A difference was that the Aeolian culture of Lesbos evidently gave women more freedom and opportunity for education than in Athens, which was strongly male oriented. Lesbos was also the birthplace of Megilla, the heroine in Lucian's *Dialogues of Courtesans*. Plutarch in *Lycurgus* said that lesbian affairs were also common in Sparta. However, it cannot be assumed that lesbianism was confined to certain cities or places.[6]

Roman life had much in common with Greek life, but they differed greatly in quality. Homosexual relationships were common enough in Rome, but pedophilia, using the word in its broadest sense, was not viewed as an exalted way of life as in Greece.[7] A young Roman would commonly have sexual relations with a good-looking male slave, called a *concubinus*, but such relations were generally not permissible with a man of free birth, although the custom and law varied from time to time. The practice of homosexuality was generally looked on with disfavor, and during some periods it was severely punished. Roman works of poetry, like those of the Greeks, sing the praises of love in lengthy lyrics, but it is almost all about heterosexual love, with only an occasional reference to men and boys. Catullus, the first Roman love-poet, was primarily heterosexual, but the following verse to Juventius, a beautiful boy, reveals a bisexual nature:

> Juventius, if I might kiss
> Your honeysweet lips as I liked,
> I'd kiss them both five hundred
> Thousands of kisses. . . .[8]

Another bisexual poet was Tibullus, who wrote an elegy in which Priapus, as the god of boy-lovers, told his worshipers how to win the affection of boys who are beautiful but cold. The earthy poet Martial describes sexual life in Rome in explicit detail, including all imaginable varieties of sexual conduct. His was a bisexual nature in which the homosexual side came out occasionally in verses to a boy he called Dindymus:

> So soft the bloom upon your cheek,
> It fades before a sunbeam or a breath.[9]

The important men of Rome displayed a spectrum of humanity, from the most upright and just to human creatures so dissolute, cruel, and sadistic that stories of their behavior stretch the limit of credulity. Hardly any of the emperors escaped stories of having been loved by some man in their youth, but it is not now always possible to separate fact from gossip. Julius Caesar was no exception. But he was probably a victim of the rumor mill, for it was well known that in adult life he had many affairs with women, including Cleopatra, and according to Suetonius, "seduced many women of high rank."[10] Caesar's heir and grand-nephew Octavian, who became Emperor Augustus, was accused in his youth of being effeminate and to have been stained by Caesar and Aulius Hirtius. He was married three times and often had affairs, and it is certain from the record that, as a man, he was totally devoid of any homosexual tendency.[11]

Tiberius, the successor of Augustus, is seen as a man of impressive intellect and high moral character. Stories about him of debauches and vulgar activities are discounted by scholars, and can probably be viewed as equal to or below the kind of gossip carried in today's scandal sheets.[12] However, Tiberius's successor, Gaius Caesar, better known as Caligula, set a record for vulgar excesses, depravity, cruelty, and sadism that probably has no equal in human history. As a boy he committed incest with his sister, and in his adolescence his grandfather, Tiberius, lamented, "I'm nurturing a viper for Rome." His degenerate acts of insane sadistic cruelty are too numerous to describe here. He demanded sexual relations with every attractive woman he met, including his own sisters, and had sexual relations with men, notably with the pantomime actor, Mnester, and Valerius Catullus, a young man of high rank.[13] When disgusted army officers murdered Caligula, the fifty-year-old Claudius became emperor. Claudius was an unlikely choice.[14] Unlike his stalwart brother Germanicus, he was weak and sickly as a youth, a stammerer, quiet, shy, and thought by most people as being not too bright. As an adult before he became emperor he led a withdrawn, scholarly life. His sexual life was described succinctly by Suetonius: "His passion for women was immoderate, and he cared nothing for men."[15] In contrast, the Emperor Nero, who habitually engaged in acts of sadistic cruelty, had innumerable extramarital relations in addition to a strong homosexual tendency. Nero had both a wife and a mistress, and was clearly bisexual.[15]

The most famous of the ancient homosexual love affairs was between the Emperor Hadrian and his beautiful male concubine and constant companion, Antinous, who died in Egypt on a visit with Hadrian to the Nile. The circumstances of Antinous's death remain a mystery. Hadrian said that Antinous fell in the river, but others suggested that he was Hadrian's sacrifice to one of the gods. In any case, in a show of unparalleled grief, Hadrian established a city, called Antinoopolis, where Antinous died, and made him a patron deity of the city. He had statues of Antinous erected throughout the Empire, and deified him to the point of founding a cult. He became the Egyptian Osiris in the city of Antinoopolis and the Greek Dionysus at other places, with altars and statues.[16]

Early Jewish law, apparently derived partly from the Babylonian code of Hammurabi, was explicit about sexuality. The Old Testament made it clear that homosexuality was prohibited because it was an "abomination" punishable by death as described in the Book of Leviticus.[17] Sodomy was so wicked that the practice was extremely dangerous, as God demonstrated when he destroyed Sodom and Gomorrah with a rain of brimstone and fire.[18] Before God put a stop to it, Lot had been besieged by men of the town to deliver his two male guests for their pleasure, and he had refused to allow such wickedness, offering his daughters instead. A similar incident described in the Book of Judges led to a bloody war when a man refused to deliver a male guest to the mob, and instead offered his daughter and a concubine. Deprived of their pleasure on the man, they seized the concubine, and abused her all night so brutally that she died. These rapists were obviously bisexual. The Israelites avenged the atrocity, but with the loss of tens of thousands of lives.[19]

A reason given for branding homosexuality as a sin in the Judeo-Christian view is that it seemingly violates the biblical command to use the human creative endowment to "be fruitful and multiply."[20] Also, in modern societies there has long been the stigma of being different. Although homosexuality is in some respects a matter of degree, and practices are highly variable, recent surveys indicate that roughly 3%, more or less, of the male population and perhaps a slightly lower percentage of females are predominantly homosexual. A cause of social distress is the fact that many of the so-called straight men and women view with disdain anyone not inclined to desire, embrace, or chase exclusively the opposite sex.

A striking feature of homosexuality throughout ancient time and the Middle Ages to the present is the inconsistency of people's attitude toward it, and especially their vacillation between permissiveness and condemnation. From the time of the love affair, possibly platonic, between the young hero David and Saul's son Jonathan, "the soul of Jonathan was knit with the soul of David, and Jonathan loved him as his own soul,"[21] some kings and clergymen were participants and protectors, and others were prosecutors and executioners. To complicate matters, homosexuality was caught up in the broader issue of whether sex itself is a sin. It would seem so from the story of Eve's transgression, which was punished by causing her the pain of childbirth and subjecting her to the rule of her husband. But the rules for sex became complicated and rigidly firm. Middle Eastern tradition not only demanded that men and women marry and have children, it said that a man could have as many wives and concubines as he could support. But then, as now, many men could not afford that luxury, so their only recourse was prostitutes or to engage in one of the forbidden acts of sex punishable by death: adultery, homosexuality, or bestiality.

Meanwhile, there was what G. Rattray Taylor called a "flowering of homosexuality" in the 12th century, but it is doubtful that it was much less common in other times. Kings, commoners, and clerics were caught up in the trend. Edward II was thought to be homosexual, "sleyne with a hoote broche putte thro the secret place posteriale,"[22] as were James VI of Scotland (James I of England) and Charles I of England. But Henry VIII, who ruled during the first half of the 16th century, and was noted for making his own sexual and marriage rules, made sodomy and bestiality felonies punishable by death. Thereafter, in most countries, homosexual activity was either already, or came to be, a criminal offense, even though it was claimed to be a disease by some people. This leads us to the question: why are some people gay or lesbian?

An early popular view was that homosexuality is a sickness that can be and should be cured. That opinion still persists in the minds of a significant number of people. In 1973, the American Psychiatric Association and the American Psychological Association both declared that homosexuality was not, in itself, an illness. This was considered a breakthrough by many homosexuals and some others. The psychologists retained the description "dystonic homosexuality" for people who are bothered by their homosexuality or who want to change their orientation. However, the new view enabled many homosexuals to accept their sexuality and lifestyle, and inspired a "gay pride" movement.

The predominant view of homosexuality in the modern world is strongly influenced by the religious conviction that it is a sinful perversion. Those who hold this view, as well as many other people, believe that homosexual behavior is psychological or of social origin and is a human perversity that can and should be "cured." This viewpoint conforms to the *tabula rasa* philosophy of Locke, who saw the mind of a newborn child as a blank slate that will come to have inscribed on it whatever impressions are made by experience.[23] The tabula rasa view is central to the nurture side of the perennial nature/nurture controversy. The opposite view is that homosexuals are born that way, and that while behavior can be changed by conscious will, sexual orientation is fixed by nature in the physiological and genetic makeup of the individual from conception. Recent and continuing studies suggest that neither one of these extreme views is completely true. However, studies give increasingly persuasive evidence that nature, that is, the way a person is when he or she is born, is an important determinant of his or her sexual orientation in at least some if not in most individuals. This conclusion is based both on findings in animal research and on studies of human anatomy and physiology.

To explore the question of why a gay man or lesbian is that way, we will first want to ask: what is it that attracts most men and women to the opposite sex? The French *vive le différence* is only a superficial explanation because many of the differences are not obvious. To be sure, the sexual organ is seen to be made for heterosexual mating, and visible secondary sex characteristics make men and women distinguishable. But the more significant differences that determine sexual behavior are the hormones that are present from early fetal development, the anatomy and function of nerve cells in the brain, and hormone activity in the brain.

When a baby is conceived, its sex depends on whether the egg (containing an X chromosome) fuses with an X sperm or a Y sperm, giving the baby XX (female) chromosomes or XY (male) chromosomes. The Y chromosome contains a gene called the testis-determining factor (TDF), but the effect of this gene is slightly delayed. The early fetus is neither male nor female because the tissues that are destined to form the male or female reproductive systems in the embryos are alike in both sexes. The fetus is basically bisexual or neutral, but as we shall see, more female than male in the initial stage, for if TDF is not present, the gonad develops into an ovary. If TDF (on the Y chromosome) is present, the gonad develops into a testis (testicle). Hormones will make the difference. Can fetal exposure to steroid sex hormones have any effect on subsequent behavior? Laboratory experiments with animals show that hormones determine how the fetus will develop and that their presence during this stage in the fetal period influences the animals for life.

The genetic female embryo will develop into a female whether the ovaries—the source of the female hormone—are present or not. This is because the ovaries do not secrete enough of the sex hormones at this stage to have a significant effect. However, if the male fetus is castrated, thus removing the source of male hormone, it will not develop into a male, but will develop exactly in the same way as a genetic female. If testosterone—the testicle hormone—is administered to a guinea pig fetus by injecting it through the mother's pelvic opening, it acts quickly to masculinize the fetus's external genitalia. If the fetus is a genetic female, the testosterone causes it to be masculinized to such an extent that its behavior after birth resembles in many ways that of a male. The hormone secreted by the fetal testicle inhibits development of the female reproductive structures and stimulates development of the male structures.[24]

Thus, the role of the male hormone is dominant, especially during the early life of the fetus. The result is that adult males are less affected than females by treatment with hormones of the opposite sex. This can be seen when male rats are treated with the ovarian hormone, estrogen. They show little change in behavior, nor do castrated rats show much change when they are treated with estrogen. It is evident from numerous experiments of this kind that the early secretion of testosterone "imprints" the male response on the developing fetus's nerve–endocrine system and causes it to react to testosterone later in life with typical male behavior. When feminization appears in males, it is not produced as much by the presence of estrogen as by the absence of testosterone, or by the androgen receptors in the brain being insensitive to testosterone. If a condition deprives an animal of testosterone during a critical time of sex brain differentiation, the result will be a typically female pattern of sexual behavior. Thus, hormones early in life have more influence on later sexual attitudes than previously thought.

But how about the effect of environment? If a pregnant rat is subjected to stress of one kind or another, especially near the end of pregnancy, male offspring show less male mounting behavior and more typically female posture for copulation, called *lordosis*, than offspring from unstressed mothers. This, presumably, is related to the effect of stress on the hormone output of the mother.

Because the brain is the site of action where many of the sexual functions are initiated, the question arises, do the sex steroid hormones affect the brain during fetal development? And if so, can the hormone effects on a part of the brain have any relation to sexual orientation? Simon LeVay, a neurobiologist who has done research on sex in terms of physiological processes, says in his book *The Sexual Brian* that he agrees with Gunther Dörner, a German endocrinologist, that "homosexuality, like heterosexuality, results at least in part from specific interactions between androgenic (male-producing) sex hormones and the brain during development."[25] Dörner was convinced that the effect of hormones on brain development and sexuality in animals could be assumed to be similar in humans. He injected gay men with estrogens, and found that they responded to estrogen with a surge in leutinizing hormones from the pituitary gland typical of females. This did not happen to straight men. His results led him to think that gay men had been exposed to unusually low levels of androgen during fetal life, which allowed their brain hypothalamic circuits to develop in a typical female direction. Dörner also thought that stress on the part of the mother during pregnancy contributed to a son's homosexuality, similar to what happens to rats in the laboratory.[26]

LeVay, working at the Salk Institute for Biological Research, reported in 1991 his finding that the size of a part of the hypothalamus, called the third interstitial nucleus of the anterior hypothalamus (INAH), was correlated with male homosexuality.[27] This is located in what is called the medial preoptic region of the hypothalamus, a part of the brain believed to be important in the regulation of typical male sexual behavior. LeVay found that the INAH was on average two to three times larger in presumed heterosexual men than in women. In gay men, the nucleus was on average the same size as in women, and two to three times smaller than in straight men. LeVay, homosexual himself, took his samples from homosexual patients who had died of AIDS. His results could be taken as evidence that people are born gay or straight, and not, as some people believe, that being gay is a willful perversity. It is highly unlikely that behavior, alone, would cause the difference in brain anatomy that LeVay observed.

There is evidence, further, that sexual orientation is partly genetic. In 1993, geneticist Dean Hamer and his colleagues at the National Cancer Institute reported finding a homosexual gene.[28] Of 76 homosexual men, 13.5% of their brothers were homosexual, compared to about 2% in the general population. That, in itself, does not prove a genetic link. But they also found more gay relatives on the maternal side than on the paternal side, suggesting that in at least some male homosexuals, the gene is passed through the female members of the family, and therefore probably on the X chromosome. A genetic analysis of 40 pairs of homosexual brothers revealed a region on the X chromosome shared by 33 of the 40 pairs of brothers. Seven pairs of homosexual brothers did not share that region of the X chromosome where the gene appears to be located. This led Hamer, also homosexual, to conclude that homosexuality may have both genetic and environmental causes. Further studies of homosexual brothers by Hamer and his colleagues confirmed that gay brothers share a section of the mother's X chromosome, suggesting that it contains a gene predisposing to homosexuality. Says Hamer:[28a]

Our results suggest that genes are involved in male sexual orientation, although they certainly do not determine a person's sexual orientation. There probably are other biological factors like hormones, for example, and other variables we simply don't know anything about.

In the final analysis, no one knows for sure why men and women are heterosexual, homosexual, or bisexual. We have seen evidence that in many cases, the hormone environment during fetal development is crucial to subsequent sexual behavior of both males and females. And there is evidence that sexual orientation is in some cases at least partly genetic. Thus, sexual orientation is related to both the fetal genetic influences and the fetal environment, specifically hormones, which in some cases may be modified by maternal stress.

WHAT'S COMING

Homosexual and bisexual behavior have been common throughout recorded history, with social acceptance ranging from tolerance to the death penalty, depending on culture, time, and place. Intolerance and discrimination imposes a psychological burden—and often a barrier to employment or advancement— that virtually forces many men and women to keep their sexual orientation secret. However, the trend to "come out of the closet" is bringing about a slowly building revolution in laws, customs, and attitudes affecting the gay and lesbian community. These will eventually lead to recognition of cultural and legal rights and privileges of unmarried couples, whether homosexual or heterosexual, equal to the traditional rights and privileges of married couples. Rights, privileges, and responsibilities may take the form of legally honored partner contracts.

The "coming out" of the gay community in the United States beginning in the 1970s is a well-known story. The views expressed by psychologists and psychiatrists helped to alleviate some of the stigma attached to homosexuality in the public mind, but the biggest change was that the visibility of coming out replaced the burden of secretiveness, and gave gay men and lesbians a sense of self-worth. They could openly reject the idea that being homosexual is a willful perversity or a crime.

Gay and lesbian activism brought about greater acceptance in a variety of ways. During the 1960s, 1970s, and 1980s, punitive laws against homosexual behavior were abolished in England and Wales, followed by Scotland, West and East Germany, Austria, Canada, and some of the states in Australia and the United States. Inclusion of gays and lesbians under the protection of anti-discrimination and human rights laws as a minority group is seen as an advance where they have been passed, though in many areas such proposed laws are hotly contested.

Numerous state and local laws prohibit sodomy and similar acts, with various degrees of punishment. Some states have repealed the sodomy laws, but some remain on the books. However, sodomy laws, like the mostly ignored laws against adultery, are seldom enforced. The U.S. Supreme Court, for the most part, has taken a hands-off attitude toward the states' dealing with homosexual activity. In 1986, the justices upheld by a vote of 5 to 4 a Georgia sodomy statute, reflecting little change in the Court's view ten years earlier when in 1976 it voted 6 to 3 to let stand a lower court ruling sustaining a Virginia sodomy law. In the 1986 decision, the justices reasoned that sexual activity is not protected by the Constitution, even in the privacy of one's own bedroom, that is, the Constitution says nothing about it one way or the other, so it remains a matter for the states to decide. The majority of the court made the distinction between the provisions of the Constitution and historic legality by citing laws invoked in the time of Henry VIII, when homosexual activity was punishable by death.

AIDS victims in the minds of many people are stigmatized by the documented high incidence of the disease among homosexual men. The stigma will gradually disappear for several reasons. Many gay men have learned to practice safer sex, although some young men have admitted that they pay little attention to the danger of unsafe sex; AIDS increasingly is becoming a heterosexual disease; the prospect of a cure or preventive vaccine, though elusive, remains a possibility; and there is a recognizable shift in attitude of the general public from one of indifference to sympathy for the sufferers, partly motivated, however, by awareness of the enormous costs to society of failing to control the epidemic.

Some issues remain unresolved or only partially resolved. The "don't ask, don't tell" policy of the military put into effect during the early days of the Clinton administration was only a minor gain, if any, for gays and lesbians, leaving them with their old nemesis of enforced secrecy and loss of identity. Homosexuals say they have valid reasons for demanding equal rights in the military, but the military dispute may be the toughest of all problems to resolve. Opponents of gays in the military point out that, as enlisted men know only too well, they are often under crowded, emotionally demanding conditions, virtually devoid of privacy and much of the freedom so highly prized in other walks of life. Male bonding under the rigors and stress of combat, possibly handed down through the millennia from the hunting parties of prehuman ancestors, is seen as having crucial survival value; as opponents of homosexuals see it, bonding under combat conditions has not been demonstrated in mixed heterosexual—openly homosexual groups. However, it is assumed that many men who have served valorously must have been gay.

The first major study of the family by the Church of England in 20 years concluded that "living in sin" should no longer be regarded as sinful, and should be dropped in view of the number of people who now live together before getting married. Said Bishop Alan Morgan, who chaired the study, "The phrase 'living in sin' stigmatizes and isn't helpful." The report also urged a "ready welcome" for homosexuals in the church, saying many have high-quality, loving relationships.[29] But ordination of homosexuals will remain a highly controversial question for many years in various denominations and dioceses of the church.

Other gains for gays that have not been fully realized: federal and state security clearances; discrimination in jobs, housing, and public accommodations; adoptions, foster care, and custody cases; and discrimination against AIDS victims. A goal of gay and lesbian couples is that they be given the same privileges in job benefits, such as health insurance, as spouses of heterosexual married couples. This has been done in a few instances, but to become widespread, a new code will have to be formulated. Bills have been introduced in state legislatures that would allow gay and other unwed couples to register with the state as domestic partners, requiring hospitals to grant visitation rights and modifying state laws relating to wills and conservatorships. The bills were designed to help unmarried elderly heterosexual couples as well as homosexual couples. Two attempts to pass such bills were made in California, in 1994 and again in 1995, but the bills were vetoed by the governor. In San Francisco, where 3 of the 11 members of the Board of Supervisors are openly lesbian or gay, a 1996 law went into effect that would allow lesbians and gays to hold "wedding" ceremonies at City Hall if they are registered as domestic partners and pay a fee of $30. A 1991 law had already given homosexuals and other unmarried couples the privilege to register their partnerships with the city for a fee of $35 and receive some of the rights accorded to married couples. For instance, registered city employees can share health benefits with their partners, pass on pension benefits on their deaths, and have hospital visitation rights.[30]

Another proposal is to enact legislation that will give homosexual marriage a legal standing and the same legal privileges and obligations as those of heterosexual couples. But that is not believed by all gays and lesbians to be the best way. Paula Ettelbrick argues that legalizing homosexual relationships by marriage would "undercut efforts to establish a distinctive gay identity and culture." She wants gay men and lesbians to be accepted with their differences, and she advocates making the law recognize partnerships outside marriage. She asks for societal and legal recognition of all kinds of family relationships, to recognize the right of a partner to stay in his or her rent-controlled apartment after the death of a lover, and to recognize the family relationship of a lesbian or gay couple who are jointly raising a child.[31]

Others ask further, why not recognize the right of a lesbian couple for one or both of them to have their own children, or for gay men to have children by a surrogate mother or adoption? A common objection is the supposition that homosexual parents will raise their children to be homosexual, but that has not been demonstrated to be the case.

The near future will see at least some states in the United States enact legislation to grant gay and lesbian couples virtually the same rights as those of married heterosexual couples. The legislation may go in the direction of either of two forms: establishment of same-sex marriage, with all rights, responsibilities, and privileges of conventional marriage, or legal recognition of cohabitation contracts with the same rights, responsibilities, and privileges but applicable also to unwed heterosexual couples who for various reasons are not inclined to marry, including elderly couples who for financial or other reasons prefer to remain unmarried. Even younger couples stand to benefit.

Although cohabitation contracts will apply to both heterosexual and homosexual people, some couples will prefer traditional marriages because people treasure memories of a ceremony in celebration of a bonding that may last a lifetime. And some traditions require elaborate formalities of congratulations, receptions, feasting, and dancing, depending on the customs of the group. For similar reasons, some couples entering into cohabitation contracts may cling to modified ceremonies as nostalgic reminders of ancestral rites. But many others will reject the formalities as outdated relics no longer appropriate for the brave new world and opt, instead, for signing a document in the presence of a notary public.

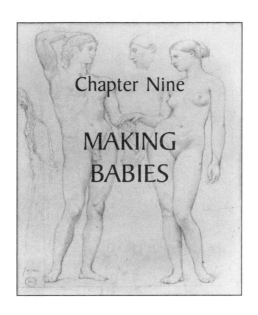

Chapter Nine

MAKING BABIES

Human fertility is a blessing and a curse. Some people are too fertile and others sterile or nearly so. There will always be some, both single and married, who want children but for various physical or physiological reasons are unable to have them. Couples who want children badly, but can't, face one of the most poignant dilemmas of family life. The inability to conceive a child affects one in six couples.

Making babies is pleasure and pain, art and science, happiness and the agony of tears. The science part can be a giver of life when all else fails. Advances in artificial insemination, *in vitro* fertilization, transfer of ova, male sperm donors, and female surrogates, make it possible for many women who would otherwise go childless to bear children. Artificial insemination is simple and relatively inexpensive, but some of the other procedures are very expensive, and often require repeating one or more times before success is achieved.

MALE FERTILITY

Artificial insemination is a practical recourse for a woman who ovulates and is capable of implanting the ovum in her uterus, but whose husband is sterile. At least 40%, probably half, of failures to conceive are caused by a deficiency in sperm, while about 10% of infertility cases are caused by a combination of male and female problems. A normal sperm output is in the range of 100–500 million sperm per ejaculate. If a man's sperm count is below an adequate count, sometimes expressed as 20 million per teaspoon (about 5 ml) or about 40–60 million per ejaculate, he will probably be sterile. Another way of expressing a satisfactory sperm count is that of Dr. Geoffrey Sher,[1] codirector of the Pacific Fertility Center in San Francisco:

> When a man has a concentration of healthy motile sperm less than 10 million per ml, its fertilization ability begins to decline because the sperm's potential for fertilizing seems to be linked to the concentration of motile sperm. The normal concentration of motile sperm in any healthy male is about 50 percent or greater; in other words, if a man has a sperm count of 100 million he could expect to have 50 million motile sperm.

When a man has a low sperm count, a special procedure can be used to pool ejaculates. For this, one way is to freeze and store the sperm from several ejaculates, and use the pooled sperm for artificial insemination.

Failure of fertilization is sometimes caused by the presence of antibodies in the semen against the man's own sperm. Some women also produce antibodies against sperm. Exposure to any of a number of chemicals can cause male sterility, but chemicals are probably only one of several causes. About 90% of men with spinal injuries are incapable of conceiving because the nerve signals do not get through to the muscles used for ejaculation. Treatment of the condition seemed hopeless until a procedure using electroejaculation was introduced at the University of Michigan in 1986 and developed by Dr. Lauro Halstead, director of the Washington, DC, hospital's fertility program, when he was working at a fertility clinic in Texas.[2] One of Halstead's patients, Michael Schneider, was paralyzed in a car accident in 1987, and was told by his doctors that he would never be able to have children. But he and his wife, Laura, longed for a child. Laura became pregnant from sperm obtained by the procedure and had a 7-pound son.

The electroejaculator is a rectal probe with electrodes carrying a small current that stimulates an erection and ejaculation of semen. It is uncomfortable but not painful. The semen can be used for artificial insemination or for fertilizing ova outside the body and inserting them into the uterus. Use of the electroejaculator has been standard practice for many years in livestock breeding, especially with bulls and rams, and according to Halstead was first used for artificial insemination in the 1940s to obtain sperm from endangered species such as gorillas and giant pandas.

The sperm in a sample of normal human semen can be seen under a microscope to be highly active, swimming around energetically in the seminal fluid with demonstrable vim and vigor. But invariably some of the sperm in an ejaculate are abnormal in one way or another.[3] Some will have irregular shapes, some will be double, some will be heads that have lost their tails, some will lack motility, and some will simply dawdle around, seemingly low in vitality. If there are too many abnormal sperm the chance of pregnancy will be low. Laboratory criteria for normality used by the American Society for Reproductive Medicine are: more than 50% of the sperm moving actively in a purposeful direction, about 50 million motile (active) sperm per ml, normal morphology, and about 50% of the initial motility surviving cryopreservation.[4]

Human spermatozoa swim in the semen at an average velocity of about 100 μm (micrometers or microns) per second, equal to about 14 inches per hour. But they do not swim in a beeline. They roll, yaw, and swerve in an arc, and some of them swim in circles getting nowhere unless perchance they get into a fallopian tube. They do not move in one plane, but rotate; a time-lapse picture of a sperm in motion looks like a miniature corkscrew.[5]

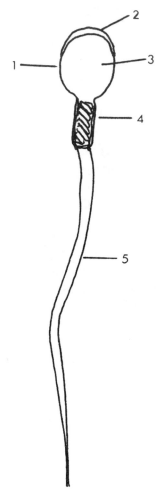

The spermatozoon carries approximately half of the genetic material received by the embryo, complementing the half in the egg from the mother. Of 100 million to a half billion sperm in a normal ejaculate, only one will normally find and penetrate a mate.

DONOR FATHERS

Insemination sans copulation was introduced scientifically in 1785 when an Italian scientist-priest, Lazzaro Spallanzani, inseminated a female dog with dog semen. Charles Bonnet, a French-Swiss lawyer-educated amateur biologist, was so alarmed by the experiment that he wrote a letter to the Italian admonishing that the procedure might someday be used in humans. But there was little general interest in it until a century later. Lori Andrews, in *New Conceptions*, tells about a Philadelphia doctor, William Pancost, who in 1884 assisted the wife of a rich merchant in getting pregnant.[6] Pancost asked the best-looking male student in the medical class he was teaching for a donation of semen, anesthetized the woman, and inseminated her. The doctor claimed that after the baby was born he worried that the child might look too much like the donor, so he told the husband what he had done. The husband was delighted but asked the doctor not to tell his wife. Even today, the perceived need for secrecy about the donor is a prominent feature of artificial insemination.

The discovery in 1949 that glycerol (glycerin) would protect sperm during freezing and thawing was a breakthrough in the development of artificial insemination. Pioneer work in livestock breeding showed that sperm could be frozen and stored for several years at liquid nitrogen temperatures with minor loss in sperm viability.[7] Improvements in freezing technique are still being made. Cryoprotectants now used include glycerol, dimethyl sulfoxide (DMS), and propanediol (an alcohol). Human sperm is put in vials or so-called straws, placed in containers of liquid nitrogen, and held at $-196°C$ ($-321°F$). Although there is a gradual loss in viable sperm and sperm motility over time, specimens can be kept usable for several years, in some cases for as long as 10 years, but with some loss of sperm. According to Robert Graham of the Repository for Germinal Choice, the half-life of sperm in cryopreservation is calculated to be about 1000 years.[8]

A husband planning a vasectomy can submit a sample to a sperm bank as a precaution in case he or his wife change their minds about having a baby. A sample of frozen sperm would

obviate the more uncertain surgical procedure of vasectomy reversal (reconnecting the severed vas deferens), or an operation to
surgically extract the semen. Formerly, only about 60% of the men
who had vasectomy reversals were able to father a child, but more
recent work results in sperm appearing in the semen of 80–90%,
and with as high as 50–80% of their wives becoming pregnant.[9]
The average sperm count after a vasectomy is lower than in men
who have never had a vasectomy, and sometimes there is an
obstruction damming the testicular fluid or trouble from antibodies that inhibit or destroy sperm motility or cause them to
clump.

It would be prudent for a young husband anticipating radiation or chemotherapy to save his undamaged sperm for possible
future use. Dr. Edward Tyler of Los Angeles tells how he used
frozen sperm to impregnate the wife of a Vietnam soldier who
wanted his wife to become pregnant while he was away, because
of the prospect that he might be gone for a long time. A New York
physician, Dr. Peter Schlegel, at the New York Hospital–Cornell
Medical Center extracted sperm from a man, Anthony Baez, about
13 or 14 hours after he died while in police custody. The man had
recently been married and the couple had planned to have children. His wife wanted to have a child of his even if widowed.[10]

In 1993, a state Court of Appeals in Los Angeles ruled that a
man had a right to bequeath his frozen sperm to a lover. The case
concerned the lover, Deborah Hecht, and William E. Kane who left
several vials of sperm with a cryobank before he committed suicide. Kane, who was divorced, left 80% of his estate to his two
daughters, 20% to Hecht, and willed the vials of sperm to Hecht to
use "should she so desire . . . to become impregnated with my
sperm." He wrote a letter to his daughters nine days before his
suicide making clear his desire that Hecht impregnate herself and
have their child. Kane's children took a dim view of the prospect
of having new siblings and potentially competing heirs. They
sued to prevent the bequest of sperm, arguing that their father had
changed his will about a month before he died, and that Hecht had
used undue influence on him. The Superior Court judge who
heard the case ordered that the sperm be destroyed, but stayed the

action pending an appeal. An appellate court unanimously reversed the decision, allowing Hecht to take possession of the sperm. USC law professor Michael H. Shapiro noted, "There is no stipulation in California law barring single women from being artificially inseminated and no prohibition on posthumous reproduction."[11,12]

Human sperm banks have been in existence since 1954. There are now sperm banks in most of the major cities. According to Diana Frank and Marta Vogel in *The Baby Makers*, the Idant Sperm Bank in New York City, with tens of thousands of specimens, has the largest supply of sperm in the world.[13] Its sperm have sired thousands of babies by so-called donor insemination (DI). In Oakland, California, the Sperm Bank of Northern California was set up in 1982 by the Oakland Feminist Women's Health Center, a group of single women. "We are, we believe," boasted administrative assistant Lisa Radcliffe, "the only woman-controlled sperm bank in the world." Within two months of their opening, about 500 men called to volunteer as donors, many of them gay men (shortly afterward, gay men were deemed ineligible to contribute to most sperm banks because of the danger of transmitting AIDS). Nearly half of the single women clients were homosexual. But more than half of their clients were husband-and-wife couples. Administrative director Laura Brown was quoted, "For years there had been a network of lesbian women racing around with fresh sperm in cold-cream jars . . . the preferred technique of insemination came to be known as the 'turkey baster method of making babies.'" She was referring to the kitchen utensil used for depositing sperm in the vagina. The Sperm Bank of Northern California from the start required donors to fill out a 10-page screening form, in addition to having physical and sperm examinations.[14]

The most exclusive sperm bank in the country was established in 1963 by cofounders Robert Klark Graham and the renowned American geneticist and Nobel laureate, Hermann Muller, who strongly advocated sperm banks so that the genetic endowment of intellectually talented men could be made available for perpetuating and spreading their genetic qualities.[15] The idea is reminiscent of a custom in ancient Sparta where men were encouraged to lend their wives to physically endowed men so that they could have children who would be perfect physical specimens. In Rome, Julius Caesar was given legal access to any wife in the Empire.

Robert K. Graham, who made a fortune as a developer of plastic lenses for eyeglasses, and was a friend and admirer of Muller, located the Hermann J. Muller Repository for Germinal Choice (RGC) in Escondido, California. At first, he invited Nobel prize winners, and later, other scientists and intellectually talented men, to contribute sperm to be made available to selected distinguished women. After the initial invitation to Nobelists, at the urging of Hermann Muller's widow, the sperm bank's screening of donors emphasized their all-around qualities. The RGC is probably the only sperm bank in the country that screens for intelligence as well as physical and personality qualities in addition to the health characteristics recommended by the American Association of Tissue Banks.

Several Nobel laureates contributed to the sperm bank; some declined. Two-time Nobel prize winner Linus Pauling, thought by many people to be the greatest chemist of the century and listed by *New Scientist* as one of the twenty greatest scientists of all time, on par with Newton, Darwin, and Einstein, opined that he preferred the old-fashioned way. In any case, Pauling was too old. One woman was publicly enthusiastic. "I'm very excited about this," she declared, "I'm tentatively going to select Number 13 because he is the youngest of the donors and has the highest IQ."[15a,16,17]

A California state assemblyman became alarmed at what he called a "master race sort of concept," and introduced a bill to regulate sperm banks. He said, "I don't like . . . the implication that the would-be mother could contract for the birth of a genius." In response, Paul Smith, research officer for the Repository, explained, "People come to us because they want the best possible sperm for their future offspring. We don't offer [sperm from] the village idiot because we don't get much demand for it."[18]

"We've had about 50 male donors," said Robert Graham during an interview in 1995. "There are many more requests for

Robert K. Graham, cofounder of the Repository for Germinal Choice, holding a child from the donor program. Photo courtesy of the Respository for Germinal Choice.

sperm than we have donations, so our inventory of frozen sperm is quite low. Women who receive sperm for impregnation through a physician must be married. We require a marriage certificate and their husband's consent."[19]

"Many of our donors make sperm donations several times

which we encourage," said administrative director Anita Neff. "It costs about $1000 for the initial laboratory screening. Follow-up tests after six-month's quarantine of the donor's sperm will run around $400. We've had between 400 and 500 women applicants resulting in more than 200 children. The oldest is now 13½."

To some people, the "germinal choice" project is a fanciful waste of time and human energy. But to others it is simply common sense to know and to have a choice in the qualities of a prospective father. A similar well-documented plan may have a place for women who want to be more selective in their choice of sperm than to take a catch-as-catch-can supply from an unknown donor picked by an anonymous person. Ilona Sherman, who owns a public relations firm in Los Angeles, was 43 and divorced when she decided to have a child on her own. She opted for artificial insemination. "I was getting older," she said, "I wasn't going to wait to meet someone to do it." She gave birth by DI to a healthy son, Adam Robert.

If there were sperm banks from which aspiring mothers like Sherman could personally select sperm from anonymous men with thoroughly documented ancestral, genetic, health, and other characteristics, they might prefer to do so instead of relying on a physician's more or less random offering, however good his spur-of-the-moment pick might be. Informed women will be at least as picky in their selection of a sperm donor as in selecting a husband. The practice of carefully planned selection is routine among livestock breeders, who are willing to pay large sums of money for sires of known desirable characteristics. In one of many such instances, Brocco, a Santa Anita Derby winner with earnings of over $1 million, was retired to stud and sold by his owners, Mr. and Mrs. Albert Broccoli, for a price reported to be $2.5 million. When a more celebrated racehorse, Northern Dancer, was retired after a spectacular career, a syndicate reportedly paid $40 million for the stallion, and were said to be expecting $1 million per stud service.

In the early days of DI, medical students, interns, and young doctors were the most common source of sperm. A survey made in 1977 by a University of Wisconsin research team showed that in

SUMMARY:	Cytogeneticist currently conducting research in clinical genetics
ANCESTRY:	Austrian
EYE COLOR:	Blue-green
SKIN:	Fair
HAIR:	Golden blonde, naturally curly
HEIGHT:	6'4"
WEIGHT:	225 lb
GENERAL APPEARANCE:	Very handsome; superb physique
PERSONALITY:	Warm; happy; confident
BORN:	Late 1960s
I.Q.:	142 on Binet scale
HOBBIES:	Member of an Olympic team; genetic research; acting
MUSIC:	Plays piano proficiently
MANUAL DEXTERITY:	Excellent
GENERAL HEALTH:	Excellent
BLOOD TYPE:	A−
COMMENTS:	Comes from a long line of talented professional individuals and has the energy and ambition to match his exceptional gifts

Description categories used for all donors to the Repository for Germinal Choice. This is a description profile of a donor designated Orange/Red #5. Courtesty of Repository for Germinal Choice, Escondido, California.

almost all cases, it was the physicians who selected the donors; 62% of them were medical students or hospital residents. Thus, the doctors were mostly choosing to reproduce themselves, that is, people of their profession, instead of a cross section of the population. One physician used a single donor for 50 pregnancies. Screening by doctors who personally selected their donors was haphazard, although most physicians were careful to see that the donor was a good fit for the nominal father and mother. Several Denver doctors who specialized in DI reported that they created their own donor registry. But others used criteria that were superficial and slipshod. In either case there was apt to be personal bias. It's an open secret that some doctors, unable to find a suitable donor when wanted, furnished their own sperm. One California physician was found to have used his own fresh semen for nearly all of his many DIs, possibly for reasons of convenience, but more probably the ego satisfaction of fathering many children. Now, with rare exceptions, donors are selected differently. Until recently, nearly all of the sperm used for DI was used fresh, but with the development of the freezing technique and the belated awareness of the danger of disease transmission, there has been a proliferation of commercial sperm banks using donors from all walks of life.

The lack of standardization and quality control of sperm donations is abetted by the aura of secrecy surrounding DIs. Both the woman who wants a DI and her husband are almost always under emotional stress. She worries about whether it's all right with her husband for her to have a baby that is not his, and he may have unexpressed reservations about the arrangement. Both of them worry about whether the child will look anything like the nominal father, or like either of them. The tensions of uncertainty generally result in their letting the doctor make all of the decisions— unwise for several reasons.

Donors' feelings about donating sperm cover a spectrum of emotions. One donor bragged, "I get a kick out of being able to father a large number of children." Others are embarrassed because they have to masturbate to provide the sperm. Said another, "What the hell, I'm getting paid for what I'd probably be doing anyway." Most sperm banks provide a small, sterile-like room, some of them with visual stimulation in the form of "girlie" magazines and male-oriented books. When sperm is brought to a doctor's office from home, the specimen should be delivered within about 30 minutes to avoid chilling. However, human sperm keeps well at room temperature for days or even weeks. If the man has trouble producing sperm by masturbation, a special condom can be used during intercourse.

Sperm banks differ in the amount of information they require from donors. Until recently, at some sperm banks the donors had only to pass a simple screening test, the most important thing being the sperm count because a sperm bank wants a record of successful DIs. The pregnancy success rate probably averages around 20%, close to that from natural coital fertilization. Other required information was usually height, weight, color, education, and age. The younger the better, above the minimum age 21 specified by most sperm banks, because with advancing age there is apt to be an increasing chance of abnormal sperm and harmful mutations. At the large sperm banks the donors' qualifications are now entered in a computer file for quick reference when getting a call from a doctor.

In the absence of legislative standards or medical profession oversight of the sperm industry, the mother-to-be and her husband will be happier, more confident, and relaxed if they know they are getting the right stuff for the genes of their child. They will insist on a complete profile of the donor—in writing. They will ask whether the donor screening adhered to the guidelines established by the American Society for Reproductive Medicine (formerly the American Fertility Society) or the American Association of Tissue Banks. They will be specific in asking questions about the donor. The profile will include information on age (maximum 35), education, occupation, height, weight, color of skin, eyes, and hair (and whether straight or curly), health, history of and tests for venereal diseases (including genital warts, herpes, gonorrhea, syphilis chlamydia, trichomonas, and AIDS), hepatitis B (chronic hepatitis tests within six months before donation), a chromosome analysis for genetic diseases, including recessive

DONOR TESTING

The following tests are to be performed on all donors.

INITIAL TESTS:	Blood typing, Rh factor
	FTA-ABs for syphilis
	HBsAg, & core anitbody
	HCV
	HIV-1, HIV-2
	HTLV-1, HTLV-2
	Blood chemistry panel including alanine aminotransferase (ALT)
	CMV-IgG & IgM
	CBC
	Urinalysis & culture
	Urethral cultures for: gonococcus, chlamydia, mycoplasma, streptococcus B, ureaplasma
	Tay–Sachs
	Cystic Fibrosis
	Karyotype (if requested or indicated)
EVERY 6 MONTHS	FTA-ABs for syphilis
	HBsAg, & core antibody
	HCV
	HIV-1, HIV-2
	HTLV-1, HTLV-2
	CMV-IgG & IgM

Requirements for sperm donation. Courtesy of Repository for Germinal Choice, Escondido, California.

ANNUAL TESTS:	SMAC-21 (to include alanine amino-transferase)
	CBC
	Urinalysis
SPERM TESTS:	Chlamydia—culture
	Neisseria gonorrheae—culture
	Streptococcus B—culture
	WBC

A semen analysis is performed on all specimens. This includes: Sperm count, morphology, motility, and cultures. All semen testing is performed on postfrozen specimens.

All vials of semen are quarantined for 180 days as a control against HIV and hepatitis B & C. Donors are tested initially and are retested at the end of the quarantine period. If the results remain negative the specimens are approved for use.

Our schedules for testing are the guidelines directed by the American Assoication of Tissue Banks and American Fertility Society with additional testing to meet our high standards.

Requirements for sperm donation. (Continued)

genes for any disease, marital status, children (evidence of reproductive ability), drug use, sexual orientation, hobbies, music, athletic or other special talents, religion, national origin, ethnic background, causes of death of each of his parents, and possibly a
photograph. The prospective parents will inquire whether special
procedures have been followed to screen for AIDS. The sperm
bank should have ejected anyone who has engaged in behavior
known to be high-risk for AIDS, and the donor should have been
screened for AIDS and/or HIV, and the sample of semen held in
quarantine for six months before the donor is again given an AIDS
antibody test.

This, of course, rules out the use of fresh donor semen. The
American Society for Reproductive Medicine and other health
agencies, including the FDA and Centers for Disease Control,
recommend the use of frozen semen exclusively. As late as 1986–
1987, according to a U.S. Office of Technology Assessment survey
of artificial insemination practices, 22% of 11,000 doctors used only
fresh semen. Fewer than half of the doctors using fresh semen
screened for AIDS or genetic defects, and only about one-fourth of
them screened for other sexually transmitted diseases.

Should there be federal controls and regulations setting standards for sperm quality similar to the authority of the FDA over
the quality of foods, drugs, cosmetics, and medical devices? The
FDA could probably find reasons to delve into the sperm business,
but they've shied away from dabbling in the affairs of such sensitive and personal enterprises. If sperm customers become alerted
to the problems with DIs, future recipients will demand that more
attention be given not only to the qualifications of the donors, but
also to the less obvious but ever-present risk that a boy and a girl
will meet, marry, and have children without knowing that they are
half brother and half sister. Often a donor supplies multiple samples of sperm to a physician who may have a large number of DI
recipients in a neighborhood. Inevitably, some of the children will
meet, and they will have much in common, but no knowledge of
their relationship. The California doctor who routinely used his
own semen was a notable threat to the community by fathering
dozens of half brothers and half sisters among his clientele. The

objection to half brothers and half sisters marrying and having children is more than a societal taboo. Geneticists have known for a long time that children of closely related parents are more apt to have genetic defects than children of distantly related parents. It is a practice at some sperm banks for donors to continue to make donations week after week for several years. An ideal program would limit the number of specimens from a donor to a total of 24, enough for three pregnancies, to avoid a large number of unknowingly related children, but a limit that strict is seldom practiced. The American Society for Reproductive Medicine recommends a limit of about 10 pregnancies per donor.

Secrecy is both good and bad. Doctors typically give as little information as they can to recipients, asking them in effect to trust them. The most controversial question is whether there should be strict anonymity or if the child should have the right to know the identity of the biological father when she or he reaches adulthood (taken to be age 18), similar to the practice in Sweden. In the United States it is often not possible because many of the sperm banks don't keep adequate records, and in some cases there is no attempt at all to match the characteristics of the donor to the recipient. Moreover, information of any kind is usually hard to get from a doctor's office. In fact, there is no requirement that either doctors or sperm banks keep records of any kind on DIs. England and several other European countries require sperm banks to keep records on the identity of donors in case they are needed for medical or other reasons. There would be no supposition of financial responsibility.

Annette Baran and Reuben Panner, clinical social workers and authors of *Lethal Secrets*, are outspoken advocates of a child's "right to know." They believe that a DI child's knowledge of both genetic parents contributes to his or her identity and self-concept in a way that connects the child to its biological and historical past vital to the child's health and well-being. They say a child has a right to know, at an appropriate age, the identity of the donor father, as well as his medical, social, and family history, and even a right to meet the donor father if he or she ever wants to have personal contact.[20]

FEMALE FERTILITY

Experience has shown that a woman's ability to conceive decreases with age, especially after 40. A common cause of female sterility is blockage of the fallopian tubes, often resulting from earlier infection. Procedures for manipulation of sperm and egg outside the body and manual placement of the fertilized egg in the uterus or fallopian tube are called *assisted reproductive technology* (ART). The ART procedure that has received the most publicity is *in vitro fertilization and embryo transfer* or IVF for short. Fertilization *in vitro*, from the Latin word *vitrum* meaning glass, simply means fertilization in glass. IVF is sometimes the only hope of an otherwise infertile woman.

First, the woman is given fertility hormones to stimulate her ovaries to produce as many eggs as possible. The mature eggs (technically oocytes) are sucked out through a needle that is inserted into the ovary. The eggs are placed in a petri dish where they are mixed with sperm from her husband, or a donor if the husband is sterile. The resulting embryos are transferred by a catheter inserted through the vagina into the uterus, where it is hoped that one of them will become implanted and become a baby.

In natural fertilization, the egg is fertilized in the fallopian tube, and the fertilized egg undergoes cleavage while traveling along the fallopian tube toward the uterus. Cleavage is a series of rapid cell divisions by which an increasing number of cells, each called a *blastomere*, is produced. By the time the cleaving embryo has reached the uterus, it is 4–5 days old, and consists of more than 100 cells. It has become a hollow sphere of cells, one layer thick, called a *blastocyst* or *blastula*, about 0.1 mm in diameter. By this time, the protective covering of the egg, called the *zona pellucida*, has ruptured, and the embryo is ready to implant in the uterine lining.

The fertility drugs used to stimulate ovulation typically produce as many as a dozen eggs. A common method of collecting the eggs is to extract them by laparoscopy (a laparoscope is a thin telescope with a built-in light source), or preferably by the less

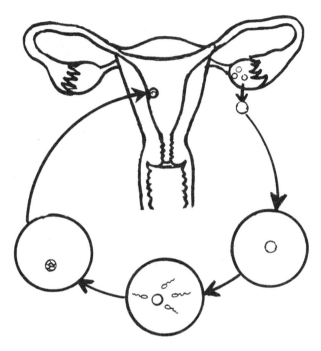

In vitro fertilization. An oocyte (egg) is surgically removed from an ovary and placed in fluid in a petri disk. Fertilization takes place when sperm is added. Cleavage (cell division) produces a multicell embryo, which is mechanically placed in the uterus where the embryo becomes implanted. Drawing by Vicki Frazior.

invasive ultrasound technique. The sperm are first washed free of seminal fluid, which·contains an inhibitor that prevents capacitation of the sperm, i.e., the process that enables the sperm to penetrate the egg.[21] Capacitation takes place naturally during coital fertilization in the female oviduct where the inhibitor does not penetrate in appreciable amount. Washing also removes potentially antigenic proteins, prostaglandins, and infectious agents that might be present.

Prepared sperm can be seen penetrating the oocytes (unfertilized eggs) in a petri dish within a few hours. The embryos are allowed to develop for 48 to 72 hours before several of them are introduced into the woman's uterus. An average of about 80% of

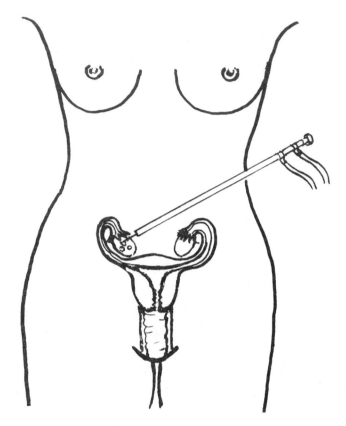

The laparoscope, a narrow, lighted instrument equipped with a lens, is used in one method of collecting eggs from the ovary. Drawing by Vicki Frazior.

the oocytes mixed with sperm in a petri dish become fertilized and form embryos. They develop into a blastocyst or blastula (the stage in which there is a single layer of cells surrounding a liquid-filled core) in about 6 days, which is the embryo stage that normally becomes implanted in the uterus. Not all of the embryos obtained in culture are usable because usually some of them are abnormal. Implantation in the lining of the uterus leading to an eventual birth takes place in no more than about 17% of the trials, so several embryos are always used to improve the odds.[22] But it is inadvisable to use more than three embryos because of the possibility of the potential mother becoming too pregnant—multiple implantations resulting in twins, triplets, or more. Some parents, however, consider multiple births a bonus blessing.

Another procedure is to bypass the *in vitro* step and place a mixture of eggs and sperm directly in the fallopian tube where fertilization takes place under natural conditions after coitus. This method is called *gamete intrafallopian transfer* (GIFT). The GIFT technique is used primarily to treat women who are still producing eggs but for one reason or another have not been able to become pregnant. In those cases, doctors harvest the eggs from the woman's ovaries, mix the eggs with her husband's sperm, and immediately inject them through a catheter into her fallopian tubes.

If the woman is menopausal, extensive hormone shots are needed to replace the hormones she is not producing. The ovaries can be made to produce multiple eggs by treating the woman with a fertility drug, like Perganol or the antiestrogen clomiphene citrate (Clomid). A method of concentrating the sperm is sometimes used by a procedure that isolates highly motile sperm. This is useful because the lumen of the uterus is limited to a volume of only about 0.25–0.5 ml of the inseminate.

The pregnancy success rate averages from less than 20% to 30%, although Dr. Ricardo Asch, who developed GIFT, used donated eggs twice with 100% success.[23] In another modification of IVF, called zygote intrafallopian transfer (ZIFT), the eggs are fertilized *in vitro* and the zygotes (already fertilized eggs) are placed in the fallopian tube. A slight modification of ZIFT is a procedure in which the embryo is in the pronuclear stage—an early developmental stage of the fertilized egg. Another modification of ZIFT, called tubal embryo (stage) transfer [TE(S)T], uses an embryo in an even later stage of cell division.

A more recent development is a micromanipulation technique in which a single sperm is injected directly into the egg before transferring it to the uterus or fallopian tube. The method, called intracytoplasmic sperm injection (ICSI), pronounced "icksee," is useful if the man has a very low sperm count, and greatly improves the chance of fertilizing the egg.[24] If a man does not produce sperm at all, a technique, still largely experimental, is to surgically remove cells from the seminal (seminiferous) tubule of a testicle and fertilize an ovum *in vitro* by injecting one of the cells into it by micromanipulation. A baby born by this method was reported in January, 1996.[25] The use of cells other than sperm is made possible by the fact that sperm are produced directly from cells that carry the genetic material in the correct number of chromosomes for fertilization. Ordinary-looking cells called *primordial germ cells* form in the human embryo long before any sex organs exist. These germ cells divide at a great rate, increasing to 600,000 during the second month when the human embryo is only 16–25 mm in length, and to almost 7 million by the fifth month. By further cell division, they form cells called *primary spermatocytes*, and when these divide, forming secondary spermatocytes, the chromosome pairs separate, leaving one-half the previous number in each daughter cell—the same as in sperm. All of this takes place in the lining of the seminal tubules of the testicles.

One thing that escalates the cost, as well as the stress, of IVF is the disappointingly high failure rate of implantation. The cost is now excessively expensive—as much as $12,000 or more per try. However, progress in having children by using IVF, so-called test-tube babies, is proceeding so rapidly that it shows promise of bringing the cost in the future within reach of many more people.

A way to increase the odds was discovered by Dr. Geoffrey Sher of the Pacific Fertility Medical Center in San Francisco where Sher and his associates achieved a 49% pregnancy rate by treating the women with aspirin and heparin (an anticlotting substance). They believe that antibodies called *antiphospholipid antibodies* are responsible for women having difficulties becoming pregnant. The antibodies are thought to form platelets around the developing placenta, cutting off its function so it fails to implant. The antiphospholipid antibodies are thought to be especially prevalent in women who have abnormal tissue growth in the uterine lining from infection, surgery, or endometriosis. The blood-thining properties of aspirin and heparin prevent the clotting that can stop implantation. Another possibility for this purpose is immunoglobulin to combat the damaging antibodies.[1]

A major advance in IVF technique was the use of frozen embryos. The big advantage of freezing is that the excess embryos do not necessarily have to be discarded, but can be used in succeeding trials if needed, thus obviating the surgical procedure of harvesting more oocytes. Embryo freezing is done in a computer-controlled refrigerating device that lowers the temperature 0.3°C per minute until it reaches −76°C. The containers of embryos are then immersed in liquid nitrogen and stored at −196°C. Thawing is done by reversing the procedure. However, the survival rate of cryopreserved embryos is not as great as the survival of frozen sperm.

The question of potential risks to babies reared from frozen embryos was raised by a study by French researchers at the University of Paris Bicetre Hospital and the Centre National de Recherche Scientifique, published in January, 1995, in the *Proceedings of the National Academy of Sciences*. The study found that adult mice born from cryopreserved embryos differ from those born from nonfrozen embryos in both morphology and behavior. Only short-term studies have been made of babies from frozen human embryos, and these are mostly of pregnancy and miscarriage rates. Says Maurice Auroux of the Bicetre Hospital, "We are in a human experiment." There is the possibility that free radicals (particles of matter carrying a positive or negative charge) caused by the thawing process or the kinds of salts used in freezing might cause mutations. But frozen embryos have been used for many years in livestock breeding, with no adverse effects. Gary Hodgen, president of the Jones Institute for Reproductive Medicine at East Virginia Medical School, was quoted by *Science*: "there are no apparent consequences [of freezing] that I am concerned or suspicious about."[26]

SURROGATE MOTHERS

Surrogate motherhood has an ancient origin. The Book of Genesis tells how Abraham's wife, Sarah, volunteered to have her handmaiden, Hagar, have a child by Abraham. Sarah was an old woman. "Look now," she said to her husband, "the Lord has kept me from bearing a child. I want you to have sex with my maid; it may be that I can obtain children by her." Hagar was an Egyptian in bondage, so being a slave, she had no choice in the matter. But the honor apparently went to her head, for she became so uppity that Sarah had to get tough with her, making life for her so unbearable that Hagar ran away into the wilderness. She had a son, Ishmael, who turned out to be what the writers of Genesis described as "a wild man." Abraham was 86 when Ishmael was born. Later, at the age of 99, he finally got Sarah pregnant, much to her amazement—and amusement.[27]

In today's world, the most common and technically simple form of surrogate motherhood is exactly comparable to the method used by Sarah and Abraham nearly 4000 years ago, except artificial insemination is deemed to be more appropriate than coital sex. When a woman is infertile or physically frail, she and her husband may decide that they would like to have a surrogate mother to carry a child for them. Sperm from the infertile woman's husband is used to impregnate the surrogate mother, who will carry the fetus to term and turn the child over to the couple. This is the only medical solution, for example, for a woman who has had a hysterectomy and removal of the ovaries. Other reasons for using a surrogate mother could be premature menopause or the risk of passing on a known genetic defect, although a more satisfactory solution to the genetic problem would be an oocyte or embryo donation.

Egg Donor

A woman can help make a baby by merely furnishing ova. When fertilized *in vitro*, the resulting embryos are implanted in the mother-to-be, the wife, who will make no genetic contribution, but the child she carries will be her husband's. This is genetically comparable, though gender-reversed, to artificial impregnation of a woman with sperm from a donor. But it is more difficult to find ova donors than sperm donors. Ova can sometimes be collected from a woman who is undergoing surgery for another purpose, and payment for the ova can help with the cost of the operation. Selling ova is just as ethical as selling sperm.

Rent-a-Womb

If a woman's ovaries are healthy, but she is unable to carry a child for various reasons such as a hysterectomy, severe cardiac disease, diabetes, or hypertension, an extracted ovum fertilized *in vitro* with her husband's sperm can be implanted in another woman.[28] The child will be the genetic offspring of both of its natural parents and will have no genetic relationship to the surrogate mother. The surrogate in this kind of arrangement is sometimes referred to as a *surrogate gestational mother*. She will furnish only the womb. Both the egg and the sperm will be furnished by the biological parents. In early 1987, a Cleveland, Ohio, surrogate mother gave birth to a so-called test-tube child. In this case, the genetic mother was fertile but was unable to carry a child because of a diseased uterus. The surrogate gestational mother was a married woman with children.

One of the biggest difficulties in getting IVF babies is implanting the fertilized egg in the uterine wall. The stage of the egg's development must be synchronized with appropriate changes in the lining of the uterus. In the case of a surrogate gestational mother, the difficulty was at first compounded by the fact that the ovulations of the two women had to be synchronized to occur at the same time. However, the problem can be solved by IVF and freezing the embryos to make them available when needed.

Another way is by a technique of ovum transfer already mentioned—that of bypassing the IVF stage by injecting the donor eggs and the husband's sperm simultaneously into the fallopian tubes where the eggs are fertilized naturally. Dr. Ricardo Asch pioneered the technique, GIFT, at the Brownsville Medical Center in Texas. In November, 1986, Asch announced the delivery of twins from GIFT, the world's first twins born from donor eggs. "It was a regular delivery of twins with excellent signs of vitality," said Dr. Asch, "They are beautiful, normal babies." The mother was a 32-year-old woman who had gone through menopause at age 20.[23]

MOTHERHOOD AFTER MENOPAUSE

It was once thought that women could not become pregnant after menopause. But it is now known that the uterus is capable of implanting an embryo long after the ovaries have shut down production of eggs. This makes it possible for older women to have babies by using an ovum donated by a younger woman. The first woman over 50 to give birth in the United States with the help of egg donations and IVF was Joni Mosby Mitchell, a grand-mother, who at the age of 52 gave birth to a baby boy on March 31, 1992. The oldest woman to give birth by this method, in a fertility program sponsored by the University of Southern California, was 55. In another program at the Martin Luther Hospital in Anaheim, Mary Shearing, a 53-year-old grandmother, had twins from do-nated eggs fertilized by her younger husband's sperm.[29]

Pregnancy by a donor ovum makes it possible for a woman to give birth to her daughter's child (the older woman's grandchild), as in the case of a mother whose daughter could not carry to term.

WHAT'S COMING

The use of sperm by DI, better known to most people as artificial insemination, has progressed from fresh sperm, by a system of more or less haphazard selection of donors, to organized procedures for handling frozen sperm by sperm banks. Examina-tions and tests have been adopted to ensure reliability and safety. Frozen sperm has practically replaced fresh sperm to allow time for testing of viability and freedom from disease microorganisms. The future of DI will see a shift to even greater control of sperm selection by the recipients. Enlightened prospective parents will demand documentation of the qualifications, history, and characteristics of the donors and will evaluate them in relation to the probable compatibility with their own inheritable qualities. They will ask for evidence that tests have been given to ensure protection against both diseases and genetic disorders. Sperm banks will more actively seek donors with outstanding qualities, both intellectual and physical, in response to demands of recipients for that kind of information.

The technique of freezing sperm, which revolutionized the screening process for potential disease transmission, also made it possible to preserve sperm or embryos months or years in advance of when a child is desired. A young man who expects to have chemotherapy or radiation therapy will be advised to have sperm cryopreserved if he and his wife think they might want subsequent children. And if a man and wife are separated for a lengthy period, she can become pregnant by airmail, from frozen sperm shipped in a dewar flask (similar to a vacuum bottle). If impregnation is carefully timed, it may be necessary only to keep the sperm at room temperature during shipment.

Although IVF and related methods of making babies have increased dramatically in the span of a few years, further expansion of the procedures is restrained by continued high costs. Some of the costs are already being assumed by some medical insurance plans, and some of the insurance companies may assume full costs in the future. Methods are being developed and refined constantly; improvement in technique will, in itself, reduce costs. An increase in the success rate, i.e., a reduction in failures to conceive, will further reduce the cost.

The most dramatic innovation will be further development and availability of genetic testing of embryos, now confined largely to cases in which the parents are known or suspected carriers of inheritable defects. Genetic testing will become routine for all IVF embryos. Ultimately, genetic profiles of a wide range of inheritable characteristics will become available. The most revolutionary sexual and social development in the next century will be genetic. Several thousand diseases and disorders are known to be caused by mutated genes. Says W. French Anderson, Director of

Gene Therapy at the University of Southern California School of Medicine:

> More than 4,000 conditions . . . are caused by inborn damage to a single gene. Many other ailments—the scourges of cancer, heart disease, AIDS, arthritis and senility, for example—result from impairment of one or more genes involved in the body's defenses.

Some of the genetic diseases are a cause of miscarriage, and some are fatal early in life before the victims can have progeny. More facts on inherited defects and their loci on chromosomes are discovered regularly. A new disease-causing gene is discovered at least every week, some of them causing susceptibility to cancer, for example breast cancer, and the pace of discovery is accelerating. Genes are made up of sequences formed by about 6 billion coding entities—nucleotides—containing so-called nitrogen bases.[30] Because the DNA is composed of double strands forming paired nucleotides, there are about 3 billion nucleotide (base) pairs. Sequences of the base pairs form roughly 100,000 genes in the human genome (complete set of human genes). One mutated nucleotide in the DNA can have profound effects.

Eventually, many people will want to have a genetic profile that will pinpoint genetic diseases and afflictions such as Tay–Sachs, muscular dystrophy, cystic fibrosis, hemophilia, Down's syndrome, Huntington's disease, severe combined immunodeficiency (SCID), Gaucher's disease, familial hypercholesterolemia, alpha-1 antitrypsin deficiency, Fanconi's anemia, Hunter's syndrome, and others, including some forms of cancer. The cost of improved techniques for determining whether a defective gene is present in the parent may be reduced in the future to the point that screening will become routine. At present, a pregnant woman can wait for the procedure called *amniocentesis* or a procedure called *chorionic villus sampling* (CVS) during pregnancy. Amniocentesis is a surgical procedure usually done about the fourth month (16 weeks) of pregnancy in which the physician inserts a hollow needle through the abdominal wall into the uterus of the pregnant woman and withdraws a small amount of amniotic fluid to be sent to laboratory for genetic analysis. The fluid will contain some cells of the developing fetus, which are centrifuged out and cultured, requiring an additional three or more weeks. The cells' chromosomes can be examined for genetic and congenital defects and gender. The procedure is so routine that it is no longer considered experimental. Many doctors recommend the procedure if the pregnant woman is over 35 because the chance of conceiving a child with Down's syndrome increases with age. The chance is 1 in 60 if the mother is over 45. If a defective gene is found, the parent is faced with the agonizing decision of whether to abort the pregnancy. CVS can be performed earlier than amniocentesis, as soon as 9 weeks into pregnancy. The chorion is the membrane surrounding the early fetus that develops into the placenta. Cells taken from the chorion contain the same genetic information as those from the amniotic fluid. However, IVF and preimplantation genetic screening, when possible, would make that surgical step unnecessary.

Recently developed techniques make it possible to be selective in picking embryos with less likelihood of having genetic defects, giving IVF an important advantage over natural impregnation. Many people, if they know that they carry certain defective genes, may in the future elect to use IVF instead of relying on the unreliable, emotionally devastating, old-fashioned way. Scientists at the New York Hospital–Cornell Medical Center reported in 1993 that they had successfully produced for the first time in the United States a pregnancy and birth following embryo biopsy. The mother in this case delivered a healthy baby girl weighing more than 9 pounds.[31]

Embryo biopsy consists of removing a single cell from the *in vitro* embryo before it is implanted in the mother, and analyzing it for genetic defects. The technique was pioneered in this country by Dr. Jaime Grifo and his colleagues at New York–Cornell's Center for Reproductive Medicine and Infertility. In this procedure, the embryo is biopsied at the eight-cell stage before it is ready for implantation and before there is any differentiation of tissue to form a recognizable fetus. Embryo biopsy, also called *preimplantation genetic diagnosis*, does not impair the ability of the embryo to develop normally.

Many people are troubled by ethical questions that arise from assisted reproductive technology (ART). Unfortunately, such concerns may delay innovation and the introduction of some promising techniques. We will explore possible and probable innovations and the associated ethical questions in the following chapter.

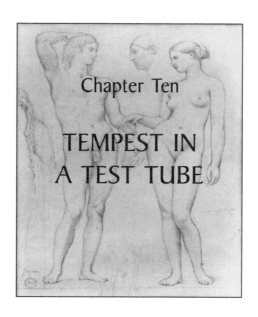

Chapter Ten

TEMPEST IN A TEST TUBE

The scientists' compulsion to fiddle with nature and change the course of natural events makes people, including many scientists, uneasy about the future. This is nowhere more evident than when dealing with human reproduction. The numerous taboos surrounding sexuality, including secrecy, and reticence toward openly discussing personal sexual matters create a tension that intensifies differences about the morality of sexual practices and innovations in fertility techniques.

Scientists were the first to raise questions about fertility techniques that would inevitably require ethical, moral, and legal decisions. Robert Edwards, the geneticist–embryologist–immunologist who later teamed up with Dr. Patrick Steptoe in the first IVF birth of a human baby, repeatedly raised ethical and social questions about the consequences of the projected research and resulting clinical practices.[1] Many others joined the debate, including the World Council of Churches.

The more or less subdued debate became a tempest after the

birth of the first so-called test-tube baby, Louise Brown, in 1978. A flood of articles appeared in the press volunteering opinions, pronouncements, prognostications, and the fears of journalists, theologians, philosophers, ethicists, theorists, scientists, doctors, lawyers, and politicians. Rhetoric came easy: "the slippery slope," "the unconsenting fetus," "who should play God?" "the sanctity of human life," "the sacredness of human personality," "human dignity and family solidarity may be debased," and "the brink of tampering with our own evolution."

People tended to confuse IVF with genetic engineering or to lump them in a package of dangerous science. A group of fifty theologians called for a halt in all efforts to change the transmission of inheritable human traits. Where to draw the line? Said the Rev. Jerry Falwell of the Moral Majority, "Scientists are delving into an area that is far too sacred for human beings to be involved in." Columnist George F. Will wrote, "Biology now stirs a fear, never stirred by physics. . . . Biology, with its threat to 'improve' the species, jeopardizes mankind's sense of dignity."[2] The American Fertility Society issued ethical guidelines.[3] The U.S. government established a de facto moratorium in 1972 on federal support of IVF that lasted for more than a decade.[4] In 1994, President Clinton announced a policy against using federal money to create human embryos solely for research purposes.[5] Meanwhile, by the 1980s IVF had become accepted medical practice.

Birth control and abortion are ancient practices that continue to arouse emotional debate over strongly held beliefs of morality and religious convictions. These, as well as the more recent practices of artificial insemination are in conflict with the long-held view of the Roman Catholic Church that sexual reproduction is a sacred gift not to be tampered with, and that even ova and sperm are untouchable entities of human reproductive life, not pieces of tissue to manipulate. Back in 1948, the Archbishop of Canterbury, leader of the Anglican Church, said he thought that artificial insemination should be made a criminal offense.[6] Even today in England, children conceived by DI are illegitimate, and their donors potentially (but not actually) have rights and responsibilities, while the husband, in theory, has none. In the United States, however, the mother's husband is routinely signed to the birth certificate, and he is considered to be the father unless it is shown that he had no access to the mother.

In 1982 in England, a Committee of Inquiry was set up to consider recent and potential developments in human fertilization and embryology and to recommend "what policies and safeguards should be applied." The report of the committee, known as the Warnock Report, after the chairperson, Mary Warnock, Mistress of Girton College, Cambridge, was mainly common sense, but left crucial questions unanswered. Seven years later, a subsequent study called the Glover Report was made available,[7] and in the United States, a Human Life Amendment to the Constitution was proposed. The Roman Catholic Church in a wide-ranging 40-page document issued by the Vatican in March, 1987, stressed that the natural transmission of life is not to be interfered with and that human procreation can rightfully occur only through the sex act by married partners. Thus, it ruled out artificial insemination and IVF. The Vatican approved prenatal diagnosis and treatment, but strongly opposed preselection of sex or other "predetermined qualities." It condemned the production of embryos "destined to be exploited as disposable biological material," and fertilization outside the human body. "Artificial insemination of an unmarried woman or a widow, whoever the donor may be, is not morally justified," the document said. Anticipating future fiction-like scientific intrusions, the Vatican condemned any attempt to clone human beings, the creation of animal–human hybrids, or gestation of human embryos in artificial or animal uteruses.[8]

The view of scientists generally was summed up by Robert Edwards:

> Now that we have demonstrated that human conception can occur outside the human body, many investigations can be done that were impossible before. These are challenges which we should not fear, though we must be on guard against abuses.[9]

Some people see ethical problems in manipulating embryos because they perceive these, even in the earliest stages of cell division, as living human beings. But the humanitarian advantage of eliminating the birth of agonizingly defective babies has thus far prevailed. The question of using aborted fetuses for medical experiments or surgical therapy is more difficult because they are more recognizable as living organisms. As the pressure grows for the use of human tissue to achieve medical advances, the clash between science and the emotional and moral issues will have to be resolved.

A highly emotional issue is the morality of *creating* human embryos in the laboratory for the specific purpose of using them in research. However, the usual production of embryos by IVF is for implantation, not research. The perceived ethics of IVF is crucial to long-term success of the method. The technique of IVF is to obtain more ova than needed for a single implantation because failure to implant, that is, become embedded in the uterus, is common. The extra embryos are simply frozen and held as a backup supply for future use if needed. If never needed, they are discarded. Some people think that the inevitable discarding of unsuitable or unwanted embryos is comparable to early abortion. Others think that it is stretching the facts to call these microscopic aggregates of a few, largely undifferentiated, cells human beings.

The U.S. government does not now prohibit the use of human embryos or fetuses for experimentation but refuses to financially support such work. Publicly funded research on human embryos was put on hold in the United States in the early 1980s. Because of politics of the abortion debate, the National Institutes of Health (NIH) had banned such research. When it was decided that the moratorium should come to an end, a science advisory panel to the NIH recommended some guidelines for keeping research on embryos within ethical bounds. They recommended approval of research on *in vitro* unused embryos up to the 14th day, following a widely used international rule, or up to the appearance of the "primitive streak," which is the first indication of a nervous system. They said that in no case should research go beyond the stage of embryo development characterized by neural tube closure, which will come at about the 18th day or later. They said that no embryo if used for research of any kind should be transferred to a woman for gestation.[10] Research may take several forms, for example, dividing an embryo into two or more embryos.

The panel approved the research use of human eggs that have been made to grow without fertilization, called *parthenotes*. Such eggs, which have not had their DNA altered by "genetic imprinting" by sperm, disintegrate without forming embryos, but are useful in research because they could yield information about cell division and other physiological features. The panel approved biopsy of blastomeres (very early stage embryos) for the purpose of removing a cell and using it to examine the DNA for genetic defects. The technique had already been used in England to screen out an embryo that had two copies of the gene for cystic fibrosis, and to select a normal embryo, which was implanted and led to the birth of a healthy baby girl. The method could also be used to test for Duchenne's muscular dystrophy, Tay–Sachs disease, Lesch–Nyhan syndrome, and several other diseases. The panel said that separation (splitting) of blastomeres for the purpose of biopsy should be permitted, but it would be forbidden to separate (divide) blastomeres to be used for implantation. They said it would be morally objectionable. Some members of the panel also opposed, on ethical grounds, creating permanent cell lines from embryos, even though selected embryos have great potential for treatment of some diseases. The panel listed several procedures as not acceptable, including:

- Transfer of human embryos to animals for gestation
- Transfer of research embryos or parthenotes to humans
- Research on embryos beyond neural tube closure (18th day)
- Twinning for gestation by separation of blastomeres
- Cloning of embryos by transplanting nuclei
- Creation of human–human or human–animal chimeras
- Creation of embryos strictly for research, such as to obtain stem cells
- Fertilization of other species with human gametes, except for clinical testing of sperm penetration, as now done with hamster eggs
- Transfer of embryos to a body cavity other than uterus

- Sex selection of embryos, except to prevent X-linked diseases
- Use of eggs, sperm, or embryos from donors without consent
- Use of sperm, eggs, or embryos for which donors receive more than reasonable compensation

There were rumbles from outside the NIH. The International Foundation for Genetic Research, located in Pittsburgh, filed a lawsuit to prohibit a list of people from advising NIH because they had conflicts of interest. And Congressman Dornan sent a letter signed by 35 members of Congress to NIH Director Harold Varmus demanding to know what authority he had to revise research guidelines.[10]

While the recommendations of the NIH panel will probably be adopted and strictly followed for NIH research and NIH funding, the guidelines will likely be too restrictive for the 200 or 300 private fertility clinics operating in the United States. Advances in fertility methods are taking place at a rapid rate, and guidelines that are too restrictive could hamper innovation and valuable improvements.

A storm of controversy arose over using surrogate mothers to produce children not their own, and in highly publicized cases, the surrogate mothers sued to keep their children even though they had signed contracts with the biological parents to give them up. The 1987 celebrated case of Baby M in New Jersey was one of the first to bring the problem to public attention. Mrs. Mary Beth Whitehead was vaginally impregnated with the semen of William Stern after Mrs. Whitehead had signed a contract to give the baby to the Sterns in return for a $10,000 fee. But when the baby was born, Mrs. Whitehead refused to give up the baby. The Sterns filed a lawsuit to force Mrs. Whitehead to comply with the contract. After a lengthy court battle that received worldwide media coverage, a Superior Court judge ordered Stern to pay Mrs. Whitehead the $10,000 and awarded custody of the baby to the Sterns. Mrs. Stern eventually adopted the baby and named her Melissa. Mrs. Whitehead's lawyer appealed the case to the New Jersey Supreme Court, which unanimously voided the contract with the reasoning that the surrogate contract conflicted with laws that prohibited the use of money in connection with adoptions, and that paying a woman to have a baby was contrary to public policy. On the other hand, the justices upheld the decision of the lower court to award custody of the child to the Sterns because they thought the Sterns would be able to provide a more stable home. The state Supreme Court also restored Mrs. Whitehead's parental rights and ordered a lower court to set visiting rights for her. While the ruling applied only to New Jersey, it illustrated the legal complexities of surrogacy and was viewed as having an impact on similar cases in other states.[11]

Donation of eggs is thought by some people to be subject to abuse. Criticism of using donated eggs to make older women pregnant is directed not only at the problem of aging of the parents as the child grows older, but also at the risk to the donor. She is given high doses of a fertility drug to produce excess eggs, which are harvested from the ovary. There are always risks common to major surgery as well as the danger of a tubal or ectopic pregnancy resulting from one or more of the eggs getting into the fallopian tube or the body cavity. The donor ordinarily receives small monetary compensation considering the inconvenience and risks.

Infertility and the overpowering desire of a vast number of people to have babies are highly personal problems that many of them are reluctant to talk about openly. But the compelling urge to have babies is a force behind the creation of a vast, largely unseen industry in the medical profession—the fertility industry—taking in millions of dollars annually. The desire to conceive is in many women so compelling that they return for treatment time after time following repeated failures. One Los Angeles couple, Susan and Tim, spent $60,000 over a period of four years that included two IVF attempts before they had a successful pregnancy using micromanipulation. A less typical experience in some respects was that of Milagros Olarve and her husband Florante, both 50. After surgery to unblock her fallopian tubes and removal of scar tissue from her abdomen, they still had no luck, so they resorted to IVF. It took two trials at about $18,000 each, then she gave birth to triplets. "*Milagros* in Spanish means *miracles*," the elated mother said, "now I have three miracles." The Olarves were lucky. It took only two tries.[12]

On the mundane level of everyday medical ethics, disturbing rumors tell of doctors who offer fertility services despite inadequate training and experience, and tales of some who repeatedly take patients without ever producing a pregnancy or live birth. The most flagrant abuse of fertility services is to harvest eggs from a woman and use excess eggs or embryos to implant in other women without the consent of all parties. A scandal erupted in 1995 at the medical school of the University of California in Irvine when doctors at the Center for Reproductive Health were alleged to have harvested eggs from women and used them to implant in other women without the donors' knowledge or consent, nor the recipients' knowledge of the origin of the eggs or embryos. Some of the implants were reported to have resulted in pregnancies and childbirths. At least 17 legal claims were filed against the doctors and the university. Early in the case, U.C. Irvine officials acknowledged that more than 30 patients were believed to have been involved in improper transfer of eggs and embryos. Later, papers came to light showing that eggs and embryos of at least 60 women may have been stolen and given to others.

The scandal broke when it became public knowledge that the university had paid three whistle-blowers a total of more than $900,000 in compensation for improper and discriminatory treatment. Part of the settlement was that the whistle-blowers would not publicly spill the beans, "to protect the patients," university officials said.[13]

FUTURE FERTILITY

What does the future hold for assisted reproduction? Clearly, the biggest obstacles to widespread use of IVF or GIFT are cost, inconvenience, discomfort, and time. The cost per try (called per cycle) probably averages a minimum of about $12,000. Often several tries are needed, and even then, there is no guarantee of success. The American Society for Reproductive Medicine estimated the 1994 cost of surrogacy, not counting IVF, at $30,000. The Center for Surrogate Parenting, Inc., gave a figure of $40,000 for the total cost to an infertile couple. The Genetics & IVF Institute of Fairfax, Virginia, gave estimated 1995 costs for steps of *in vitro* fertilization and embryo transfer (IVF/ET):

Preliminary consultation	$300
Preliminary laboratory tests	
Female	1600
Male	600–1300
Consultation, if needed	300
Complete IVF cycle	9353
(If canceled or no oocytes obtained	4494)
Cryopreservation of embryos	1642
Cryostorage, per month	30
Micromanipulation/donor sperm	2535
Frozen embryo transfer cycles	3502
(If monitored but no transfer	1229)

Improvements will continue to be made in technique and probability of success, but for the foreseeable future, IVF will continue to be costly. Fortunately, a few health insurance companies pay up to half the total cost, including the operating room and anesthesiologist fees. At present, most of them will not cover laboratory, fertilization, or embryo transfer costs, but it is expected that insurance coverage will increase, especially as improved techniques and success rates make it possible to reduce costs. Currently there is wide variability in the success rates of different clinics.

Embryo Biopsy

Experience with IVF embryos shows that up to 30% of the embryos should be discarded because they have chromosome abnormalities. However, the usual procedure is to use whole embryos for embryo assessment, and this does not permit a genetic analysis without destroying the embryo. Genetic assessment is especially desirable to determine whether the embryo has a chromosome abnormality known to be carried by one of the parents. The usual IVF technique produces an excess of embryos, but wastage can be reduced by embryo biopsy, which will make it possible to predict some heritable characteristics in addition to determining the presence or absence of important congenital and genetic diseases. This can be done, as described in Chapter 9, by removing a single cell for genetic analysis by micromanipulation during the early development of the IVF embryo.

There will be benefits from embryo analysis in addition to a reduction in the need for prenatal genetic diagnosis and therapeutic abortions. The human genome project, a study to determine the complete human genetic profile, is well under way, and the discovery of genetic markers is accelerating. The knowledge eventually may enable biopsy analysts to make virtually a complete profile of the kind of individual the embryo will become. While use of the technique at present is confined to determining genetic defects before implantation of the embryo, a future application of micromanipulation of the early embryo may well be to introduce normal genes into the embryo to take over from defective genes that if left alone would cause disease or fatality.

Correction of Genetic Defects

Foreign DNA can be injected into pronuclear (very early stage) embryos, and the DNA will proliferate along with cell divisions and growth of the embryo. DNA can also be inserted by injecting retroviral vectors (carriers) that have been produced to contain the desired genes. The potential use for these methods will be to correct genetic abnormalities. In the present state of knowledge, the result of incorporating foreign DNA in the human genome is unpredictable, so for the time being, the major emphasis will be on correcting genetic defects later by introducing normal DNA into somatic (body) cells of the defective tissues. For the present, the most practical way to get foreign DNA into the tissues is to use embryonic cells, which in some tissues can be expected to differentiate into the tissue of their environment and proliferate themselves along with their new DNA.

The potential for use and misuse of this kind of genetic engineering is so vast that ethical questions may impede but not prevent its development in a responsible manner. In a news conference held in Washington, DC, on May 19, 1995, a coalition of nearly 200 religious leaders took a stand against allowing patent rights on human and animal life forms.[14] While their objections were directed mainly toward patenting human genes *per se*, which is also opposed by many scientists on pragmatic grounds, their position seemed to be motivated more broadly by a fear of producing life forms other than those found in nature. "What's at stake here," said Richard D. Land, head of the Southern Baptist Convention's Christian Life Commission, "is a defense against the attempt to modify into a marketable product human and animal life." In the worst case scenario, according to Land, the time could come when human genes are used to develop "designer humans" to conform to someone's idea of the ideal human. "At that point," said Land, "we've started to play God."[14a] A different view probably held by most scientists is that expressed by Alexander M. Capron, an ethicist at the UCLA Law Center. "The objections are tapping into people's fears of Frankenstein monsters and wild-eyed scientists with no respect for human beings," says Capron.

Embryonic Cells for Transplantation

Embryonic and fetal cells have advantages over adult cells in their ability to become established and grow in the organism receiving them. The possibility of using embryonic cells is suggested by the earlier interest in using fetal tissue for transplantation to correct serious or lethal diseases, injuries, or genetic abnormalities. A highly publicized case was the attempt to treat Parkinson's disease, a degenerative brain affliction, by transplanting tissue taken from parts of the fetal brain, the substantia nigra and corpus striatum, believed to be affected by the disease. The operation was pioneered by a South American physician who reported good results, but attempts to confirm the method in the United States were not uniformly successful.

Early injection of normal cells into embryos, fetuses, or developing children with injured or genetically defective tissues or organs might reverse development of the defect. Juvenile diabetes is believed to be one affliction probably susceptible to transplantation of normal cells into children. Insulin, a deficiency of which causes diabetes mellitus, is produced by cells in a part of the pancreas called the islets of Langerhans, which are easily accessible. Conceivably, benefits could accrue to adults as well.

Embryo Splitting

Splitting embryos—separating the cells—before they differentiate into tissues would make it possible to produce genetically identical embryonic cells, in other words, clones of the original embryo. It happens frequently in nature, resulting in identical twins. In the laboratory, an embryo in the four-cell stage, for example, can be used to produce four identical embryos. These could be used immediately by IVF to produce identical quadruplets or frozen for future use. A woman could use the frozen split embryos to have identical twins, triplets, or quadruplets, not necessarily all at once but over a period of years at her choosing. Although split embryos conceivably can be used to produce identical twins, the more common experience in IVF is the inadvertent occurrence of fraternal twins, caused by implantation of two separately fertilized eggs.

Because the cells from a split embryo are all identical genetically, the genetic makeup of the entire group of split embryos could be determined by making a genetic analysis of only one of them. Cells from the remaining identical embryos could be used for transplanting if the clone were found to be free of injuries, diseases, or abnormalities. The cells being all the same genotype, immunological rejection would be minimized. The embryos would also be useful in fundamental research on abnormalities that might occur, their causes, and possible cures or preventive measures, but there are strong ethical objections to the experimental use of embryos. However, there are potentially multiple uses for split embryos. Besides genetic analysis, the embryos could be cultured and stem cells (cells that differentiate into different tissues) could be used for transplanting to correct for diseases or abnormalities.

The number of embryos that can be obtained from embryo splitting is limited. Beyond a few cell divisions, the embryo is preprogrammed to start the formation of a blastocoel (fluid-filled ball), beyond which splitting to form new embryos is not possible. Four embryos from splitting is the practical limit.[9]

Twinning

A celebrated case reported nationwide and described in *Redbook* magazine was the story of Jane and Terry Mohr. Jane entered an IVP program at UCLA on June 26, 1986. Ten eggs were retrieved, of which nine became fertilized. Two days later four of the fertilized eggs were implanted into her uterus, and the remaining five were frozen. On February 15, 1987, a son was born by cesarean section. About a year later, March, 1988, Jane decided to have her frozen embryos transferred to her. Three of the five had survived the freezing and thawing, and were implanted into her uterus. On November 29, 1988, twin girls were born. The boy and the two girls are technically twins, all conceived *in vitro* on the same day but born almost two years apart. They were fraternal twins, not identical twins as would be the case if split embryos had been used.[15] Dr. Arthur L. Wisot, of the UCLA IVF program, reported, "More recently we have had two further 'twins,' the second being born forty months after the first retrieval."

It has been suggested that split embryos could be cryopreserved for producing an identical twin years later from which organ transplants could be harvested if needed. Organ transplants from an identical twin would be ideal because there would be no organ rejection problem. However, the idea is so repulsive ethically that there is little chance of using the method, even if the embryo could be gestated in the womb of a species other than human.

However, if a grown man fell heir to frozen split embryos identical to those from which he was produced, he could have them implanted in a woman, for example, his wife, in which case the child would be an identical twin whom he could raise as his son.

Gender Selection

The desire to have a child of one sex or another—most commonly a male—dates from biblical times and the early Greeks. Dr. Joel Batzofin gives a brief review of the bizarre and irrelevant sexual practices that were advocated to increase the odds of conceiving a child of predetermined sex. The early Greeks thought that the male-determining sperm came from the left testicle, so tying off the right testicle would produce boys. Hippocrates taught that if a woman would lie on her right side, "the seed would give birth to a boy," and vice versa. In the 18th century, French noblemen were told that if they had their left testicle removed, it would guarantee a male heir. As late as 1970, a physician, L. B. Shettles, described several coital positions and practices that would give either a male or a female offspring.[16]

Determining the sex of a single embryo before implantation is now possible without injuring the embryo. With improved techniques it may become possible by removing a single cell during the early development of the embryo and subjecting it to genetic analysis for gender determination and other genetic qualities. Sex determination could be the main objective or it could be a by-product of overall genetic analysis. A practical procedure will be to determine the sex of one of the clones of split embryos. By analyzing only one of the embryos, the sex of the children from the remaining clones would be predetermined.

A modern method uses a sperm processing technique combined with a biopsy of preimplantation embryos, sexing the blastomeres, and using only those of the desired sex for completing the IVF. In 1973, R. J. Ericsson and co-workers reported that they were able to enrich samples of semen with Y-bearing sperm by using a bovine serum albumin technique. They were able to increase the Y-bearing sperm from an average of 48.5% to about 67%, and the separation yielded a higher percentage of motile sperm. In a 1993 survey of 65 centers that used the Ericsson technique, of 1034 births 72% were males and 28% were females.[17] Several methods have been tried for enhancing the X-bearing sperm. One frequently cited is the use of clomiphene citrate for ovulation induction in women who want girls. The drug has an effect on the cervical mucus that is presumed to change the permeability of the mucus to sperm with different swimming patterns and surface charges. According to Dr. Joel Batzofin of the Huntington Reproductive Center in Pasadena, California, "An analysis of 97 sex selection treatment cycles that resulted in live births which were performed in our Center since 1989 showed that a desired sex outcome was achieved in 74, or 76.2% of cases."[18]

The Roman Catholic Church strongly opposes preselection of sex, and a science panel of the National Institutes of Health said that sex selection of embryos is not acceptable, except to prevent X-linked diseases. However, the motivations for desiring a boy or a girl are so compelling that ethical restraints will probably have little force. For example, in the United States, a couple with four boys may desperately want a girl, and if they have four girls they may want a boy. In India and some other countries where girls are considered a financial liability, many families want only boys.

Cloning of Adults

There would be few technical obstacles to removing the nucleus from an embryo and replacing it with a nucleus from an embryo to be cloned. Cloning in the usual sense means producing progeny that are genetically identical to the parents or parent. Although adult humans have never been cloned, it's theoretically possible to remove the nucleus from a human oocyte and replace it with a nucleus taken from a body cell of an adult person (male or female), and when this is cultured to the blastocyst stage, and implanted in the uterus of a woman, the child would be an exact replica of the adult from which the body cell nucleus was taken. This basically was the method described by novelist David Rorvik in his fictional account, *In His Image*[19] In practice, adult nuclei lack the ability to stimulate embryonic cells into normal development, and practically nothing is known about the reason for this incompatibility. A great deal of research will be needed to make cloning in this way a reality, although there is no reason to think that scientists could not resolve the mystery.

A more practical way to create clones is by embryo splitting. In this way, at least four identical embryos can be produced at a time. Assuming that refinements in technique would yield close to 100% implantation, gestation, and birth, preferably in four different mothers, "litters" of four identical children could be obtained. With advanced knowledge and expertise in genetic analysis, embryos can be selected with any known genetic profile, having specific physical, mental, and behavioral characteristics. Theoretically, a woman could produce a family of children having predictable qualities. She could do this by having them serially from frozen embryos. Or she could have identical twins by implanting more than one embryo at the same time with the help of hormone treatments. Or she could employ a surrogate mother. A woman, by using a frozen embryo, could give birth to her own sibling—an identical twin. The method of harvesting multiple embryos from a valuable animal and implanting them in less valuable surrogate mothers has potential advantages in livestock breeding.

There could develop great demand for human embryos having genes for different qualities depending on the choice of prospective parents, thus requiring large computerized inventories of cryopreserved embryos in embryo banks, forming a worldwide industry. Large-capacity cryobanks for storing pedigree sperm, ova, and embryos will come into existence, with a cash flow large enough to be listed on the New York Stock Exchange. The genetic integrity of the embryos will be crucial, so a new insurance industry will develop to protect clients against mistakes or fraud, similar in function to real estate title insurance companies. But the central feature of the industry will be a proliferation of cloning laboratories, which will specialize in receiving eggs and sperm from certified donors, fertilizing eggs, screening embryos for defects, micromanipulation for sexing and determining the presence or absence of desirable genes, and cloning for maximum production. The cloning laboratories and cryobanks will furnish brochures of their services, and catalogs of embryos and their genetic characteristics.

Ethical questions about producing large numbers of clones will have to be dealt with. A flood of publicity followed the announcement in 1993 that a researcher at George Washington University in Washington, DC, had cloned human embryos. It became known in December, 1994, that they had done the work without prior approval of the university committee charged with approving research on human subjects. Also, the researcher did not obtain informed consent from the egg and sperm donors. The funding agency, the National Institutes of Health, found the work to be in "serious noncompliance" with its guidelines on human subjects research. University president Stephen Trachtenberg said that he had ordered all of the research data to be destroyed.[20,21]

Opposition to this kind of biotechnology will inevitably come from religious groups and others. And objections based on the fear that some dictator might try to change humanity in his image will make the practice politically impossible until plans can be set in place for controlling abuses of the procedure.

Hybridization

Some people have suggested that human eggs might be fertilized *in vitro* with sperm from other species, thereby producing new types of beings that would be useful in industry for special tasks. Conversely, eggs from other species might be fertilized with human sperm, a procedure that would be much easier. According to the theory, the embryos might be gestated in domestic animals, making it possible to produce large numbers of the hybrids. Different strains of hybrids would be developed for different tasks. Much of human work consists of routine or repetitive tasks that can be quickly learned, for example, operating automatic machines, assembling simple components, stapling packages, and loading and unloading cargo. There are several qualities, however, that would be hard to obtain in hybrids, one of the most important of which, besides speech, is manual dexterity comparable to that of humans. The anatomy of the chimp hand, for example, does not permit it to perform a delicate task such as threading a needle.

The hybrids would undoubtedly be sterile, so there would be no need for breeding pens, but hybridization would develop into a huge industry consisting of both production and research organizations. New strains would be constantly developed to meet new needs.

While it might be economically profitable to have human–animal hybrid strains, technical and ethical obstacles are enormous. Speculation on hybridization ignores the reason one species is different from other species. The classical definition of a species is that its members do not regularly interbreed with other species. One of the reasons is that the zona pellucida (the external barrier) of the oocyte ordinarily cannot be penetrated by sperm from a different species (there are exceptions among lower organisms). In addition, the lining of the uterus has a specific immunological capability of rejecting a foreign embryo, making it impossible for it to become implanted. However, there are also exceptions to this exclusion among closely related species, and it is sometimes possible to produce hybrids by human intervention. The sterile mule, the progeny of breeding a mare to a jackass, is a well-known example. But there is no species of animal related closely enough to humans that could logically be expected to hybridize. In fact, our closest relative, the chimpanzee, is not in the same genus nor even in the same family. We are classified as being in the family Hominidae, the genus *Homo*, and the species *sapiens*. Chimps are in the family Pongidae along with the other great apes, the orangutan, and the gorilla (chimps are given the genus and species name *Pan troglodytes*).

The equines on the outside (near) row are all mules, hybrids from mating a mare with a jackass. Before the advent of tractors and trucks, mules were widely used as farm and draft animals, valued for their remarkable strength and endurance. Unfortunately, mules are sterile. Mating a jenny (female donkey) with a stallion gives a smaller, and less useful hybrid. Attempts to hybridize humans with closely related species are regarded by most people as unethical, and in any case are probably not possible. However, it is theoretically possible to modify some animals in a way that would endow them with some human physiological qualities by introducing human genes into their embryos, also held to be unethical.

Despite obvious similarities, and the claim that only 0.4% of human DNA differs from that of chimps,[22] there is actually an enormous gap between the two species in inheritable characteristics. The human genome has 3 billion base pairs (6 billion nucleotides). If 60 million (1%) are actually active, and 99.6% of them are common to humans and chimps, we still have 240,000 nucleotides (genetic units) that are different from those in chimps.

A human–chimp hybrid domestic animal is an extremely remote possibility unless or until a way is found to overcome the technical obstacles, an accomplishment that would require intensive research and a reversal of present-day ethical convictions. Aside from ethical objections, a proposal to produce legions of hybrids would likely raise a storm of protest similar to that of the Luddites of the early 19th century in England, who objected to the jobs and opportunities lost because of technological advances.

But how about genetic engineering to insert human genes into the DNA of animal embryos? This would not only obviate the hybridization problems but would open up a vast field for producing not just half-and-half hybrids but almost an infinite number of combinations. What can be done with mice can be done with men. We could engineer animals to produce human milk, human enzymes, and human hormones, many of them difficult to produce synthetically, yet needed for treatment of some diseases. Much of that is being done already using bacteria, but microorganisms cannot produce mammalian organs. There is an urgent need for human transplant organs. Attempts have been made to use ape organs, but with little success because of rejection. A recent attempt was made to transplant ape bone marrow. If genetically engineered hearts, lungs, kidneys, livers, and other organs and glands with essential human characteristics to avoid rejection could be produced in animals, the demand would create a new major industry.

But moral and ethical objections as well as fear of disastrous consequences will place severe restraints on fiddling with the human genome, either in humans or using parts of the genome, that is, specific genes, in other organisms.

Male Gestation

A blue sky idea is to plant human embryos in men treated with hormones to enable them to carry the offspring to term in their body cavities. There is little chance of this succeeding in view of the fact that most ectopic pregnancies in women that escape detection are fatal because of the development of hemorrhaging. But even if it could be done, and there is the possibility that a way could be found to do it, an advantage to the manipulation is not clear except for giving women the satisfaction of seeing men go through the irritation of pregnancy and the pain of childbirth. It's doubtful that enough men would volunteer to make the endeavor worthwhile, although some transvestites might offer their services. In that case the purpose would be defeated because the experiment would be on women, not men.

Ectogenesis

The most ambitious of all projections for the future use of embryos from IVF is to find a way of culturing the embryos to term outside the human body—truly *in vitro* babies. The idea, called *ectogenesis*, was thought of by an imaginative writer more than 150 years ago. A scene in Goethe's *Faust* (1749–1832) has Mephistopheles and his protégé, Wagner, in the laboratory examining a flask.[23]

MEPHISTOPHELES: What's going on here?
WAGNER: A human is being made!
MEPHISTOPHELES: A man? Do tell! What lovesick couple
    have you put in that misty bottle?
WAGNER: God forbid! Reproducing as people used to do,
    Is both vain and senseless.
    The essence of how life used to begin,
    Simply repetition of original sin,
    The urgency to make themselves a clone,
    To have and to hold as their very own,
    All that has lost its primitive appeal.

The beasts are known to be addicted still,
But man with his great talents must gain
A higher, even higher origin . . .
HOMUNCULUS (in the flask to Wagner): Hi, Daddio!
How are you? It's not a jest.
Come, press me tenderly to your breast,
But not too hard; the glass might break.
That's the way it is with things we make,
For what is natural goes out in space,
But the artificial stays in place. . . .

Goethe's *homunculus* may have inspired Aldous Huxley to write his 1932 novel *Brave New World* in which he depicts a laboratory-style baby factory.[24] Knowing as we do that science often outdoes fiction, what is the chance that ectogenesis will become a reality?

Our ignorance of what controls embryo implantation, as well as growth and development, leaves an enormous gap in our ability to predict what steps would have to be taken to bring a human fetus to term outside the body. With birds, all we have to do is incubate the eggs, but mammals are cut from different tissue. Scientists have tried it on mammals with only partial success. Yu-Chih Hsu, at the Johns Hopkins School of Hygiene and Public Health in Baltimore, Maryland, succeeded in culturing mouse embryos from the blastocyst stage to about one-half of the normal 21-day gestation period. But the amount of research needed for more than a mere beginning of ectogenesis of embryos of placental animals staggers the imagination.

For the foreseeable future, ectogenesis of humans remains beyond the horizon. However, we can look to basic research to reveal clues of how it could be done. If a way is found to bring a mammalian embryo to term *in vitro*, it would surely be possible to do the same with human embryos. The specter of a scheming dictator, a devious scientist, or an ambitious terrorist cloning a cadre of human robots, bringing them to term in bottles, and grooming them to goose-stepping discipline in a remote training ground, is a scenario for science fiction. But if scientists ever unravel the mystery of gestation to the point that *in vitro* birth of mammalians becomes a reality, bringing one or a few human embryos to term in secret places would not be beyond the realm of possibility.

Morality

A fundamental unresolved moral issue is the question: Is an embryo a human being? Slightly less controversial is the question: Is it immoral to tamper with reproduction? There is a solid biological basis for the belief, according to one view, that a new generation begins at the moment an oocyte is fertilized by a spermatozoon. But is an embryo in the two-, four-, or eight-cell stage a person—with rights, privileges, and legal status of a citizen? If so, can creating and discarding (killing) an embryo be viewed as murder? Unfortunately, there is no chemical, physical, or biological guideline to answer these questions, nor a simple answer to the question: When does life begin? In a contemporary context, life has no beginning and no end. Why is this so? In humans, as in all animals that reproduce sexually, there is a continuous cycle of two alternating kinds of life: a somatic (body) stage and a gametic (sex-cell) stage. It is futile to point to either stage as the beginning, for the cycle has continued without interruption since shortly after the creation of life several billion years ago. The conclusion is inescapable that life as we know it is continuous, with no beginning and no end within the time frame of *Homo sapiens*. Life is a continuous cycle from generation to generation—a cycle superimposed on the birth and death of individuals.

Whether it is justifiable to take a life at any stage in the cycle depends on the laws and customs of the place and time. Killing in warfare is legal, socially acceptable—even required—and usually morally justified and religiously sanctioned. Infants are not spared, nor pregnant women. The wastage of sperm and potential sperm is enormous. Which brings us back to the laboratory. Is the wastage of embryos in the laboratory justifiable? For guidelines to answer this and the other questions we have to depend on either an instinct within or a higher sense of justice. In the end, the weight of human harm or benefits and the causation or alleviation of human suffering will determine which way the balance tips.

Legal Matters

The legal status of fertility manipulation is even more contorted than the moral and ethical issues, as hard as that might be to believe. Artificial insemination has been pretty well standardized by law and custom. The more complicated legal questions surrounding surrogate motherhood are vague, confusing, and contentious. The strong emotional attachment of a woman who bears a child to what she perceives as her baby is an invitation to litigation despite prior agreement and the promise of payment in money. A complication is that the father must legally adopt the child born to a surrogate mother, while in some states payment to a mother for adoption is prohibited. There is little that can be done about the risk that a paternity test might reveal that the child is not the offspring of the man who contracted with the surrogate, in which case the surrogate would have to take the child or put it up for adoption. If the child were born with a defect so severe that neither the surrogate nor the couple contracting with her would want the child, litigation could ensue. The psychological effect on the surrogate of giving up a child she comes to consider her own can range from grief to severe distress, unless she can participate in rearing the child.

The Ethics Committee of The American Society for Reproductive Medicine reported in 1994 that legislation dealing with commercial surrogacy had been introduced in 39 states and the District of Columbia. Several states, Virginia for one, adopted statutes requiring a court order for each surrogate procedure. Whether legislation will improve the relations between prospective parents and surrogates or make them more difficult is impossible to say. Meanwhile, let the buyer beware, get a good lawyer, and insist on a well-researched contract.

The Long View

Aldous Huxley envisioned producing assembly-line human beings having qualities predetermined to be suitable for specific kinds of work. Fetuses were reared in drastically different environments calculated to make them become ideal tropical workers, chemical workers, rocket engineers, and so forth. Some of the female fetuses would be given hormone treatments to make them into freemartins—sterile masculinized workers. Fetuses were rated in intellectual capacity from alpha to epsilon, depending on the environment they were subjected to. An alpha would be a future sewage worker, a beta-minus would become a mechanic. If Huxley had known in 1932 about the phenomenal discoveries in biotechnology later in the century, he probably would have ignored the comparatively crude effort to modify human beings by manipulating their fetal environment, and instead would have used the manipulation of genes in accordance with genetic engineering methods.

It is now possible to remove one cell from a developing embryo and determine the genetic makeup in any region of the DNA. Thus, genetic screening of embryos before implantation in IVF procedures is possible, and may become routine. It may become possible to predetermine the structure and function of proteins, and the regulation of their expression in various tissues, to the point of making it possible to predict from the sequence of genomic DNA alone the morphology, physiology, and behavior of the person who develops from the embryo.

Harvey F. Lodish, at the Whitehead Institute for Medical Research, Cambridge, MA, predicts:

> All this information will be transferred to a supercomputer, together with information about the environment—including likely nutrition, environmental toxins, sunlight, and so forth. The output will be a color movie in which the embryo develops into a fetus, is born, and then grows into an adult, explicitly depicting body size and shape and hair, skin, and eye color. Eventually the DNA sequence base will be ex-

panded to cover genes important for traits such as speech and musical ability; the mother will be able to hear the embryo—as an adult—speak or sing.[25]

Thus, one can envision the time to come when parents-to-be, by punching the keyboard of a computer, will be able to pick and choose among thousands of genes and determine what combination of qualities they want their progeny to have. These, in turn, will determine the child's growth and development, health, capacity for education and mental growth, and aptitude for sports, intellectual pursuits, and vocational preference. In short, parents will be able to predetermine what kind of person their child will become.

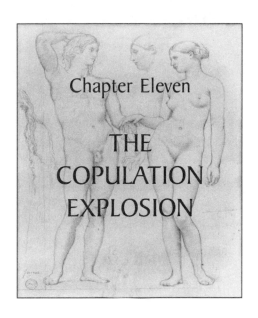

Chapter Eleven

THE COPULATION EXPLOSION

A sign of the times is the number of kids having babies out of wedlock. The unblessed event is so common that the word *bastard* has almost disappeared from the English language. Roughly one-third of the births in the United States are fatherless, and the number is increasing. Unfortunately, as Donna E. Shalala, Secretary of U.S. Health and Human Services, wrote in 1994, "four out of five children of teen-age mothers who drop out of school live in poverty."[1] Other Western countries are experiencing a similar proliferation of fatherless children: 29% in Canada, 33% in France, 46% in Denmark, and 50% in Sweden. The rate of out-of-wedlock births in England is 31%, slightly higher than in the United States at 30%, and the rate is climbing in all Western countries.

Most teenagers—both boys and girls—speak openly about their sexual activity. Schools hand out free condoms as nonchalantly as if they were sticks of bubble gum. Grades might benefit if schools would issue pencils and erasers as generously. Another phenomenon that would have been shocking in former times is that parents accept their children's sexual behavior as a normal part of life, and often see to it that the kids are supplied with contraceptives with the same solicitude as when they take them to little league or dancing school.

According to a Carnegie Council report issued in October, 1995, based on a 1988 survey, 27% of the girls and 33% of the boys engaged in sex by their 15th birthday, and the number was steadily climbing.

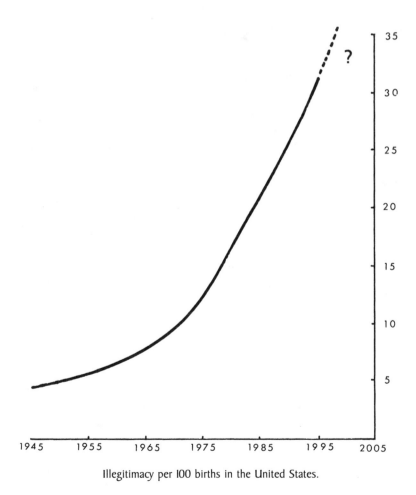

Illegitimacy per 100 births in the United States.

The reason for the spectacular proliferation of sexual activity among children is obscure. Some people blame it on television, where couples are shown almost nightly on one show or another going to bed for sex. Another influence on kids is said to be the role models of unwed older women having children. Vice President Dan Quayle, in a speech extolling "family values," created a flap when he criticized actress Candice Bergen for setting a bad example by choosing to have a baby out of wedlock on her television show *Murphy Brown*.

"It's no secret that a lot of TV characters have sex," says an advertisement of the Planned Parenthood Affiliates of Southern California.

> The only secret is how they keep from getting pregnant . . . the networks usually won't allow the word "contraception" on the air unless it's part of a news report . . . our kids don't have a clue. . . .
>   If they're going to show sex on TV, after all, the least they can do is do it right.[2]

In other words, why don't they show the passionate couple doing "safe sex"?

The stigma of teen pregnancy that prevailed in former times prompted embarrassed parents to send their pregnant daughters to homes for unwed mothers. Now, at some high schools, students can leave their babies at campus day-care centers.

It has been said that the cheapest and most effective birth control pill is an aspirin tablet held firmly between the girl's knees. In the absence of such unrealistic restraint, the number of unwed mothers has increased phenomenally. The inevitable result is that abortions have increased, although not in proportion to pregnancies. In the minds of many people abortion is an act of violence against a living human, and labeled murder. Others contend that bringing a child into the world unwanted, unloved, and probably destined for squalor, poverty, resentment, and abuse is the greater crime. Although the technology is widely known, neither schools nor parents have, as yet, come up with a strategy for letting the kids have their uninhibited fun without a high probability of their getting pregnant, many of them having their own baby kids, and others getting and spreading diseases, including AIDS. "No wonder," say pediatric specialists, "adults, themselves, have a dismal record of birth control." More than 60% of women 20 to 24 say their pregnancies are unplanned, and 77% of women older than 40 say their pregnancies were surprises.[3] Dr. Helen Rodrigues-Tuas, a pediatrician and member of the government-sponsored Institute of Medicine (IOM), was quoted, "Teens are responsible for only 20% of the unintended pregnancies." People of all ages simply dislike the bother of contraceptives, and even when they think of it seriously, they often fail to communicate to their partners what needs to be done to avoid an unwanted pregnancy.

AIDS

Although still primarily a disease of male homosexuals and intravenous drug users within the United States, the AIDS virus is increasingly infecting heterosexuals, and according to some predictions is expected to become a major worldwide venereal disease epidemic. The director of the Centers for Disease Control and Prevention (CDC) told a gathering at the World AIDS Day conference in Atlanta, Georgia, on December 1, 1994, that AIDS is the leading cause of death among Americans between the ages of 24 and 44. "In December, 1984," said CDC Director David Satcher, "three-fourths of AIDS cases were men who have sex with men. This year [1994], this group makes up only a little more than half of all cases, so you see the epidemic is changing."[4] However, others say that predictions of a heterosexual AIDS epidemic are exaggerated. They point out that a high proportion of heterosexuals are monogamous or nearly so in contrast to homosexuals, who during and preceding the early stages of the epidemic had an average of more than 1000 lifetime sexual contacts.

The promotion of so-called safe sex may not do as much good as people think because condoms are not as safe as many people are led to believe. The latex device for preventing sperm and germ transfer from one person to another was made possible by Charles

Goodyear in 1844 when he invented a way to vulcanize rubber and a new way to process it. But the idea of a condom originated with Gabriel Fallopius, who by 1560 invented a linen sheath to be worn under the prepuce. Fallopius, an Italian anatomist, was noted for his studies of the inner ear and the genital system. He coined the word *vagina* and described the clitoris, and is remembered for his description of ovarian tubes, or fallopian tubes. Linen condoms, later made of "gold-beater's skin" for the wealthy, became popular not for contraception, but as protection against venereal diseases. They came to be sold widely, brothels stocked them, and they were advertised in the press. But the thick, tough materials did not have the appeal of later models made of lambskin (animal intestine tissue) or modern condoms made of latex. Rattray Taylor quotes Daniel Turner, writing in 1717 in a book on syphilis:

> the *Condom* being the best, if not the only, Preservative our Libertines have found out at present, and yet by reason of its blunting the Sensation, I have heard some of them acknowledge that they often chose to risk a Clap.[5]

Even with modern production and testing, there is a significant rate of failure, from holes or more often breakage, which was well known before the onset of AIDS. But after AIDS became a feared epidemic, condoms, in the mind of many authorities, mysteriously became "safe." They are not safe, only safer, and if AIDS becomes an epidemic among heterosexuals, a better method of protection will have to be found and used. However, reliable statistics on safety are hard to come by.

The federal Food and Drug Administration (FDA) started a program of testing condoms in April, 1987.[6] Out of 219 batches comprising a total of 54,000 latex condoms, 20% of the batches failed to pass inspection and were ordered withheld or withdrawn from the market. Thirty percent of the foreign batches failed to pass inspection, and 10% of the American-made batches were rejected. In subsequent testing, 12% of U.S. and 21% of foreign batches failed to pass. FDA deputy commissioner John Norris said that the average failure rate of individual latex condoms made in the United States was 3.3 per 1000, a rate the FDA considers acceptable. The FDA rejects a batch of condoms if more than 4 per 1000 fail in water-leakage tests after being filled with 300 ml of water. If two or more batches of foreign-manufactured condoms fail to pass inspection, future shipments from that source into the United States are stopped.

Carter-Wallace, Inc., supplier of Trojans, a widely used brand of latex condoms, describes the testing procedure.[7]

> Before packaging, every condom is electronically tested for defects, such as holes or areas of thinning. To detect defects, every latex condom is passed through a water bath on an electrically charged metal mold (mandrel). If water comes in contact with the mandrel through a hole or defect, an electric charge signals that the condom must be discarded.

Carter-Wallace cites a 1988 National Survey of Family Growth which emphasized the importance of consistently correct use of contraceptive methods.

> For example, the typical pregnancy failure rate during the first year was 8% for oral contraceptives, 15% for male condoms, and 26% for periodic abstinence . . . women who always use oral contraceptives will have a near zero (0.1%) failure rate, and consistent male condom users, who tend to be more knowledgeable and careful than casual users, will have a 2% failure rate. For prevention of HIV infection and STDs, as with pregnancy prevention, consistent and correct use is crucial. . . . Prevention messages must highlight the importance of consistent and correct condom use.[8,9]

Some people have questioned how effective condoms actually are in preventing the spread of the AIDS virus—in the absence of clinical proof in human tests. However, laboratory tests show that latex condoms—when they don't fail—are effective barriers to the AIDS virus, hepatitis B, gonorrhea, chlamydia, and other sexually transmitted diseases (STDs). But the CDC cautions, "Individuals likely to become infected should be aware that condom use cannot completely eliminate the risk of transmission." According to the CDC,[9] reported breakage rates in the studies were 2% or less for vaginal or anal intercourse. One study reported complete slippage off the penis during intercourse for one (0.4%) of 237 condoms and complete slippage off the penis during withdrawal for one of 237 condoms. The greatest concern is about lambskin condoms, made from animal intestine membranes, which represent only about 5% of the condom market, but are said to be popular among gays because the lambskins are thought to be resistant to breakage during anal intercourse and to enhance sexual sensation. Preliminary research in the United States and Canada indicated that lambskin condoms allowed dangerous leakage of the human immunodeficiency virus (HIV) as well as hepatitis B and herpes viruses. It was suggested that lambskins be required to carry a warning statement to that effect.[10]

But the bigger problem is the number of people who do not use condoms at all. According to Carter-Wallace, more than 454 million condoms were bought by U.S. consumers in 1993, roughly 1 million per day. Still, in one study, only about 20% of sexually active American women reported that their male partners used condoms. Some people think that by teaching the kids how to do it, sex education has encouraged carefree sexual activity, and therefore pregnancies. In truth, many children are either unconvinced or irresponsibly careless. Susan Carpenter McMillan, who is spokesperson for the Woman's Coalition, and founder of ShE List, a conservative women's political action committee, says, "Fifty-eight percent of young girls still refuse to use contraceptives despite billions of tax dollars spent on sex education programs." It must be conceded that sex education, such as it is, has not done the job of preventing either copulation or pregnancies.

Clearly, until better contraceptives and methods of use are developed, more than chemistry is needed, namely, restraint, which may or may not be forthcoming. Meanwhile, there's no reason to think that technology has exhausted the possibilities for safe, effective, and cheap birth control drugs and vaccines, abortion drugs similar to RU 486, and protection against diseases. Research in these areas will increase as people become more aware of the seriousness of having the burden of child mothers, STDs, and unwanted population growth.

THE SILENT EPIDEMIC

The threat of a worldwide pandemic of AIDS has alerted people to the danger of careless sex. But throughout the din of talk and flood of ink on AIDS, the experts have been strangely silent on the currently most ominous by-product of the copulation explosion, especially among sexually active teenagers: STDs. According to Dr. William L. Roper and co-workers at the CDC in Atlanta, Georgia, "An estimated 12 million other [than AIDS] sexually transmitted diseases occur annually in the United States."[11] Despite the fact that these are serious health threats, beginning soon after intercourse or often years later, young people are prone to ignore the danger; many of them are only vaguely aware of it.

The STDs, besides AIDS and infection by its causative virus, HIV, are primarily chlamydia, gonorrhea, genital herpes, hepatitis B, human papilloma virus, syphilis, trichomoniasis, and cervical cancer, the latter probably caused by sexually transmitted human papilloma virus.

In a survey by the Gallup organization in which about 1000 adults were interviewed in each of several European countries, one-third of them could not name an STD other than AIDS. The American Social Health Association (ASHA) sponsored the survey. Peggy Clarke, president of ASHA, said that an estimated 55 million people in the United States have STDs.

One of the hottest debates of the century relating to sex, probably second only to the abortion argument, is how to control the epidemic of illegitimacy. According to a 1991 Rockefeller Commission study, a family headed by a single female is six times more apt to be poor than a two-parent family. Critics say that giving welfare to jobless teenage single mothers is a financial subsidy that merely encourages more of the same.[12] Black illegitimacy, ranging from 50% to 80% in inner cities, is often cited as a worst-case example of the corrupting effect of subsidizing irresponsible sex. But columnist Charles Krauthammer, in an article in *The Washington Post*, wrote of the emergence of a white underclass: "In raw numbers, European-American whites are the ethnic group with the most people in poverty, most illegitimate children, most women on welfare, and the most arrests for serious crimes."[13]

Elijah Anderson, a professor at the University of Pennsylvania, made a five-year study entitled *Sex Codes Among Inner-City Youth*, in which he describes the intergenerational poverty and social chaos accompanying the peer-group ethic of "hit and run" sex, leaving as many as 80% of the teenage mothers without fathers for their babies. "In cold economic terms," says Anderson, "a baby can be an asset, which is without doubt an important factor behind exploitation sex and out-of-wedlock babies." One woman disagreed, "Taking care of a baby is not easy, even if you get a little money for it."[14]

The dilemma of unwed mothers was summarized by William P. O'Hare, coordinator of Kids Count at the Annie E. Casey Foundation in Baltimore:[14]

> the homes that many of these girls live in are so crummy that having a child and getting [welfare] is a way of getting out— an escape of sorts. Also, $500 or $600 a month seems like a lot of money to a kid.

When, in spite of everything, there are too many kids with children, there will be a strong incentive to put the children up for adoption. Unfortunately, with roughly one million babies born of single women each year in the United States, many of them would not be adopted. Orphanages have been proposed as one solution. Charles Dickens's descriptions of the horrible workhouses for orphans in early 19th century England raise visions of a decadent and heartless society tossing innocent inner-city children into human warehouses and factory workshops worse than the grimy pockets of poverty and crime many of them would be taken away from. Frank F. Furstenberg, Jr., professor of sociology at the University of Pennsylvania, proposes instead of orphanages, "residential family centers" to house low-income parents and their children, run as cooperatives. In his plan, the families would be given supportive services such as parent education, health services, day care, and recreation.[15] Failing that, reformers declare, unless single mothers want to care for their children on their own, the best thing for the children is to have care provided for them in foster homes or similar kinds of child-care homes.

If reform movements fail, the future will see, at first experimentally at the option of the mothers, nursery schools and academies that will give children an environment of life and learning removed from poverty and crime, and which at the same time will give unwed mothers freedom to pursue education or work.

THE PROFUSION OF PEOPLE

The most important sexual advance in terms of human welfare will be finding a way to control the runaway increase in births over deaths that is presently creating misery and despair in many parts of the world, and threatens to drag even the advanced societies over the precipice into a degraded, productively sterile, and declining civilization. Millions of television viewers have seen the suffering by starvation and disease in overpopulated regions of the world. And many people have seen firsthand the insufferable congestion in megacities. Probably typical—although not the largest—is Cairo, home to about 9.5 million people. Three million of them lack sewers, half a million live in rooftop shelters, and another half a million inhabit the tombs of the so-called City of the Dead in the most degrading conditions imaginable.[16]

As Thomas Robert Malthus predicted 200 years ago, a runaway growth in global population leaves millions of people in squalid and filthy conditions, living on the ragged edge of starvation. Thousands die of malnutrition and diseases every year.[17] Malthus contended that the unbridled reproductive urge would outstrip the capacity of the earth to produce food and provide for human welfare. He recommended a preventive method that seems naive by today's standard of conduct: sexual restraint. More recently, Paul Ehrlich, a biologist at Stanford University, reminded people again of the adverse effects of too many people, and organized Zero Population Growth to promote birth control.

People pushed the worldwide population up in 1991 by a record 92 million, to a global total of 5.2 billion. The increase in

	Millions
World total	5718
Africa	728
North America[a]	455
South America	320
Asia[b]	3459
Europe[c]	727
Oceania[a]	29

World population, 1995 provisional midyear estimates. [a]Hawaii, a state of the United States of America, is included in North America rather than Oceania. [b]Including both the Asian and European portions of Turkey. [c]Excluding the European portion of Turkey, which is included in Asia. Source: Population and Vital Statistics Report, Statistical Papers Series A Vol. XLVII, No. 4, United Nations.

population resulted from 143 million births against 51 million deaths for the year.[18] By 1994, the breeding population had added another 200 million, putting the world total at 5.6 billion, and by 1995 pushed it to 5.7 billion.

The rate of population increase peaked in the late 1960s at just over 2% per year, and has since fallen further to 1.6% per year. The decline came from a drop in fertility in developing countries from an average of six children per woman to slightly under four. Still, the population growth in most of the developing world is remarkably high. The "doubling time" is only 24 years in Africa and 35 years in Asia and Latin America. Those rates compare with 98 years, or less than a century, in North America and 1025 in Europe.

In view of the fact that an unprecedented number of women will be entering their reproductive years, how many people will the world have to support by the end of the next few decades?

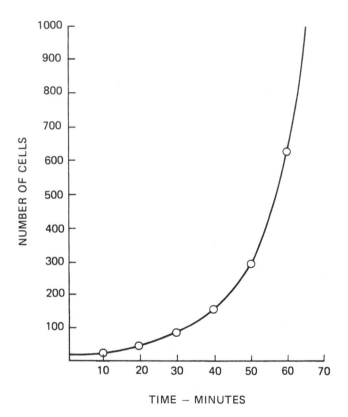

TIME — MINUTES

A hypothetical colony of yeast cells, each reproducing itself every ten minutes in a microbiological "Utopia" where there is unlimited food and space, resembles the present phase of the human growth curve. The yeast curve starts off innocently enough, but as time goes on, the curves bends more sharply upward, until at ten minutes after the hour, it disappears from the chart, careening off into space toward infinity. Within a short span of time, yeast would overwhelm the earth. Actually, nothing of the sort ever happens. The curve levels off mainly because of the food supply. Scarcity of food and other resources, accumulation of toxins, and the onslaught of predators and diseases eventually cause a sharp bend downwards, often approaching near extinction.

According to UN projections, by 2050 the global population will have grown to between 7.8 and 12.5 billion depending on the rate of decline in fertility. Even if the fertility rate could be reduced to the so-called replacement level of 2.1 children per woman before the turn of the century (which few people think will happen), the world population would still climb to 7.7 billion in 2050.[19]

In contrast to much of the world, the population of the former Soviet Union and western Europe, representing 9% of the world population, has nearly stabilized, and in Russia there is fear of a dangerous decline in births.[20] But the population growth worldwide staggers the senses. In the span of half a century, we have seen the world population more than double. The impact of 2.5 billion more people diminished the resources of the planet and the quality of life in many parts of the world.[21] What can, or should, be done to put a damper on runaway human reproduction? People with different viewpoints have been arguing about it for decades.

Lester Brown, a renowned specialist on population growth, says:

> Time is not on our side. The world has waited too long to stabilize population. The decline in seafood supply per person and in grain output per person is already underway. This is not something that might happen. It is happening. . . . Unless we act quickly and decisively, neither history nor our children will judge us kindly.[21]

In September, 1994, about 180 nations meeting in Cairo at a UN-sponsored International Conference on Population and Development, approved a program to limit the world's people to 7.2 billion over the next two decades.[22] This will be close to double the increase in the previous half century. And that's just a hopeful goal! The additional 1.6 billion people (a 29% increase)—even if that limitation can be achieved—will use up a lot more of the world's resources or create suffering from deprivation, probably both. Many of the 1.6 billion, as many of those in the past, will starve in agony, and many will silently die of nutritional-deficiency and microbial diseases.

In effect, it appeared that the International Conference on Population and Development threw in the towel. But despite the gloomy projection, many individual countries are trying to improve family planning. The surprising fertility decline in East Asia, though still high, may be the prelude to a similar trend in other parts of the world.

Population control will not be most effective, as commonly supposed, by imposing birth control on the overly fecund people of the world, but instead, will be initiated in the more advanced societies such as those in western Europe and North America in a more enlightened way. Recent history shows clearly that the more affluent nations have lower birth rates than poor nations. Measures to increase the economic welfare of people in impoverished countries will be more rewarding and more effective than the practice of simply sending food, medicine, and condoms to starving populations. Reduction in population growth will not necessarily depend entirely on new discoveries, although biotechnological advances will come into play.

The world is now divided between the breeders and the feeders. The breeders will continue to deplete the resources of both themselves and their feeders until they become self-sustaining by limiting their fecundity.

A curious dichotomy of purpose exists in advanced countries, including the United States: subsidizing a high birth rate with a tax deduction for each child. Money incentives are the strongest form of persuasion. A procedure that will eventually be adopted for reducing the birth rate in advanced countries is simple, direct, and quick: instead of providing subsidies for births either by direct welfare payments or in the form of tax credits for dependent children, tax credits will be provided for having fewer than two children until a satisfactory balance between birth rate and death rate is achieved. In China, the one child per family policy is enforced by the government. In democracies people will continue to be free to have as many children as they want, but they will have to pay for more than one. People whose economic status does not provide a tax break would be given free contraceptives, advice, and moral persuasion, but no financial incentive for carelessness.

To be sure, there will be opposition to tax incentives for fewer children. Many politicians and businessmen view growth—any kind of growth—as synonymous with progress. More people mean more customers, more voters, and more taxpayers. But there is no virtue in growth *per se*. City dumps, urban blight, and cancers grow. True progress is unrelated to growth except that it may be smothered and suffocated by the burden of too many people.

ABORTIONS

Worldwide, ovariectomy, tubal ligation, and abortion are widely used methods of birth control. Unsafe (illegal) abortions have become an alarmingly common method of birth control in developing countries. A study made for the World Health Organization estimated 50 million artificially terminated pregnancies—30 million legal abortions plus another 20 million illegal abortions—annually.[23,24] In Ukraine, Russia, and other ex-Soviet parts of the world, there are two abortions for every birth. One estimate is that the average Ukrainian woman has four or five abortions in her lifetime, and some have ten or more. The UN Population Fund and the International Planned Parenthood Federation, the most important international sources of family planning assistance, were effectively supporting birth control in developing countries when the United States withdrew financial support because people said it was promoting abortion programs. The result was an increase in unwanted pregnancies and, some people maintained, an actual increase in the number of abortions.[21]

A practice that, perversely, has the effect of increasing the birth rate is a cruel form of female mutilation, incomprehensible by Western standards, that is common in some parts of the Islamic world. The mutilation ranges in degree from drawing blood to complete removal of the clitoris. In an article published in *Ms.* magazine in March, 1979, coauthors Robin Morgan and Gloria Steinem estimated that 30 million women were suffering the results of genital mutilation.[25] But an official estimate of the World Health Organization (WHO) increased the number to 75 million.

The mutilation takes several forms. They are mainly: Sunna,

or female "circumcision," which consists of removal of the prepuce and/or tip of the clitoris; "clitoridectomy," removal of the entire clitoris (both prepuce and glans, plus the adjacent part of the labia minora); and an operation called "infibulation," from the Latin *fibula*, meaning "clasp," in which the clitoris, labia minora, and labia majora are removed, plus an operation in which the forward two-thirds of the labia majora are scraped raw before being sewn together with catgut or metal wire or held together with a thorn from the acacia tree. A stick is inserted into the wound to preserve a small opening to allow passage of urine and menstrual blood.

The operation in one form or another is widely practiced in various parts of the Middle East, Africa, India, western Asia, the Malay archipelago, Australia, and New Guinea. Infibulation is common in the Sudan, Somalia, and Nigeria. The operation is usually performed by a midwife, but it is often done by a member of the family, in that case usually the father. In addition to severe bleeding, intense pain, and trauma, there is great danger of tetanus or other infection leading to death. According to *Intercom*, a publication of the Population Reference Bureau, as many as 20 million women in black Africa are said to be victims of the practice. A Nigerian journalist, Esther Ogunmodede, who campaigned for an end to the barbaric practice, explained the reason for it. "To keep the young girl 'pure' and the married woman faithful," says Ogunmodede, "genital operations are maintained as one of Africa's most valued 'traditions.'" One rationale given for the operation by those who defend the practice is that it reduces the frequency of sexual intercourse and keeps the birth rate down. But others point out that it actually increases the birth rate. The woman is apt to find intercourse so painful that she becomes pregnant as quickly and as often as possible, even though an operation is needed at childbirth, because it enables her to avoid sexual contact during pregnancy and a customarily long period after giving birth.

The need to avoid unwanted children is only one part of the maternal problem. Hemorrhage during childbirth and complications from unsafe abortions are reported to be the principal causes of maternal death in developing countries. According to Jodi L. Jacobson, writing for the Worldwatch Institute:[26]

> At least 500,000 women die annually from pregnancy-related causes. Ninety-nine percent of them live in developing countries.
>
> Complications of pregnancy, childbirth, and unsafe abortions are thus the leading killers of women of reproductive age throughout the Third World. . . .
>
> For every woman who dies, many others are left with illnesses or impairments that rob them of their health and productivity, often for the rest of their lives. . . .
>
> In the majority of countries with data, hemorrhage and complications of unsafe abortion are the two most important causes of maternal death. . . .
>
> Unsafe abortion and hemorrhage together account for more than 30 percent of maternal deaths in Ethiopia, India, Tanzania and Zambia.

People in developing countries have had a fleeting glimpse of what life is like in the more affluent parts of the world, and they yearn for more than the grubby existence of the past. The realization is beginning to dawn on people in poor circumstances that the rocky path to deprivation, poverty, even starvation, is to have more mouths to feed. Barring more benign ways to limit offspring, abortion is often a last resort. Abortions in many of the Third World countries are performed by poorly trained or untrained midwives. "Scraping," a crude form of surgical curettage, is common, often causing hemorrhage or infection. Sometimes women, in desperation at the thought of feeding another child, will do drastic things to abort the fetus themselves. Mutilation with a knitting needle is one way.[23]

In countries where abortion is legal, and therefore apt to be done under more sanitary conditions, a common procedure is that the doctor, after giving the woman a shot of local anesthetic, will insert a thin plastic tube into the uterus. A vacuum pump at 250 millimeters of mercury sucks out the embryo and deposits it as a formless mixture of fluid and tissue in a bottle.

The plight of women is aggravated by discrimination against females in the allocation of food, health care, and education. Many of them suffer from malnutrition and anemia. Simply put, females have less "value" than males. Male children are preferred not only because they can contribute more economically, but also because a marriage dowry in some parts of the world may impose a crippling burden on the family to the point of ruin. In India, the 1971 Medical Termination of Pregnancy Act permits any woman to end a pregnancy during the first 20 weeks. Many couples, to avoid having daughters, get sex determination tests and abort the fetus if it is a female. Even though the Indian Parliament made it a crime punishable by three years in prison for operators of ultrasound clinics to reveal the sex of a fetus to an expectant mother, the economics are so compelling that the law is probably unenforceable.[23]

In China, abortion has long been less an option than a duty to satisfy the Communist Party policy of limiting couples to one child, imposed if necessary by salaried state functionaries and family planning cadres. Reportedly, family planning cadres will sometimes force abortion as late as the sixth month of pregnancy.

The U.S. Supreme Court's 7 to 2 ruling of January, 1973, in the case of Roe vs. Wade removed all federal restrictions on abortion. The Court said that the states could not place restrictions on abortion during the first trimester—the first three months of a pregnancy. During the second trimester, or up to six months of pregnancy, when the danger of medical complications are greater, the justices said that the states would be justified in imposing controls "reasonably related to the preservation and protection of maternal health," such as requiring the abortion to be performed in a licensed hospital. Once the fetus becomes viable—capable of surviving outside the womb, usually considered to be between the 24th and 28th weeks or about six months of pregnancy—the states may prohibit abortion as long as they leave open the possibility of terminating the pregnancy when it is necessary to preserve the mother's life or health. Thus, a woman and her physician can legally decide whether a pregnancy should be aborted if there are no state or local laws that prohibit it and, in any case, women have the unrestricted constitutional right to an abortion during the first three months of pregnancy.

Several European and Far Eastern countries permit abortions with various restrictions. Abortion is usually permitted in the countries of the former Soviet Union and every country of western Europe except Ireland and Malta where it can be done only to save a mother's life. Many other countries throughout the world prohibit abortions except for strict exemptions, such as for the health of the mother or in case of rape. But laws are not as effective as lawmakers intend. In Chile, abortion carries a 15-year prison sentence, but the country has the highest abortion rate in Latin America. One study estimated that Chile has 450,000 pregnancies annually and that 35% of them are terminated artificially, often crudely by amateur abortionists. Many of the women end up in hospitals or worse. In the Republic of Ireland, abortion is prohibited but is said to be actually more common than in The Netherlands where there is no legal restriction.[23]

Religious views on abortion differ widely, even between denominations of Christians. The Roman Catholic Church holds that abortion is always a sin and an "abominable crime." Protestant churches are more lenient to various degrees. Islam views are fragmented. Traditional Islam holds that abortion is a sin and illegal, but some leaders allow it in cases of rape or even poverty. Muslim leaders say that ensoulment occurs 40 days after conception, and that the sinfulness of abortion depends on how long after conception it is done. After 120 days it is murder. Judaism permits abortions in some cases. In Israel, abortion is illegal but there are many exemptions and it must be authorized by an official committee.[24]

Buddhism seems to have a humane view of abortion. Although it is viewed as a misdeed, the happiness of the "living human being" may be considered. The view of Hinduism on abortion seems to be evolving in adjustment to modern thinking. The traditional teaching is that abortion is a sin, but many leaders think that it is needed for population control. The prevailing view of Hindus is that a person has a soul only after being born.

Despite a growing tide of abortions, strong religious forces oppose any kind of effective birth control that would otherwise be available to women in poor circumstances. The International Conference on Population and Development held in Cairo in September, 1994, was nearly untracked by wrangling over the wording of a resolution dealing with abortion. Most of the 180 nations represented were willing to settle on a compromise calling for individual governments to deal with the health risks of illegal abortion while not promoting abortion as a family planning measure. Legalization of abortion would be up to each nation to decide for itself. But the Vatican vehemently opposed any faint suggestion of support for abortion, and many of the Muslim countries objected as well. The conference ended with approval of an anemic proposal to limit world population to 7.2 billion in the next two decades, called a new category of "reproductive rights." The conferees emphasized improving health, education, and living standards for women, anticipating that women would then elect to have smaller families.[22] The Vatican joined the consensus with reservations. Said Archbishop Renato Martino,

> Especially, nothing is to be understood to imply that the Holy See endorses abortion, or has in any way changed its moral position concerning abortion, or on contraceptives, or on sterilization, nor on the use of condoms in HIV/AIDS prevention programs.

Many countries, including most of the Latin-American countries that shared the Vatican's views joined the consensus but recorded objections.[22]

It is an irony of human psychology, and a symptom of ethical confusion, that some people who accuse abortion doctors of murder advocate the murder of the doctors as justifiable homicide. The divisive and inflammatory controversy over the morality of abortions may, at some time in the future, largely disappear because birth control measures can be expected eventually to be so effective, safe, cheap, and universally available that unwanted pregnancies will be virtually a thing of the past. It would be overly optimistic to think that this would come about quickly. "Not one of these methods [several under study] will be used by people before the year 2010," says Carl Djerassi, inventor of the modern oral contraceptive pill.[27] But it is the belief of some researchers that technology has reached nowhere near the limit of dealing with birth control. The contraceptive implant, Norplant, and the controversial abortion pill, RU 486, are only a start. Implants are highly effective, but costly and inconvenient, and RU 486 has met with strong opposition on religious and moral grounds. Some of the contraceptive pills can be used in large doses as "day after" preventives, but instruction on how to use them is not widely available, and they would be too expensive for women in poor countries.

One approach is to develop a contraceptive vaccine. It is theoretically possible to immunize a woman against implantation of a fertilized egg in the uterine wall. The hormone chorionic gonadotropin (hCG) helps implant the blastocyst (fertilized egg). Inducing the formation of antibodies to the hormone would interrupt the process of implantation and prevent pregnancy.

Most of the effort in the past has been to find a method that can be conveniently used by women. But researchers have speculated for a long time that a method of treating men would be more effective.[27] Vaccines for men are a promising lead. A vaccine under study as a treatment for prostate cancer induces the body to make antibodies against gonadotropin-releasing hormone (GnRH) secreted by the pituitary gland, the function of which is to stimulate the production of testosterone and sperm. It could be useful as a male contraceptive except for the fact that it also causes men to lose their libido.[28] Another approach is to target the follicle-stimulating hormone (FSH), which is also required for sperm production but doesn't affect the release of testosterone. Some scientists believe the best approach would be to target antigens in the sperm, but any method of tinkering with the immune system is fraught with the danger of side effects.[27]

Scientists at the World Health Organization gave men testosterone, which in higher than normal concentrations signals the body by a feedback mechanism, to slow down sperm production. When the sperm count of 300 men fell from at least 20 million per cubic centimeter to less than 3 million, their female partners had only four pregnancies in a year. In another study, George Gerton, a reproductive biologist at the University of Pennsylvania School of

Medicine, says, "If we can find proteins unique to sperm and egg cells that orchestrate sperm–egg binding and fusion, we may be able to design specific reagents to interrupt the process."

There is reason to be hopeful that we will have a universally available over-the-counter pill to prevent embryo implantation. It will be given free to schoolchildren along with their "safe" condoms. But this state of perfection in chemistry and behavior may take many years to achieve. Even today, the problem of birth control is not lack of scientific knowledge. We know now how to control the population but we lack the determination to do what is needed. The tragic AIDS epidemic may serve one useful purpose. If the worldwide use of condoms becomes popular, birth control may be a bonus benefit. The breakthrough will come with the inevitable development of safe, effective, and cheap birth control drugs that can be used worldwide, including poor countries, to replace the crude methods now employed: withdrawal, condoms, abortifacients, surgical sterilization, and surgical abortion.

ENVIRONMENT

Degradation of the environment is directly related to human population density. An easily measured indicator of the changing environment is the effect on the earth's forest cover, which is declining rapidly. The UN Food and Agriculture Organization reported that in 1992 the loss was at an annual rate of 17 million hectares (about 42 million acres). The loss is most evident in the tropics where forests are being converted to pastures and other agricultural uses, and mining the forests for hardwood for shipment to the affluent countries. Although cutting is selective for valuable trees, according to agricultural experts, logging typically destroys 30 to 60% of the economically unwanted trees. But that is not all. Everywhere there can be seen devastation of grasslands, soil erosion, soil nutrient depletion, water shortage, water and air pollution, and dwindling energy supplies, including firewood that much of the world's population depends on. And the dwindling resources have to be divided among an ever larger number of people. David Pimentel and co-workers at Cornell University point out, "With the addition of a quarter of a million people each day, the world population's food demand is increasing at a time when per capita food productivity is beginning to decline."[29] J. G. Seth, reporting for the United Nations, says that about 80% of the world's agricultural land suffers moderate to severe erosion, and 10% suffers slight erosion.

Many people who think of themselves as ecologists or environmentalists never give a thought to one of the most basic principles of ecology: the *carrying capacity* of the environment. Traditionally, carrying capacity refers to the maximum number of individuals of a species that can be supported by the environment. In the traditional sense, and the one that many people have in mind when they oppose population control, we are nowhere near the carrying capacity of the earth because if we ignore scarcity, congestion, pollution, and the law of diminishing returns, we will be able to crowd more people into the finite space of earth for decades to come. But in human terms, the carrying capacity is constrained by the *quality of life*. In that context, many parts of the world, including the United States, are well over the carrying capacity for the maximum quality of life. David Pimentel, Cornell University professor of ecology and systematics, says that even if we learn to use our dwindling resources more efficiently, the planet cannot sustain 2 billion more people with a quality of life for everyone. "Continued rapid population growth," says Pimental, "will result in even more severe social, economic and political conflicts—plus catastrophic public health and environmental problems."

World population growth is out of control, and is the basic cause of environmental degradation. The global demand for material goods of all kinds, from washers to weapons, even in the so-called developing countries, is bringing about the destruction of natural resources at an accelerating rate. Environmental damage in Third World countries is not as much from their own consumption as from the increasing demand for their products by the wealthy nations, which have about 22% of the world's population but consume two-thirds of the production. It will soon be too late to initiate the drastic measures in population control that are needed to forestall a disastrous worldwide decline in resources and, therefore, human welfare.

DISEASES

It must be admitted that if left unattended, the population problem will eventually take care of itself in a way that would be biologically successful but humanly disastrous. A fact of nature is that most species are subject to cyclic fluctuations in population, most dramatically seen in insects, mammals, and other forms of wildlife as well as in microscopic organisms. When conditions are favorable, a species will soar to a peak of enormous population density. As all mathematicians know and anyone can observe, exponential growth in a finite world must come to an end. At that point, one of several things can happen. The population may become extinct. Having consumed most of the available food, or as a result of a buildup of predators, parasites, disease, or polluting excretion the population will decline precipitously to numbers that can be sustained by the environment, often verging on oblivion. The human population is now on the upward slope of the curve, and appears to be rapidly approaching the peak at which the high population density, especially the concentration of millions of people in the close quarters of megacities, many of them living in poverty and squalor, forms a virtual incubator for diseases and disastrous epidemics.

Laurie Garrett, an immunologist and fellow at the Harvard School of Public Health, thinks that as megacities with 10 million or more people proliferate in economically disadvantaged countries, and as environmental conditions deteriorate worldwide, microbes will get the upper hand.[30] In her book *The Coming Plague: Newly Emerging Diseases in a World Out of Balance*, she says, "[H]umans are actually aiding and abetting the microbes."

Responsible sperm control, though technically possible, is a worldwide failure, while germ control in the recent past has been a phenomenal success, leading to what Garrett calls "The Age of

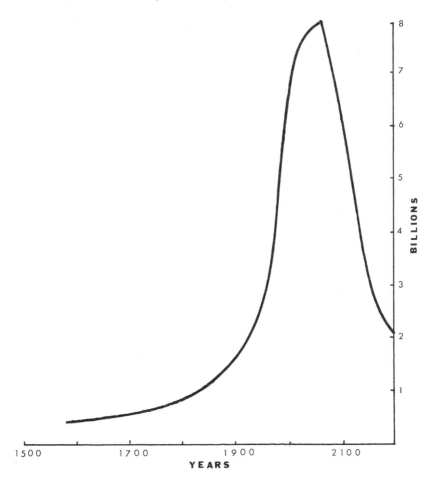

Population in billions, postulating a typical crash from exceeding the carrying capacity of the earth in the late twenty-first century if breeding is not voluntarily controlled.

Optimism"—that turned out to be an ephemeral dream. A dark shadow of disaster portends a catastrophic future unless the deterioration in living conditions in much of the world can be reversed by economic advances made possible by population control. New diseases and new strains of old diseases spread rapidly in an era of fast global travel, and find their way to the microbial incubators of megacities. Joshua Lederberg, professor and president emeritus of Rockefeller University, opined that the most important changes that led to this situation are the unprecedented movement of people and the "sheer expansion of our species."

The capability of microbes to become resistant to antibiotics adds to the agony. Says Dr. Stuart Levy in *The Antibiotic Paradox*, "Antibiotic resistance is not constrained by local or even national borders. It confronts all individuals and populations around the world."[31] Trying to defeat antibiotic-resistant microbes by switching antibiotics or developing new ones is a losing game because the microbes stay one jump ahead by mutating to strains that are resistant, or quickly become resistant to anything the microbe fighters come up with.

Besides more judicious use of antibiotics by using them only when needed, most authorities advocate aggressive immunization programs. But another dark shadow looms ever larger. Modern medicine's nullifying the process of natural selection—aggressive germ control versus slipshod sperm control—is both a blessing and a potential curse. Germ control makes it possible for millions of people to survive and reproduce who otherwise would die early in life from natural causes, many of them before reproductive age. Natural selection, a brutality of nature though it seems, does the job of weeding out those who are susceptible and leaving those who have natural immunity. The inevitable result of saving large numbers of people devoid of natural immunity is the build-up of populations lacking resistance to diseases and possibly other environmental hazards. People who are not immunized will be vulnerable to pandemics of calamitous proportions in the event of disruptions such as a worldwide war or similar disaster during which vaccines and nutritional needs might be quickly exhausted. However, the danger of a catastrophic dying from a particular disease is minimized by the demonstrable fact that when the incidence of a disease is reduced by the immunization of a large part of the population, the sources of infection are also reduced. That is the way the virus that causes one of the worst diseases of all time, smallpox, was brought to its knees, and finally to extinction. The two remaining tightly guarded laboratory cultures of the virus are scheduled to be destroyed. The World Health Organization's governing board agreed to set June 30, 1999, as the destruction date if the 190-nation World Health Assembly approves. It will be the only case of ridding the earth forever of a dangerous pest or pathogen by human intervention.

WHAT'S COMING

Elimination of population congestion and resultant improvement of economic conditions and nutrition will alleviate the danger of disease organisms bringing the human species to its knees. Enlightened and rigorous population control, worldwide, will go far to ensure the survival of *Homo sapiens* in good health and economic well-being. Whether action will be taken soon enough to avoid disaster is not certain.

It was not long ago that humans were a minor species on earth, competing more or less on equal terms with other predators, but in far fewer numbers than most of them. Skill at hunting, cleverness in making lethal weapons beyond stones and clubs, and the invention of agriculture gradually enabled people to band together in ever larger societies, and above all, to increase in numbers. The urge to reproduce remained a powerful driving force, so to avoid chaos in tightly knit societies, social constraints on copulation, such as marriage, were put in place by common consent. As today, they were not always honored, sometimes hardly at all.

There is little evidence, apart from swings in puritanical mood, that people have changed their breeding habits from one millennium to the next. What has changed are the number of people to do it with, and the survival rate of the offspring through medical and nutritional advances, together resulting in an astonishing exponential rate of increase in peopling the earth. As Lester Brown points out, people born before the middle of the 20th century saw the world population more than double from 2.5 billion to 5.5 billion, and it is predicted to double again in the next 20 years.[32]

> The environmental effects of adding 2.5 billion people are
> highly visible, especially in the Third World. They can be seen
> in the loss of tree cover, devastation of grasslands, soil ero-
> sion, crowding, poverty, land hunger, water pollution, and
> swelling streams of environmental refugees. (p.16)

Homo sapiens, as the most prolific of primates, and the least
sexually inhibited, is fast approaching the moment of truth when
nature will determine whether our species can continue to occupy
the earth in comfort or descend in a spiral of decline from the peak
of its exponential rise into a grubby, atavistic life of savagery,
clinging by tooth and claw to the remnants of our depleted planet
for survival. In short, *Homo sapiens* is in peril of copulating itself to
extinction.

Despite the gloomy expectation of billions of more people,
more congestion, more deforestation, more soil erosion, more pollution, fewer mineral resources, and less food production capability per person, there are encouraging signs. There is currently a
slight decline in the *rate* of population increase, the result of several social changes. Most importantly, there is an increasing
awareness among families in Third World countries that more
children mean less food to share instead of being a form of social
security as in the past. And many of the world leaders are belat-
edly becoming aware of the problems of population growth, resulting in official actions to reduce the birth rate in some of the
most heavily congested countries. Finally, scientists are working
diligently to discover methods of birth control that will be more
effective and cheaper, and there is every reason to think that they
will be successful.

The most pessimistic scenario is one in which people will
continue to populate the earth and consume its resources in an
orgiastic frenzy without restraint, disregarding congestion, depletion of resources, and pollution until the world is reduced to a
menagerie of monkeylike primates scrambling for the scraps of a
decayed civilization on the brink of extinction. It doesn't take a
mathematician to compute the result of delay. Respect for simple
arithmetic may teach us how to save humanity from Thomas
Malthus's prediction that we will outbreed our ability to survive a

dwindling supply of resources. The story is told of the Arabian merchant who contracted with the sultan to work for one grain of wheat the first day, two the second day, four the third day, and so doubling with each day to the 64th day corresponding to the squares on their chessboard—and how he bankrupted the kingdom. Most sultans would have seen the light and beheaded the merchant by the 12th day. Assuming a population of 1 million people at the end of the Ice Age (some say far fewer), since then the human population has doubled 12 times with the curve heading off the top of the chart into space.

The most optimistic scenario is one in which common people and political leaders will soon have a revelation of vision beyond next week's ball game or next year's election, and find ways to transform the world from an orgiastic human breeding farm without limits to a level of population low enough to sustain people in universal prosperity and harmony.

The most probable scenario is something between the worst and the best. In the near term, people will continue to increase at a near-exponential rate, forests will continue to disappear, more productive land will be lost to soil erosion, energy and mineral resources will become more dear, congestion and pollution will get worse, health services will be overextended, and diseases will become rampant until we, in desperation, exhaustion, or disgust, turn to the only recourse we'll have for a dignified life. After the agony of too little and nearly too late, we will learn the secret of responsible global sex—don't overpopulate when you copulate.

Chapter Twelve

CYBERSEX

A remarkable thing about the information superhighway is how quickly people seized on cyberspace to express one of the oldest forms of art and literature—pornography.

On-line services came on strong in the early 1990s and have become the fastest growing segment of the world media market. America Online, Prodigy, CompuServe, and Delphi grew in double-digit figures. Microsoft's on-line service followed. The Japanese pitched in quickly. Niftyserve, co-owned by the giant electronics firm NEC, doubled its growth to half a million subscribers in less than two years. Fukitsu's PCVAN is almost as big. The World Wide Web became one of the most popular on-line services. Collectively, they carry a heavy traffic of every imaginable kind of communication on the international Internet.[1]

The value of porn on the Internet was demonstrated when two enterprising graduate students at Stanford University created a list, which they named Yahoo, of favorite sites on the Internet of interest to a wide range of users.[2] Popular categories, each with their own sublevels and sub-sublevels, were such items as entertainment, dating, multimedia, regional information, and businesses. They had to drop the erotica category because the sites under it kept crashing, overwhelmed by inquiries as soon as they were listed. Music-oriented sites are by far the largest single category on the World Wide Web according to the Yahoo index. But some people think that pornography is even bigger.

Music is easier to transmit over computer lines than the moving pictures of television and movies. By comparison with video, sound takes up less than one-tenth as much bandwidth—the capacity of a line to carry data. Still, there is plenty of porn on the Internet. An operator at the Livermore Laboratory of the University of California was found to be using its powerful computer system to collect, distribute, and exchange a massive amount of pornographic material. Games are an important part of all of the large on-line services. But often overlooked in the glamor of the fast track highway is the proliferation of resources available by modem: namely, the neighborhood computer bulletin boards, commonly called BBSs. There's a BBS for nearly every taste, fancy, and life-style, from acrobatics to Zen Buddhism. Several networks serve to tie local BBSs together, one of the best known of which is Fidonet. Thus, a local forum on Arabian horse shows might tie in with equestrians all over the country, or the world. With an estimated 50,000 to 100,000 BBSs throughout the United States, they are useful to people in isolated locales who share a common interest. They offer a chance to chat on-screen with other users, and offer unlimited electronic mail and various commercial services. For users who just want e-mail from an on-line service, they can adopt a BBS as their main post office.[3]

Many BBSs, especially the biggest and most expensive, are adult oriented, offering sexually explicit material. Cyberspace writer Daniel Akst tells us that BBSs are "a font of pornography." Most of them disclose their area of interest upfront, so the user can be forewarned. Many of them offer personal ads. Some lesbian and gay BBSs are connected by a service called GayCom.

Writer Robert A. Jones examined the history and status of computer porn. An example of the developing segment of the interactive cyberspace industry that deals in erotica is an organization called New Machine Publishing, set up by a group of four 25-year-olds to digitize, that is, to convert video images into the digital language of CD-ROMs.[4] A videotape is loaded into one side of a computer, which converts it into digitized images. (CD-ROM stands for "compact disc—read only memory.") It is essentially the same as a music CD, but with more capacity, being able to store an hour of video plus stereophonic sound. But the most valuable feature of CD-ROM is that the viewer can pick optional commands on the screen, thereby determining the course of action. For example, the video may show a fully dressed pretty girl strolling onscreen beside a swimming pool. The screen gives you a choice. Do you want her to lie down on the chaise? Do you want her to dive into the pool? Do you want her to strip and dive into the pool? (She may or may not do everything you ask, because it's impossible to program every one of the hundreds of possible interactions, but you have an input.)

The young men of New Machine were on the threshold of a new category of major corporate enterprise. One estimate is that producers of erotica enjoy 20% of the fledgling CD-ROM business, which translated into 1994 sales in the United States is about $260 million. Writer Paul Tharp says that CD-ROM has turned the smutty side of cyberspace into a $1 billion-plus business.[5] Tharp says, "Explicit X-rated porn that once was available only in sleazy side street shops is as easy to get on a PC as ordering a pizza."

"And if you have children playing upstairs on the family PC, watch out," he says. "They may not be doing their homework."

The first commercial CD-ROM interactive erotica was "Virtual Valerie," produced by a Chicago firm called Reactor. However, Valerie was an animated character. The first interactive erotica on CD-ROM with live actors was New Machine's debut product, "Nightwatch Interactive." Nightwatch, introduced in 1992, took off rocketlike, and shot New Machine into the New Age. New Machine followed up with "The Interactive Adventures of Seymore Butts" and "Dream Machine." A slick CD-ROM entitled "Man Enough" says in the blurb that it's a first-person interactive simulation with beautiful characters in the boudoir whose expression and demeanor change in response to the user's dialogue.[6] The quick intrusion of erotica into CD-ROM interaction is reminiscent of how quickly it invaded earlier innovations in communications: printing of the numerous erotic stories in the Gutenberg Bible, pornographic tracts, and an illustrated guide to lovemaking put out by the early printing presses, "French postcards" used for trading like modern baseball cards following the introduction of improved photo printing, and one of Thomas Edison's first, the bland movie "The Kiss."

The oldest and the newest have come together on the Internet in some cities—prostitutes setting up appointments through cyberspace. Another indication that use of the superhighway may be getting out of hand is the complaint of some women users of the Internet that they're being cyber-raped with vulgar messages.

Some users of the information highway are almost universally condemned. In one case, a 41-year-old man was charged with possessing child pornography, a misdemeanor that was punishable by up to a year in county jail and a $1000 fine. If convicted, he would have to register as a sex offender. Police said he had placed an ad in a magazine called *Loving Alternatives*, seeking an "open relationship" with one or two couples interested in "family nudity." Police said that "family nudity" is a code phrase used by pedophiles to signal an interest in child pornography. The police found numerous electronic photos on the hard disc of the man's computer that depicted child erotica and pornography. The porno photos were of boys under 14 engaged in sexual activities such as masturbation and oral copulation.[7]

One of the first police busts of purveyors of electronic porn was in California, where a man and woman were put in the lockup for transmitting kiddie porn—sexually obscene pictures of children—through interstate telephone lines to an undercover agent in Memphis.

Parents and police are deeply concerned about the ready availability of porn to children and the use of the Internet by pedophiles to make contact with potential victims. Anyone, even small children, with access to a computer can obtain it, and this gives pedophiles the ability to communicate freely with them. There is the real possibility that children could be lured into illicit sex, prostitution, or worse. Cases of pedophiles making the acquaintance of minors and luring them away from home are increasing. In 1994, a Massachusetts man was charged with statutory rape of two young boys he had met through a computer bulletin board. The same year, a California computer engineer pleaded no contest to a charge of molesting a 14-year-old boy after setting up a meeting with him through e-mail.

In 1995, a 51-year-old Seattle postal worker was sentenced to six years in prison after pleading guilty to having sex with a 10-year-old girl and to making graphic sexually oriented e-mail contacts with adolescent and teen-age girls in several states. Prosecutors alleged that the man talked girls into exchanging nude photos of themselves. He was arrested after the mother of a 14-year-old girl saw him talking with her daughter at a shopping mall. He had lured her via e-mail by posing as a 13-year-old boy.

In another Washington case, a 15-year-old boy picked up a bus ticket from the mailbox and slipped away. The boy's frantic parents tried to locate him by searching the boy's vacant computer, and found the name of a man with whom their son had exchanged messages. When they looked up the man's listing in America Online's subscriber directory, they found that he had given his hobby as fellatio. They were able to contact the man on America Online, and he contemptuously described to them in graphic detail some acts he had done with the boy. After several days, the boy was found alone at the San Francisco International Airport. He told his parents that his contact was an older teenager.

Only days after the episode of the missing Washington boy a 13-year-old Kentucky girl disappeared after exchanging messages on America Online with a man in California. The girl had left a computer printout that said, "We can run around our room naked all day and all night." About two weeks later, the frightened girl was taken into protective custody in Los Angeles after she contacted the local FBI office from a phone booth on Hollywood Boulevard.[8]

Various remedies have been proposed to shield children from the unprecedented dangers and temptations transmitted through computers, but none of them seems to offer much protection. Some computer experts suggest that on-line services set up standards for subscribers, requiring all players to disclose fully their identities. A suggestion was made that on-line computer services restrict children's access to undesirable material such as photos and indecent chat lines by requiring users to verify their age with a personal verification number. Both proposals were opposed by civil liberties groups, and proponents did not say how it could be policed and enforced.

After many months of debate, the U.S. Congress enacted a sweeping revision of the outdated Communications Act of 1934, removing much of the monopoly protection in the industry. A provision of the bill was to outlaw transmission of indecent and sexually explicit materials to minors over computer networks. The measure, signed into law on February 7, 1996, calls for fines of as much as $250,000 and jail terms for as much as five years for anyone who makes indecent or sexually explicit material available to children in a public on-line forum. The law bans display of material that is "patently offensive," as measured by prevailing community standards, in places accessible to minors. Another provision of the law requires all television manufacturers to include in new sets a computer chip, called the V-chip or violence chip, that will enable parents to block out programs they consider objectionable. To aid them in making decisions, the law further calls for a rating system. President Clinton announced that he would meet with entertainment industry executives to propose that they initiate a voluntary rating system for television programs, similar to those used for movies.

The ink was hardly dry before a coalition of human rights and civil liberties groups filed suit in Philadelphia seeking to block the law's provisions. Many rights activists as well as some legal experts believed that prohibitions in the law were overly broad. The ACLU, Planned Parenthood, and other organizations asked the court to overturn parts of the law that would prevent on-line dissemination of information about abortion.

The new measures raised a howl of protest from those who fear censorship and violation of constitutional freedom of speech guarantees. But protests may be a waste of energy because no one seems to have the vaguest idea how an enforcement agency could monitor the flood of information on the net, much of it cyberjunk. To use an old radio expression, they wouldn't be able to hear the signal for the noise.

Those who want voluntary control of porn on cyberspace say that laws are not needed because parents can already protect their children from on-line lewdness with electronic controls offered by some of the services, including America Online, CompuServe, and Prodigy. They advocate old-fashioned parental involvement and supervision. Representative Mark Foley of Florida opined that parents already have a V-chip, "the on–off switch." However, it is unrealistic to expect parents to stand around while their children are on the Internet waiting to push a button whenever something objectionable shows up. Some services provide a way to block out certain news groups. In fact, dealers carry software known as "twit filters" that can block any name or handle that the user finds offensive. The user keys in the offending name or handle and that person becomes a nonentity that you'll never see or hear from again. SofWatch Software has developed software that will bar children from Internet areas that contains sexually explicit material. Computer expert Lawrence J. Magid wrote a booklet, *Child Safety on the Information Highway*, which can be obtained free by calling the National Center for Missing and Exploited Children at 800-843-5678.

WHAT IS PORNOGRAPHY?

Defining "pornography" is like trying to catch a greased pig. Webster is clear enough, but everybody else uses the word to describe anything from free speech to whatever it is they don't like. *Webster's International Dictionary* says that pornography is any depiction, such as writing or pictures, intended primarily to arouse sexual desires. According to Nadine Strossen, law professor and president of the American Civil Liberties Union, the term *pornography* is of no legal significance. The U.S. Supreme Court zeroed in on *obscenity*, another slippery word, to describe sexually oriented expressions that are legally restricted. *Obscene* is from a Latin word meaning "filth." Webster says that an obscenity is something offensive to one's feelings or to prevailing notions of modesty or decency, or something that is disgusting or repulsive. Legally, according to rulings of the Supreme Court, obscenities are expressions such as those in books, films, and other art, that appeal to a prurient (excitement of lust) interest in sex, are patently offensive when judged by contemporary community standards, and have no serious artistic, scientific, or social value. By the Court's definition, obscenities can range all the way from talk that is politically incorrect to urinating on the street or copulating in public. In the Fanny Hill (Roth) case of 1957, the Supreme Court ruled that obscenity is not protected by the constitutional guarantee of free speech, but also ruled that sexual representations are not obscene, and are therefore protected if taken as a whole the dominant theme of the work does not appeal to prurient interests.[9]

Many people equate erotica with pornography, but there is a difference in emphasis. *Pornography* is from the Greek root *pornē*, meaning "prostitute," and *graphos*, meaning "description of," so the word has come to mean any depiction related to sexual arousal. *Erotica*, on the other hand, is from the Greek word *erōtikos* or *eros*, meaning love. Eros was the god of love, son of Aphrodite, the goddess of love and beauty.

In practice, pornography is any erotic material that a group of people does not want anyone else to see or hear. The word has been bastardized by people who object to all sorts of expressions, ideas, and activities. One of the most ingenious uses of the word was by law professor Patricia Williams in an endorsement on the jacket of a book, *Only Words*, written by University of Michigan law professor Catharine MacKinnon. Williams categorized criticism of MacKinnon's idea as "intellectual pornography." MacKinnon is a crusading advocate of suppressing all forms of what she views as pornography.[10]

A figurine of Peruvian erotic art in the Alfred M. Kinsey collection. Courtesy of The Kinsey Institute for Research in Sex, Gender, and Reproduction.

Feminists are polarized in their views of what should or can be done about pornography. Law professor Catharine MacKinnon and writer Andrea Dworkin vigorously promote legislation that would crack down on pornography. Their model legislation defines pornography broadly as "sexually explicit subordination of women through pictures and/or words." "But this definition," counters Nadine Strossen, "is so amorphous that it can well encompass any and all sexual speech." Strossen says in her book *Defending Pornography*,

> We are in the midst of a full-fledged "sex panic," in which seemingly all descriptions and depictions of human sexuality are becoming embattled . . . students and faculty have attacked myriad words and images on campus as purportedly constituting sexual harassment. Any expression about sex is especially dangerous, and hence is especially endangered.

Strossen castigates those she calls "pornophobic feminists" for fomenting the sex panic, especially among liberals and on campuses.[11]

An attack on a wide spectrum of sexual expression, mainly sexual harassment on campuses, was basically unrelated to the pornophobe movement. Sexual harassment codes were adopted by many campuses around the country in the early 1990s, outlawing among other things, "sexual innuendos," "suggestive remarks," "leering, ogling, and physical gestures conveying a sexual meaning," "sexually suggestive looks," and, of course, physical attacks such as "pinching or fondling." Unfortunately, some administrators got carried away in their zeal to enforce the rules. Extreme measures were taken against teachers in several cases for discussing sexually related matters. In one episode described by Dick Johnson in *The New York Times*, May 11, 1994, Graydon Snyder, professor at the Chicago Theological Seminary, was disciplined for reciting a lesson from the Talmud in a religion class.[12] The Talmud story is about a man who falls off a roof and lands on a woman in a way that causes him to have accidental intercourse with her. The lesson is that the man is innocent because the act was unintentional. Although Snyder had been using the passage for 30 years in a discussion of Jewish and Christian ideas of responsibility and guilt, the gentle humor of the ridiculously hypothetical incident and its lesson were lost in the uproar that followed. Maybe sex-tainted humor had something to do with the turmoil. Under the new concept of politically correct speech, a female student filed a complaint of sexual harassment. Among other strong actions taken by an administration that fell under the spell of the new order was the ruling that henceforth Snyder's lectures would have to be monitored by a school official sitting in his classroom with a tape recorder. Thus, we saw the innovation of "word cops" and "sex police" on campuses.

Depictions of nude and seminude bodies are favorite targets of the pornophobes. Says Andrea Dworkin, "It's very hard to look at a picture of a woman's body and not see it with the perception that her body is being exploited." Strossen tells of the 1992 removal of a painting of the statue of Venus de Milo from a Springfield, Missouri, shopping mall because the managers thought it was "too shocking." The painting of the statue, sculpted about 150 BC, and a longtime centerpiece display of the Louvre Museum in Paris, was replaced by a painting of a woman wearing a long, frilly dress. Strossen describe many such incidents.

Andrea Dworkin and Catharine MacKinnon drafted a pornography law that was adopted in 1983 by the Minneapolis City Council. The law authorized lawsuits for damages and injunctive relief for several offenses described as "graphic sexually explicit subordination of women through pictures and/or words." Although the Council passed the law twice, it was vetoed each time by Mayor Donald Fraser on the ground that it violated the First Amendment. Both Fraser and his wife had long been known as champions of women's rights.

In 1984, the city of Indianapolis also passed a law modeled after the one drafted by Dworkin–MacKinnon. Immediately after it was signed by Mayor (also minister) William Hudnut, the law was challenged in federal court by a coalition of several plaintiffs. The ACLU filed a brief arguing that the law "unconstitutionally introduced gender-based discrimination into the First Amendment." The courts, all the way to the Supreme Court, agreed that the antipornography law violated the First Amendment Free Speech guarantee. This was so obvious to the Supreme Court justices that they did not even bother to ask for briefs, hear arguments, or even issue an opinion.[13]

Nadine Strossen strongly opposes antipornography legislation, especially what she calls the "MacDworkin style law," which she says, "authorizes civil lawsuits that trespass beyond the permitted realm of private persuasion into the forbidden territory of governmental coercion." She argues that, clearly, such laws would be unconstitutional censorship.

Feminist Gloria Steinem takes a position different from either the Dworkin–MacKinnon stance or that of Nadine Strossen. Steinem, in her book *Outrageous Acts and Everyday Rebellions*, decries the confusion from lumping together "pornography," "obscenity," "erotica," and "explicit sex," because, she says, "sex and violence are so intertwined." Though having no objective to erotica, *per se*, she sees pornography and its violence as an "antiwoman weapon" and holds men responsible.[14] "Men are the purchasers of pornography," she says, "and the majority of men are turned on by it, while the majority of women find it angering." She is outraged at the multibillion dollar industry that features such monstrosities as "snuff" movies and related pornographic literature that features slow death from sexual torture as the "final orgasm and ultimate pleasure." *Snuff* is the porn word for killing a woman for sexual pleasure. Steinem notes that snuff movies in which real women were eviscerated and finally killed by slow or related torture were driven underground partly by the discovery of the graves of murdered women around the house of a filmmaker in California. But she says, movies of simulated torture murders of women are still thriving. So-called "kiddie porn" or "chicken porn" movies find a lucrative market, as well as magazines that show adult men undressing, fondling, and sexually assaulting children. According to Steinem, some chicken porn magazines give explicit instructions on how to violate a child sexually without leaving visible signs of rape, the assumption being that a child's testimony has little chance of being believed.

Sexual violence is featured in some video games. Gloria Steinem tells of a game called *Custer's Revenge* that features a smiling, rope-bound Indian woman and a male figure with an erection representing General Custer. The idea is to rape the woman as many times as possible.[15] Steinem sums up her outrage, ". . . until we finally untangle sexuality and aggression, there will be more pornography and less erotica. There will be little murders in our beds—and very little love." Steinem admits that, "Obviously, untangling sex from aggression and violence or the threat of it is going to take a very long time. And the process is going to be greatly resisted as a challenge to the very heart of male dominance and male centrality."

Throughout most of the 20th century, any expression related to sex was obscene. Margaret Sanger began a movement in 1913 that led to the American Birth Control League. In the early days of flouting abusive censorship, Sanger and other pioneer birth control advocates were vilified and prosecuted for violating obscenity laws. In some cases prosecutions culminated in fines and imprisonment.

Two recent presidential commissions made surveys of pornography and issued recommendations. In 1970 the President's Commission on Obscenity and Pornography, which had been appointed by President Johnson, reported its findings to President Nixon. The Commission recommended repeal of all laws that prohibited the distribution of sexually explicit material to consenting adults. It also advocated a nationwide sex education program. The Commission thought that censorship of sexually explicit material might actually increase their desirability. Present Nixon emphatically denounced the report. And subsequent court rulings left the determination of obscenity ambiguous, vague, and subjective.

People high in government thought that additional facts should be accumulated. On May 20, 1985, Attorney General Edwin Meese III announced the appointment of a committee to determine "the nature, extent, and impact on society of pornography in the United States and to make specific recommendations to the Attorney General concerning more effective ways in which the spread of pornography could be contained consistent with constitutional guarantees." The final report was a gargantuan compendium of information and statements acquired from innumerable sources. The Commission made 92 recommendations, the general focus of which was on more restrictive laws and more stringent enforcement.[16] Four of the eleven commissioners were women. Three of them filed independent statements, one of which, co-authored by Dr. Judith Becker and Ellen Levine, said, among other statements,

> We believe it would be seriously misleading to read this report and see a green light for prosecuting all pornographers. . . . and we stress the need for non-governmental solutions and tolerance for the views of others. . . . a need for massive public reeducation about potential problems associated with them seems strongly indicated. . . . [T]o make all pornography the scapegoat is not constructive. . . . In conclusion we repeat that we face a complex social and legal problem that requires extensive study before realistic remedies can be recommended.

Dr. Becker was associate professor of clinical psychology at Columbia University; Ellen Levine was editor in chief of *Woman's Day* and a vice president of CBS Magazines.[17]

WHAT'S COMING

It's clear that something new and portentous has happened to eroticism, pornography, and obscenity. These time-honored forms of art and literature now wing their way on cyberspace to all parts of the world in dissemination of all levels of erotica from benign to violent, with the added feature of children being both participants and victims. A battle of gigantic proportions is looming between the champions of free speech and the defenders of privacy. It's a battle with no end in sight. The mass of cyberporn backed up by an insatiable appetite and a free speech commitment pitted against the anger of desperation and determination to defend the honor of home and family is a no-win crusade for either side. There will be compromises in which there will be something for everyone but not enough for anyone. Users will be permitted to use the Internet for almost anything they wish, but there will be a requirement that their identity and interests will be clearly stated and available. There will be a few restrictions already covered by present laws, especially those pertaining to child pornography. Rape and other sex acts accompanied by violence that are transmitted on-line, if produced live—not simulated—will carry heavy penalties under existing laws pertaining to such crimes.

It is generally accepted that depiction of rape and violence desensitizes the viewer and can lead to violence. Children will probably be given identification numbers, which will be out of bounds for some material and some sources, and all computers will be equipped with chips or downloaded with programs to enable parents to permanently black out names, handles, and other sources.

In one of the largest mass censorships in history, in December, 1995, Germany ordered the CompuServe on-line network to shut down access to more than 200 Internet newsgroups that the authorities deemed indecent and offensive. CompuServe complied, but the action shut down access to the newsgroups by CompuServe worldwide because CompuServe said it had no way of selecting geographic coverage.[18] But experts said that attempts to censor the Internet are futile because the information is available from so many sources.

Policing the vast network of cyberspace by pornophobes is a visionary dream. Even if a computer genius comes up with a practical way of doing it, protection of privacy and defense against objectionable intrusion will not be perfect. Hackers and clever adults will continue to find ways to gain access to and transmit unauthorized material. And children will, as always, find ways to outwit their parents.

Interactive CD-ROM is the wave of the future and will be an important vehicle for juvenile, adult, family, and pornographic entertainment. The intense interaction of video games in the class of Sega and Nintendo, which were limited to personal interaction, not interpersonal-interactivity, made a slow start in converting to interactive networks. A pioneer in the field was "Doom," a violent search-and-destroy network game. Restricting access to children will be difficult, as with all other forms of art and literature. But because of the popularity of CD-ROM, special measures will have to be taken, such as age limits for access as with liquor and tobacco. A new form of erotic adventure, *virtual sex*, may soon be developed. The technique, now called "virtual reality," is envisioned as a way to enhance the pleasure of viewing a scene or action. It is not merely watching actors perform as on stage or in a movie. In virtual sex, for example, the voyeuristic pleasure of watching people engage in coital capers, or whatever, is replaced by providing the realism of the user participating in the action. The user puts on a helmet or gets into a large box, and the experience happens in the privacy of the space provided. More advanced equipment will be simpler and lighter: goggles and thin wires with electrodes taped to the wrists and scalp. A computer generates sights and sounds with other sensory accompaniments.

For a long time, we've been able to transit sound electronically, including the intense emotions of music in its various forms. And we can supplement and intensify the feelings with visual imagery. How primitive! There is a vast store of sensations still untapped electronically, including odors, tastes, touch, pressure, and kinesthetic sensations. For instance, odors. It can be expected that research will unravel the presently unsolved mystery of human sex pheromones (body odors and flavors). Sex pheromones— mainly aphrodisiacs—are so common throughout the animal world, including the higher primates, that it is almost certain they have a subliminal role in human sexuality even though they escape our conscious awareness. Our clumsy effort to find the answer through a multibillion dollar perfume industry will be replaced by a breakthrough in biotechnology that will find one of its benefits in virtual sex. The human nose has 10 million olfactory receptors, and with training, the nose can discriminate between about 10,000 odors. There is already available an "electronic nose," called the AromaScanner, that visualizes odors in 3D, and the odors can be precisely identified with an instrument called a gas chromatograph.[19] Instruments of this kind will lead to the identification of human sex pheromones and their action as a prelude to how their effects can be duplicated and intensified electronically. Similar determinations will be made of the senses of touch, taste, pressure, and kinesthesia in studies of how to intensify or modify them. Virtual sex will greatly enhance normal sensations, and will add some never before experienced.

Virtual sex programs *en solo* will be available but the more popular programs will be those in which the viewer can choose one or more partners from a wide selection of choices. The choices can be, but will not have to be, those offered by a programmer. A man or woman will be able to choose his or her spouse or lover.

The most advanced technique will make it possible for a couple to join in virtual sex even though separated. An e-mail message to set an agreed upon time will enable a traveling man or woman to enjoy the comforts of home. Men and women serving in the military at foreign bases will especially benefit. Because not all of the men will have wives, sweethearts, or girlfriends back home, the availability of virtual sex will not eliminate prostitution. But for the first time, it will introduce completely safe prostitution, as well as safe sex generally. Areas near military bases, as well as R and R areas, for example, are notorious for having a plethora of cafés, bars, dance halls, dives of various kinds, B-girls, and prostitutes. Standards of health and safety will improve dramatically when virtual sex parlors are established in competition with the usual places of entertainment. Sexually transmitted diseases, including AIDS, will decline dramatically. Military commanders have the authority to declare places of entertainment off-limits if they pose a threat to the health and welfare of military personnel. Commanders will be more inclined to declare the sleazier joints off-limits if wholesome recreation becomes attractive. Many of the men who do not have wives or sweethearts at home will employ prostitutes via virtual sex. The girls may come from nearby or picked from a catalog of girls around the world available at virtual sex parlors.

Virtual sex will not necessarily be confined to establishment sex parlors. If history is a guide, technical development will bring about miniaturization, as it has with other innovations, making them more personal and bringing them into the home. Movies were first shown in theaters; the theaters became larger and the screens wider, ensuring the perpetuation of the movie theater, but at the same time, home movies came into use, and finally videotapes. Interactive CD-ROM followed. Radio first came into use by amateurs, then by the military where it revolutionized communication; then came commercial broadcasting, and progressively, pocket radios, small CB two-way radios, and portable cellular phones. Virtual sex will see a similar evolution. The bulge you see in a briefcase may not by a weighty report to be read all night by the busy traveler. It might be a two-way virtual sex unit with a built-in modem that will make a business trip as much pleasure as staying at home.

Explorers, who are typically away from home for long periods of time—months, sometimes years—will find the portable units handy. Astronauts, who hope someday to take off on a mission to another solar system, will be away from home for years, even if they achieve half the speed of light. Ideally, they'll take spouses with them, but some will be single. Virtual sex will be a virtual necessity in a situation where the added stress of a lengthy period of celibacy might endanger the mission.

No one has produced virtual sex, and there is no certainty that it can be done with any degree of perfection. Still, the idea will continue to challenge electronic entrepreneurs with visions of fortunes for as long as the desire for sex persists, which will be a long time. Part of the appeal will be the privacy and safety of virtual sex in a society that is becoming increasingly aware of the threat of AIDS and other STDs. Virtual sex will be preferred by many men and women to surreptitious affairs, cocktail bar pickups, or the currently criminal patronage of prostitutes. Besides, virtual sex, as envisioned, will provide more intense sensations than actual sex, as well as sensations that are nonexistent in natural sex. Sensations will be more than additive, they will be synergistic—a system whereby the input of one sensation enhances another, or several other sensations, rather than merely adding to them. Virtual sex will have special appeal to couples, who will be able to enhance the sensations of their own style and preferences.

The more advanced devices will be able to stimulate the specific pleasure centers of the brain to enhance sensations beyond anything experienced naturally. Laboratory experiments with animals have established the fact that when a sex hormone (testosterone) is injected into a certain area of the hypothalamus, the animal is stimulated into female behavior regardless of its sex. And when the hormone is injected into another, nearby, area of the hypothalamus, the animal is stimulated into behaving as a male, again regardless of its sex. The animals were unable to communicate what their sensations were like, but it is well known that the hypothalamus, which is both part of the brain and an organ of internal secretion, is the emotional switchboard of the brain, standing in command of sexual development, performance, and emotions. The hypothalamus has connections to the eye nerves, hence its ability to reset the circadian rhythm, and to the amygdala, where at least some of the emotion signals originate. Imaging machines, more sensitive than those now used for medical diagnosis, will make it possible to map the brain in detail, and pinpoint areas of emotions and sensations.

People would not want needles stuck into their brains, even as small as hypodermics, to get their kicks. Although chemicals taken by mouth are capable of reaching the brain, the most effective way to activate the pleasure centers without side effects will be a noninvasive probe, possibly with a low-energy colored laser. People will choose between enhanced male sensations or enhanced female sensations, or both at the same time. Because of the intensity of the sensations, the sessions might have to be limited in duration, say no more than a few minutes at a time, to avoid overloading the brain circuits. But they could be repeated as frequently as the nerve cells regenerate their functional capacity.

By the time all this comes about, much of what we hail now as new innovations will be out-of-date or will have disappeared from the cyberscene. As writer Robert Jones puts it, the superhighway will be cluttered with the electronic Model T wreckage of the 20th century.[20] Cyberspace will have become SUPERSPACE powered by breastpocket devices with speed and memory beyond anything imagined or thought possible. CD-ROMs will have faded into history, the mere memories of grandparents who will regale children at the fireside with stories about the simple pleasures of earlier times, and who will barely be aware of the fun and foolishness to come in the Age of Microchips when electrons will carry the communications of mind and body beyond mere words, sights, and sounds.

When Michael Faraday, the electronics wizard of his day, demonstrated the production of electricity with a primitive generator to a group of cognoscenti, one of them asked, "But what good is it?" Faraday replied, "Someday, sir, you will sell it." Sometime in the future a precocious kid will put the components of a virtual reality generator together in a shoe box, and when he demonstrates it at a gathering of the American Association for the Advancement of Science, someone will ask, "But what good is it?" The kid will blush and stammer, "Well . . . someday, madam, you'll be intimate with it."

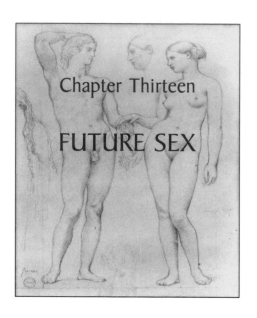

Chapter Thirteen

FUTURE SEX

Sex is basically a simple biological function, but in human experience it has branched into more behavioral tendrils than a hydra—like the mythical Hydra killed by Heracles, as soon as one head is cut off, two more grow. Equated with sin since the encounter of Adam and Eve, sexuality is emerging torturously from the dark shadows of secret shame. The hydra-head of sexuality will see some things change dramatically in the next century, while some things will stay the same depending on culture and the part of the world in which the people live. Ancient shibboleths and taboos are already yielding to a rapidly spreading mantle of enlightenment over a broad spectrum of humanity.

The most spectacular development in the near future will be a flourishing of openness and frankness in discussing sex and sexuality, comparable to the ease with which people have always discussed other facets of human behavior—food and drink, clothing, children, recreation, work, religion, physical ailments, appendectomies, and spats with the spouse. Physicians, who in the past received little or no training in sexual matters except for highly specialized problems, will be carried along with the tide, no longer confined to psychiatry. Conditioned from childhood to view sex as sinful or secret, or both, old-fashioned general practitioners will be replaced by physicians who will see sexual problems and practices as major health problems important to the welfare of their patients. Conservative medical schools will reluctantly expand their curricula to include instruction in sex, sex problems, and their treatment, and this will be followed by certified board specialties.

Sex therapy will have an expanding role as part of the physician's arsenal, creating a new category of highly trained medical assistants, both male and female. It may find a place in premarital instruction in ensuring at least an auspicious start along the rocky road of marital bliss. However, the need for premarital instruction, and in fact the need for all sex therapy, will be minimized by an enlightened view and acceptance of nudity as normal and innocuous behavior. There will be belated awareness of what the Greeks knew nearly 3000 years ago, that the human body is beautiful or ugly and good or evil only in the mind's eye. Escape from the tyranny of prudery will release the spirit of creativity and renew the joy of living.

Videotapes will be used increasingly for instruction as well as for erotic stimulation and entertainment. Many people view erotic movies and tapes as pornographic trash, and in truth, a high proportion of them are of low quality—amateurish photography, poor acting, and abominable directing. But the fact that at least a third of erotic videos now sold are used and enjoyed by married couples is an indication that an increase in demand will lead to improved quality and variety. Erotic interactive CD-ROMs are presently used almost exclusively by voyeurs for entertainment, but the technology offers possibilities for educational material of a wide variety.

Dissemination of erotic material on the Internet is worrisome to many people, especially if they have children with access to a computer and an on-line service. The 1996 Communications Decency Act made it a federal crime to transmit "indecent" material over the Internet without ensuring that children cannot see it and required software services to establish a rating system for use by parents who want to block objectionable programs. But it will take many years to resolve the problems. The American Civil Liberties Union, along with several communications businesses, immediately challenged the constitutionality of the Decency Act, with a vow to take it to the Supreme Court if necessary. If the Act is upheld, what is "indecent" will be argued interminably.

A rating standard agreed upon by a consortium of 39 software and computer companies implemented a variety of privately developed rating systems. For example, one based on the Platform for Internet Content Selection (PICS) has a scale of nine rankings from "subtle innuendo" to "explicitly for adults," with one level reserved for technical references to sex, such as medical information. The company that offers this system ranked, at last count, 30,000 of the half-million or so sites on the World Wide Web alone. Stay tuned!

The age-old search for ways to enhance pelvic pleasure has not diminished. Although most of the so-called love potions—aphrodisiacs—have no physiological value, and in some cases are dangerous, the placebo effect is real enough to keep them in worldwide demand, many of them at exorbitant prices. Modern pharmacology has already embarked on a new generation of sex drugs, but the main thrust is for drugs and ways of using them to correct sexual dysfunctions, especially to overcome impotence, problems that are more common than most people realize. So-called sex toys are of limited therapeutic value, but will have increasing use for sexual gratification. Now available in a small number of unobtrusive shops or by mail order, sex toys will come to be openly available in mall shops and will be topics of open discussion as prudery eventually becomes a topic of interest mainly for historians.

Bed roles are highly personal experiences. The domineering man and submissive woman are relics of the past, but many couples are tethered to strong childhood impressions of the idea that sex is nasty, secret, and unmentionable. Bed roles will evolve with an awakening to the fact that knowledge of intimate sexual matters is something to share and that individuals differ in their desires and needs. The inevitable decline of prudery will contribute to sexual relationships that enable man and woman to see each other as equals with differences in desires and needs openly shared.

The legal status of same-sex relationships is in a state of flux. The action of the state of Hawaii in authorizing same-sex marriages gave encouragement to gays and lesbians, who anticipated the protection of a federal law that recognizes marriage in any state as being valid in all states. Hawaii's action, at the same time, reinvigorated lively debate about states' rights and how the courts would interpret various state laws. Several states had already passed laws banning same-sex marriages, and additional states had such legislation under consideration. It remains unpredictable to what extent several thousand years of tradition that "marriage" is a union for man and woman will influence justices' decisions. But even if same-sex marriages in general are denied legal standing, there will remain a strong trend toward granting specific legal rights to same-sex couples, such as hospital visitation, inheritance of assets, health insurance, and pensions. The same privileges will be granted to committed unmarried heterosexual couples.

Prostitution, a traditional human activity since at least the beginning of historical memory, will continue to flourish worldwide. In parts of the world, such as most parts of the United States, where prostitution is a criminal offense, it will be gradually decriminalized. This will come about less through a moral awakening and sense of justice and fairness than through fear of uncontrollable disease epidemics, especially if the heterosexual AIDS epidemic materializes as widely predicted. Decriminalization will open the way to licensing prostitutes, accompanied by mandatory weekly health examinations and collection of fees and taxes, which, in turn, will create funds for public prevention and treatment of venereal diseases.

The battle of the sexes may be known to future historians as the Thousand Years' War, for it will not be resolved easily or completely. Women will achieve parity of numbers in the work force, taking into account the part of the female population that will choose to be full-time homemakers or to work part-time. And equally qualified women will receive pay equal to that of men for the same kind of work. More women will engage in politics, which perhaps they will dominate, and more women will own and be in control of businesses. But surprisingly to some, and to the anguish of many women, there will continue to be more men than women in top jobs. The reason is a well-known characteristic of *Homo sapiens* that cultural trends, politics, and crusades are not apt to change within the life span of the human species. Men produce, on average, more testosterone than women do, and testosterone has been clearly established as a prime cause of aggressiveness. Feminists readily acknowledge that men generally are more aggressive than women. In a society that glorifies "success"—typically, climbing to the top of the corporate ladder or aggressively accumulating conspicuous wealth—there is no evidence and no reason to think that aggressiveness will play a reduced role in achieving success in business.

Science and technology have drastically affected human sexuality for many years, most notably in their effect on fertility through use of the contraceptive "pill." Improved chemical contraceptives and abortifacients will have worldwide impact in the future, but widespread use and its effect will be greatly delayed until after the world population reaches such overwhelming numbers that civilization is threatened with collapse through shortages of resources—mainly fuel, forests, soil, fresh water, and food—and unmanageable pollution of air, water, and soil. *Homo sapiens*, said to be the "world's sexiest animal," will come perilously close to copulating itself into extinction and will recover only after the shock of the human dilemma sinks into the consciousness of the reputedly brainiest animal on earth.

Meanwhile, infertile couples who want babies will increasingly seek and receive help from science. Artificial insemination, known technically as donor insemination (DI), is a practice of longstanding social acceptance. DI in the future will differ greatly from the early slipshod practice of collecting sperm with minimum attention to genetic and health suitability. Careful testing for diseases is prompted by fear of transmitting AIDS, and this requires freezing the sperm and holding it for several months. In the future much more attention will be given to sperm donors' characteristics other than health and physical appearance, especially mental achievements and other outstanding qualities of donors. Other methods of overcoming infertility, including *in vitro* fertilization (IVF) and embryo transfer, will become increasingly available. Assisted reproductive technology (ART), along with its variations, and surrogate motherhood are currently so expensive that availability is limited to moderately affluent couples. While improved success rates will reduce the cost, the methods will still not be cheap.

Techniques for producing and handling human embryos have suggested the possibility of using excess embryos for scientific and medical research. But ethical questions are so serious that most such research will be delayed indefinitely. Some procedures are clearly out of bounds even if possible, such as implantation of human embryos into other species and hybridizing humans with other species. Cloning human embryos for a limited purpose such as determining genetic characteristics will encounter objections.

The greatest potential for benefits from work with human embryos is the determination of genetic characteristics and correction of deficiencies. Close ethical monitoring is predictable. Gestating human embryos to term *in vitro* is so far from present capability that even consideration of the ethical impact is in the distant future.

A quantum jump in erotic pleasure may become widely available in a form of virtual reality called virtual sex, or cybersex, when transmitted on the Internet. No one has produced virtual sex or cybersex, but it remains within the realm of possibility. The monetary and social incentives are very great, because it will introduce sensations not normally experienced, will make sexual encounters possible even when spouse or partner are separated by great distances, and equally important, will introduce, for the first time, sex that is truly safe.

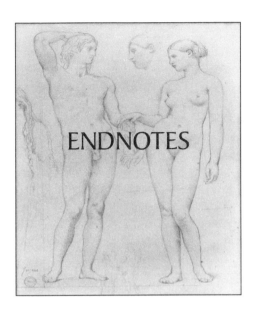

ENDNOTES

INTRODUCTION

[1]J. Hastings, *Encyclopaedia of Religion and Ethics* (Clark, 1915), cited by G. Rattray Taylor, *Sex in History* (New York: Vanguard Press, 1954), p. 255.

CHAPTER ONE: THE NAKED TRUTH

[1]Genesis 1:27, 2:25, 3:7.
[2]Genesis 9:21–27.
[3]Hugh C. Lester, *Godiva Rides Again: A History of the Nudism Movement* (New York: Vantage Press, 1968).
[4]Matthew 27:35.
[5]Lester, pp. 72–75.
[6]Quoted by Leon Elder, *Free Beaches: A Phenomenon of the California Coast* (Santa Barbara: Capra Press, 1974).

[7] Magazines relating to nudism and nudist parks: *Lee Barndall's World Guide to Nude Beaches and Recreation*, N Editions, P.O. Box 132, Oshkosh, WI 54902. *North American Guide to Nude Recreation*, 18th edition, The American Sunbathing Association, 1703 North Main Street, Kissimmee, FL 34744-3391; 800-879-6833. *Nude & Natural*, The Naturist Society, The Naturist, Inc., P.O. Box 132, Oshkosh, WI 54902.

[8] Jack D. Douglas and Paul K. Rasmussen with Carol Ann Flanagan, *The Nude Beach* (Beverly Hills: Sage Publications, 1977), p. 93.

[9] Valerie Tamis, "Did You Know? There Are Almost as Many Saunas as Automobiles in Finland," *Avenues* (July/August 1995), p. 37.

[10] Aileen Goodson, *Therapy Nudity & Joy: The Therapeutic Use of Nudity Through the Ages* (Los Angeles: Elysium Growth Press, 1991).

[11] Goodson.

Other Readings

Jan Gay, *On Going Naked* (Garden City, NY: Garden City Publishing Co., 1932).

Fred Ilfeld, Jr., and Roger Lauer, *Social Nudism in America* (New Haven, CN: College and University Press, 1964).

Frances and Mason Merrill, *Nudism Comes to America* (Garden City, NY: Garden City Publishing Co., 1932).

Maurice Parmelee, *Nudism in Modern Life: The New Gymnosophy* (Garden City, NY: Garden City Publishing Co., 1931).

CHAPTER TWO: THE IMPOSSIBLE DREAM

[1] Thomas Bullfinch, *The Age of Fable* (Garden City, NY: Doubleday, 1948).

[2] Pliny, *The Natural History of C. Plinius Secundus*, trans. Philemon Holland (London: Centaur Press, Ltd., 1962; New York: McGraw-Hill, 1964), pp. 202, 246–248, 290, 343.

[3] *The Kama Sutra of Vatsyayana: The Classic Hindu Treatise on Love and Social Conduct*, trans. Sir Richard F. Burton (New York: E. P. Dutton, 1964).

[4] M. Laurence Lieberman, *The Sexual Pharmacy: The Complete Guide to Drugs with Sexual Side Effects* (New York: New American Library, 1988).

[5] P. V. Taberner, *Aphrodisiacs: The Science and the Myth* (Philadelphia: University of Pennsylvania Press, 1985).

[6] Alan Hull Walton, *Aphrodisiacs: From Legend to Prescription* (Westport, CN: Associated Booksellers, 1958).

[7] Lucy W. Clausen, *Insect Fact and Folklore* (New York: Macmillan Publishing Co., 1962).

[8] James E. Carrel and Thomas Eisner, "Cantharidin: A Potent Feeding Deterrent to Insects," *Science* 183 (February 22, 1974), pp. 755–757.

[9] Genesis 29; 30:14–17.

[10] Shakespeare: *Antony and Cleopatra* I, v, 4.

[11] Rhazes, *Liber ad Almansorem*, trans. in the 12th century by the School of Gerard of Cremona (Venice, 1497).

[12] Martin Levy, "Medieval Arabic Toxicology," *Transactions of the American Philosophical Society* 56 (New Series), Part 7 (1966).

[13] Michael J. Goodman, "It's a Jungle Out There," *Los Angeles Times Magazine*, October 15, 1995.

[14] John J. Putnam, "India Struggles to Save her Wildlife," *National Geographic* 150(3) (September 1976), pp. 299–342.

[15] *National Geographic* 183(4) (April 1993); John Gordon Davis, "Operation Rhino," *Reader's Digest*, September 1972, and abstract of *To Save the Great Chipimbiri* (New York: Doubleday, 1972).

[16] "Dehorning Rhinos to Give Them a Future," *National Geographic* 183(4) (April 1993), unnumbered page.

[17] "Earth Almanac, Though Namibia's Seals Starve, Culling Continues," *National Geographic* 187(5) (May 1995), unnumbered page.

[18] Mary Williams Walsh, "Reindeer Herd Sits on the Horns of a Dilemma," *Los Angeles Times*, November 24, 1992, p. 6.

[19] Quoted by Reuters, "He's Out to Charm With Snake Products," *Los Angeles Times*, July 10, 1995, p. D5.

[20]Craig Turner, "Canada Discovers a Root to Wealth," *Los Angeles Times*, October 7, 1995.

[21]Chris Kraul, "Mescal Distillers in Hopeful Spirits," *Los Angeles Times*, January 22, 1996.

[22]Robert Hendrickson, *Lewd Food: The Complete Guide to Aphrodisiac Edibles* (Radnor, PA: Chilton Book Co., 1974).

[23]Louis S. Goodman and Alfred Gilman, *The Pharmacological Basis of Therapeutics*, 4th ed. (New York: Macmillan & Co., 1970), pp. 524–525.

[24]Martha Windholz, Susan Budavari, Lorraine Y. Stroumtsos, and Margaret Noether Fertig, eds., *The Merck Index*, 11th ed. (Rahway, NJ: Merck & Co., 1989).

[25]Cynthia Mervis Watson, with Angels Hynes, *Love Potions: A Guide to Aphrodisiacs and Sexual Pleasures* (New York: J. P. Tarcher/Perigee, 1993).

[26]Harold Hopkins, "Chocolate: Has a Rich History and Certain Standards," *FDA Consumer* (July–August 1981), pp. 5–9.

[27]Allen M. Young, *The Chocolate Tree: A Natural History of Cacao* (Washington DC: Smithsonian Institution Press, 1993).

[28]Barry L. Jacobs, "Serotonin, Motor Activity and Depression— Related Disorders," *American Scientist* 82 (September–October 1994), pp. 456–463.

[29]Diane Ackerman, *A Natural History of Love* (New York: Random House, 1994).

[30]Carol McGraw, "New AIDS Research Stirs Concern over 'Poppers,' " *Los Angeles Times*, March 30, 1986, p. 3.

[31]Winand K. Hock, "Unapproved Drugs Probed," *FDA Consumer* (October 1984), pp. 6–7.

[32]G. L. Gessa and E. M. Paglietti, "Induction of Copulatory Behavior in Sexually Inactive Rats by Naloxone," *Science* 204 (April 13, 1979), pp. 203–205.

[33]Alessandro Tagliamonte, Paola Tagliamonte, Gian L. Gessa, and Bernard B. Brodie, "Compulsive Sexual Activity Induced by p-Chlorophenylalanine in Normal and Pinealectomized Male Rats," *Science* 166 (December 12, 1969), pp. 1433–1435.

[34]G. L. Gessa, A. Tagliamonte, and P. Tagliamonte, "Aphrodisiac Effect of p-Chlorophenylalanine," *Science* 171 (February 19, 1971), p. 706.

[35]Richard E. Whalen and William G. Luttge, "P-Chlorophenyl-alanine Methyl Ester: An Aphrodisiac?" *Science* 169 (September 4, 1970), pp. 1000–1001.

[36]James Ferguson, Steven Henriksen, Harry Cohen, George Mitchell, Jack Barchas, and William Dement, " 'Hypersexuality' and Behavioral Changes in Cats Caused by Administration of p-Chlorophenylalanine," *Science* 168 (April 24, 1970), pp. 499–501.

[37]Judith Willis, "Drugs that Take the Joy Out of Sex," *FDA Consumer* (July–August 1981), pp. 31–32.

[38]*Chemical and Engineering News* (August 1, 1977), pp. 17–18.

[39]John Schwartz, "Depression Drug's Side Effect Has Users Aroused, *Los Angeles Times* (November 7, 1995).

Other Readings

"Another Drug Abuse Problem: Methaqualone," *Health Tips* (July 1973), Index 313, California Medical Association.

James Cleugh, *A History of Oriental Orgies: An Account of Erotic Practices Among the Peoples of the East and the Near East* (New York: Crown Publishers, 1968).

Francis Connell, "The Use of Aphrodisiacs," *American Ecclesiastical Review* 136 (1957), cited by Noonan, 1965.

John Davenport, *Aphrodisiacs and Love Stimulants: With Other Chapters on the Secrets of Venus* (New York: Lyle Stuart, Inc., 1966).

Annabel Hecht, "Aphrodisiacs," *FDA Consumer* (December 1981– January 1983), p. 11

Hippocrates, *The Theory and Practice of Medicine* (New York: Citadel Press, 1964).

"New Drugs May Relieve Sexual Disorders," *Chemical & Engineering News* (August 1, 1977), pp. 17–18.

John T. Noonan, *Contraception: A History and its Treatment by the Catholic Theologian Canonists* (New York: New American Library, 1965).

Ovid, *Ars Amatoria*, ed. E. J. Kenney (Oxford, 1961), pp. 415–423.

Physicians' Desk Reference, 48th ed. (Montvale, NJ: Medical Economics Co., Inc., 1994).

Norman Taylor, *Plant Drugs that Changed the World* (New York: Dodd, Mead & Co., 1965).

CHAPTER THREE: JOYS 'R' US

[1]James Cleugh, *A History of Oriental Orgies: An Account of Erotic Practices Among Peoples of the East and Near East* (New York: Crown Publishers, 1968), p. 128.

[2]Vern Bullough and Bonnie Bullough, *Sin, Sickness, and Sanity* (New York: New American Library, 1977).

[3]Reay Tannahill, *Sex in History* (New York: Stein & Day/ Scarborough House, 1992).

[4]*Good Vibrations* (catalog), Open Enterprises, Inc., 938 Howard Street, Suite 101, San Francisco, CA 94103-4163.

[5]*Xandria Collection, Catalog #946*, Lawrence Research Group, P.O. Box 319005, San Francisco, CA 94131.

[6]*Good Vibes Gazette*, Number XVIII, Holiday 1995.

[7]Carlene Stephens "Chastity Belt," *Academic American Encyclopedia* (1990), pp. 301–302.

Other Readings

The Kama Sutra of Vatsyayana: The Classic Hindu Treatise on Love and Social Conduct, trans. Sir Richard F. Burton (New York: E. P. Dutton, 1964).

Mail Order Catalog 1995, The Condom Revolution Erotic Giftshop, 1799 Newport Blvd., Suite A102, Costa Mesa, CA 92627.

The Sexuality Library Fall 1995, Open Enterprises, Inc., 938 Howard Street, Suite 101, San Francisco, CA 94103-4163.

O. A. Wall, *Sex and Sex Worship (Phallic Worship)* (St. Louis: C. V. Mosby Co., 1922).

CHAPTER FOUR: THE SEX WARS

[1]Isaac Asimov, *Asimov's Guide to the Bible* (New York: Avenal Books, 1981), p. 546.

[2]Aristophanes, *Lysistrata*, trans. Jack Lindsay, In *The Complete Plays of Aristophanes*, ed. Moses Hadas (New York: Bantam Books, 1962).

[3]Betty Friedan, *The Feminine Mystique*, Twentieth Anniversary Edition (New York: W. W. Norton & Co., 1983), p. 5.

[4]Gloria Steinem, *Moving Beyond Words* (New York: Simon & Schuster, 1994).

[5]Simon LeVay, *The Sexual Brain* (Cambridge, MA: MIT Press, 1993).

[6]Sharon Begley, "Gray Matters," *Newsweek*, March 27, 1995, pp. 48–54.

[7]Alan E. Fisher, "Maternal and Sexual Behavior Induced by Intracranial Chemical Stimulation," *Science* 124 (1956), pp. 228–229.

[8]Anke Ehrhardt and Heino F. L. Meyer-Bahlburg, "Effects of Prenatal Sex Hormones on Gender-Related Behavior," *Science* 211 (1981), pp. 1312–1318.

[9]Reviewed by Gina Bari Kolata, "!Kung Hunter Gatherers: Feminism, Diet and Birth Control," *Science* 185 (1974), pp. 932–934.

[10]Lionel Tiger and Joseph Shepher, *Women in the Kibbutz* (New York: Harcourt Brace Jovanovich, 1975), reviewed by Rosabeth Moss Kanter, "Interpreting the Results of a Social Experiment," *Science* 192 (May 14, 1976), pp. 662–663.

[11]Juanita Darling, "The Women Who Run Juchitan," *Los Angeles Times*, March 31, 1995.

[12]Kathleen Gerson, *No Man's Land* (New York: Basic Books, 1993), reviewed by Martha R. Fowlkes, *Science* 266 (October 14, 1994), pp. 307–308.

[13]"Women, the New Providers," study by Louis Harris and Associates, reviewed by Donna K. H. Walters, 1995.

[14]Vicki Torres, "Women-owned Firms' Hiring Outpaces Nation," *Los Angeles Times*, April 12, 1995.

[15]Vicki Torres, "State Leads in Women-Owned Small Businesses," *Los Angeles Times*, January 30, 1996.

[16]"Women on Board," *Los Angeles Times*, April 19, 1995.

[17]Jane Applegate, "Female Entrepreneurs Map Strategy," *Los Angeles Times*, April 4, 1995.

[18]Suzanne Schlosberg, "In the Name of Love," *Los Angeles Times*, May 22, 1995.

[19]Karen Kaplan, "Telecommuting Trend Hits Close to Home," *Los Angeles Times*, October 27, 1995.

[20]Elizabeth Mehren, "Going Solo," *Los Angeles Times*, March 28, 1995, pp. E1, E8.

[21]Jenifer Warren, "Panel Kills Bill on Breast-Feeding," *Los Angeles Times*, May 11, 1995, pp. A3, A30.

[22]Joyce Brothers, "Harassment Issue May Be Backlash," *Los Angeles Times*, March 11, 1995, p. E9.

[23]Katherine Dowling, "Sexual Harassment Jackpot," *Los Angeles Times*, September 7, 1994.

[24]Dennis Hunt, " 'Short, Short Man' Attacks Big, Big Sex," *Los Angeles Times*, February 4, 1995, p. F4.

[25]"Psychology Today," *Riverside Press-Enterprise*, March 10, 1995.

[26]UPI, "Sperm Bank Picketed," *Los Angeles Times*, December 2, 1975.

Other Readings

Robin Abcarian, "Truth is the Tool That Will Smash the Glass Ceiling," *Los Angeles Times*, April 2, 1995.

David Elkind, *Ties that Stress: The New Family Imbalance* (Cambridge, MA: Harvard University Press, 1994).

Jacqueline J. Goodnow and Jennifer M. Bowes, *Men, Women and Household Work* (London: Oxford University Press, 1994).

Elaine Morgan, *The Scars of Evolution* (London: Souvenir Press, 1990; London: Oxford University Press, 1994).

Martine Rothblatt, *The Apartheid Sex: A Manifesto on the Freedom of Gender* (New York: Crown Publishers, 1995).

Gloria Steinem, *Outrageous Acts and Everyday Rebellions* (New York: Holt, Rinehart & Winston, 1983).

Lisa Tuttle, *Encyclopedia of Feminism* (New York: Facts on File Publications, 1986).

CHAPTER FIVE: BED ROLES

[1]Sandra L. Bem, "Sex Role Adaptability: One Consequence of Psychological Androgeny," *Journal of Personality and Social Psychology* 31(4) (1975), pp. 634–643, cited by Douglas C. Kimmel,

Adulthood and Aging, 2nd ed. (New York: John Wiley & Sons, 1980), pp. 161–162, 173.

[2]Betty Friedan, *The Second Stage* (New York: Summit Books, 1982).

[3]Alexandra Penney, *How to Make Love to a Man* (New York: Wings Books, 1981).

[4]John Feltman, ed., *Hands-On Healing: Massage Remedies for Hundreds of Health Problems* (Emmaus, PA: Rodale Press, 1989). Lists several instructional videotapes. A tape of interest to lovers is *Massage ... The Touch of Love*, 28 minutes, nudity, "men and women massage each other from head to toe in front of a roaring fireplace."

[5]Denise Gellene, "Looking for Love but Finding Headaches," *Los Angeles Times*, March 2, 1995.

[6]David M. Buss, "Human Mate Selection," *American Scientist* 73 (January–February 1985), pp. 47–51.

[7]David M. Buss, "The Strategies of Human Mating," *American Scientist* 82 (May–June 1994), pp. 238–249.

[8]David M. Buss, *The Evolution of Desire: Strategies of Human Mating* (New York: Basic Books, 1994).

[9]Quoted by Beverly Beyette, "For Kinsey Director, It's Same Old Story," *Los Angeles Times*, May 18, 1986, p. 42.

[10]Edward O. Laumann, John H. Gagnon, Robert T. Michael, and Stuart Michaels, *The Social Organization of Sexuality* (Chicago: University of Chicago Press, 1994).

[11]Robert T. Michael, John H. Gagnon, Edward O. Laumann, and Gina Kolata, *Sex in America* (Boston: Little, Brown & Co., 1994), p. 216.

[12]Quoted by Rosalind Miles, *Love, Sex, Death, and the Making of the Male* (New York: Summit Books, 1991), p. 97.

[13]Diane Ackerman, *A Natural History of Love* (New York: Random House, 1994), 281

[14]Quoted by Beverly Beyette, "For Kinsey Director, It's Same Old Story," *Los Angeles Times*, May 16, 1995, p. 1.

[15]Leslie Knowlton, "Thigh Anxiety," *Los Angeles Times*, August 23, 1994; Denise Gellens, "Cashing in on Thigh Anxiety," *Los Angeles Times*, November 29, 1994.

[16] Ackerman, p. 128.

[17] I Kings 11:1,3.

[18] William H. Masters and Virginia Johnson, *Human Sexual Response* (Boston: Little, Brown & Co., 1966).

[19] *Reader's Digest*, March 1994, p. 180.

[20] David Stipp, "Better Prognosis: Research on Impotence Upsets Idea That it is Usually Psychological," reprinted from *The Wall Street Journal* by Potency Recovery Center, Van Nuys, California (no date given).

[21] Peter D. Kramer, *Listening to Prozac* (New York: Penguin Books, 1995).

[22] Louis S. Goodman and Alfred Gilman, *The Pharmacological Basis of Therapeutics* (London: Macmillan & Co., 1970).

[23] Beyette, 1985, p. 1.

[24] Ernest Hemingway, *A Moveable Feast* (New York: Charles Scribner's Sons, 1964), pp. 190–191.

[25] Quoted by Rosalind Miles, *Love, Sex, Death, and the Making of the Male* (New York: Summit Books, 1991), p. 15.

[26] Jeffrey Meyers, *Hemingway: A Biography* (New York: Harper & Row, 1985), p. 352.

[27] Douglas P. Shuit, "Doctor Agrees to Stop Doing Penile Surgery," *Los Angeles Times*, February 6, 1996, p. B1.

[28] Masters and Johnson, p. 260.

[29] Douglas C. Kimmel, *Adulthood and Aging*, 2nd ed. (New York: John Wiley & Sons, 1980).

[30] Kimmel, pp. 410–413.

[31] Masters and Johnson, p. 203.

[32] Melissa Healy, "At 92, Thurmond Can Still Fend Off Ouster Attempt," *Los Angeles Times*, February 14, 1995.

[33] J. R. Moehringer, "Grandfather's Sex Parties Investigated," *Los Angeles Times*, May 1, 1995, p. A3.

[34] Miles, p. 209

[35] Ovid, *The Art of Love and Other Love Books of Ovid* (New York: Grosset & Dunlap, 1959), pp. 194–195.

[36] Ackerman, p. 41.

[37] Otto Kiefer, *Sexual Life in Ancient Rome* (London: Abbey Library, 1934).

[38]Sydney Biddle Barrows, with William Novak, *Mayflower Madam: The Secret Life of Sydney Biddle Barrows* (New York: Ivy Books, 1986), p. 107.

[39]Lloyd Grove, "Southern Discomfort," *Los Angeles Times* (May 1, 1996), pp. E1, E4.

Other Readings

Simone de Beauvoir, *The Coming of Age*, trans. Patrick O'Brian (New York: G. P. Putnam's Sons, 1972).

Joyce Brothers, *What Every Woman Should Know About Men* (New York: Ballantine Books, 1981).

Vern L. Bullough, *Science in the Bedroom: A History of Sex Research* (New York: Basic Books, 1994).

Alex Comfort, ed., *The Joy of Sex* (New York: Crown Publishers, 1972).

Marilyn Ferguson, *The Brain Revolution: The Frontiers of Mind Research* (New York: Bantam Books, 1973).

Betty Friedan, *The Feminine Mystique*, Twentieth Anniversary Edition (New York: W. W. Norton & Co., 1983).

Betty Friedan, *The Fountain of Age* (New York: Simon & Schuster, 1993).

Natalie Gittelson, *The Erotic Life of the American Wife: A Survey of Her Sexual Mores* (New York: Dell Publishing Co., 1969).

Shere Hite, *The Hite Report: A Nationwide Study of Female Sexuality* (New York: Macmillan Publishing Co., 1976)

Corinne Hutt, *Males & Females* (Harmondsworth, Middlesex, England: Penguin Books, 1972).

The Kama Sutra of Vatsyayana: The Classic Hindu Treatise on Love and Social Conduct, trans. Sir Richard F. Burton (New York: E. P. Dutton, 1964).

Nat Lehrman, *Masters and Johnson Explained* (Chicago: Playboy Press, 1970).

Margaret Mead, *Male and Female: A Study of the Sexes in a Changing World* (New York: William Morrow & Co., 1949).

Michael Morgenstern, with Steven Naifeh and Gregory White Smith, *How to Make Love to a Woman* (New York: Wings Books, 1982).

Michael Teitelbaum, ed. *Sex Differences: Social and Biological Perspectives* (Garden City, NY: Anchor Press/Doubleday, 1976).

Barry Thorne and Nancy Henley, eds., *Language and Sex: Difference and Dominance* (Rowley, MA: Newbury House, 1975).

Renee Twombly, "Assault on the Male," *Environmental Health Perspectives* 103 (September 1995), pp. 802–805.

Bernie Zilbergeld, *Male Sexuality* (New York: Bantam Books, 1978).

CHAPTER SIX: THE MASCULINE MYSTIQUE

[1]Betty Friedan, *The Feminine Mystique*, Twentieth Anniversary Edition (New York: W. W. Norton & Co., 1983).

[2]Gloria Steinem reviews much of her activities in: *Outrageous Acts and Everyday Rebellions* (New York: Holt, Rinehart & Winston, 1983); and *Moving Beyond Words* (New York: Simon & Schuster, 1994).

[3]Survey figures on infidelity vary so widely that, in aggregate, they are not very reliable.

[3a]Betty Friedan, *The Second Stage* (New York: Summit Books, 1981), p. 4.

[4]Germaine Greer, *The Female Eunuch* (New York: McGraw–Hill, 1971), p. 245.

[5]Sam Keen, *Fire in the Belly: On Being a Man* (New York: Bantam Books, 1991), p. 28.

[6]Betty Friedan, *The Feminine Mystique*, Twentieth Anniversary Edition (New York: W. W. Norton & Co., 1983), pp. xxii–xxiii.

[7]Margaret Mead, *Male and Female: A Study of the Sexes in a Changing World* (New York: William Morrow & Co., 1949), p. 3.

[8]Jesse Katz, "Striptease Club Opens Its Doors to the Stock Market," *Los Angeles Times*, October 13, 1995, p. A1.

[9]David M. Buss, *The Evolution of Desire: Strategies of Human Mating* (New York: Basic Books, 1994).

[10]Mutilation of captives, slaves, and some criminals was done in different ways. A more common practice with slaves was to castrate, that is, cut off the testicles, which if done to an adult did not always completely destroy his sex drive. When a man is

castrated as an adult, there is some loss of libido, but his ability to copulate may persist for an indefinite time [William F. Ganong, *Review of Medical Physiology* (Los Altos, CA: Lange Medical Publications, 1971)]. In some cases the penis as well as testicles was cut off. A simple, cruel, and painful method was to crush the testicles, having at least the effect of a modern vasectomy.

In some parts of the ancient world it was the practice to cut off the penises of defeated warriors. An account of a campaign of the Egyptian pharaoh Merneptah, who defeated the Libyans in 1300 BC, is carved into a monument at Karnak. It brags that he returned with 13,000 penises. The tally: 6 Libyan generals, 6359 Libyan soldiers, 222 Sirculians, 542 Etruscans, and 6111 Greeks [G. L. Simons, *Simons' Book of World Sexual Records* (New York: Bell, 1955), p. 57].

The Hebrews found it more symbolically satisfying to take the foreskins of their defeated enemies. When King Saul reluctantly offered David the hand of his daughter in marriage, he demanded, in deference to the fact that David was not wealthy, 100 Philistine foreskins instead of a dowry. Secretly, Saul was hatefully jealous of David, and hoped that he would be killed in battle. But David promptly went out with his men and killed 200 Philistines. When he presented their foreskins to the King, he had earned the right to be the King's son-in-law (I Samuel 18: 20–27).

11 Diane Ackerman, *A Natural History of Love* (New York: Random House, 1994), p. 197.

12 Rosalind Miles, *Love, Sex, Death, and the Making of the Male* ((New York: Summit Books, 1991), p. 198.

13 Helen E. Fisher, *The Sex Contract: The Evolution of Human Behavior* (New York: William Morrow & Co., 1982).

14 David M. Buss, "Human Mate Selection," *American Scientist* 75 (January–February 1985), pp. 47–51.

15 David G. Savage, "High Court Case Revives Debate on Gender Bias," *Los Angeles Times*, January 1, 1996.

15a Patricia Sexton, "Schools Are Emasculating Our Boys," *Saturday Review* (June 19, 1965); cited by Vance Packard, *The Sexual Wilderness* (New York: David McKay Co., 1968), p. 353.

[16] Vance Packard, *The Sexual Wilderness* (New York: David McKay Co., 1968), p. 360.

[17] Quoted by Rosalind Miles, p. 225.

[18] Constance Holden, ed., "Winning With Testosterone," *Science* 269 (September 8, 1995), pp. 1341–1343.

[19] Paul Liben, "When Chivalry is Not Chauvinism," *Los Angeles Times*, September 5, 1995.

[20] Quoted by Rosalind Miles, p. 169.

Other Readings

Donald H. Bell, *Being a Man: The Paradox of Masculinity* (Lexington, MA: Lewis Publishing Co., 1982).

Ronald F. Levant, with Gini Kopecky, *Masculinity Reconstructed: Changing the Rules of Manhood—at Work, in Relationships, and in Family Life* (New York: E. P. Dutton, 1995).

CHAPTER SEVEN: MATING FOR MONEY

[1] Helen E. Fisher, *The Sex Contract: The Evolution of Human Behavior* (New York: William Morrow & Co., 1982).

[2] Samuel Noah Kramer, *History Begins at Sumer* (New York: Doubleday, 1959).

[3] Jeffrey H. Tigay, *The Evolution of the Gilgamesh Epic* (Philadelphia: University of Pennsylvania Press, 1982).

[4] Samuel Putnam, *History of Prostitution: Among All the People of the World, From the Most Remote Antiquity to the Present Day* (Chicago: Pascal Covici, 1926).

[5] Genesis 38.

[6] Joshua 2.

[7] Hosea 2,3.

[8] St. Luke 7:37–50.

[9] Marco Polo, *The Travels of Marco Polo* (New York: Grosset & Dunlap, 1931), p. 219.

[10] Hans Licht, *Sexual Life in Ancient Greece*, trans. J. H. Freese (London: Lund Humphries; New York: Barnes & Noble, 1932).

[11] Robert Flacelière, *Love in Ancient Greece*, trans. James Cleugh (New York: Crown Publishers, 1960).

[12] G. Rattray Taylor, *Sex in History* (New York: Vanguard Press, 1954).

[13] Herodotus, *The Histories*, trans. Aubrey de Sélincourt (Harmondsworth, Middlesex, England: Penguin Books, 1954).

[14] Otto Augustus Wall, *Sex and Sex Worship* (St. Louis: C. V. Mosby Co., 1922).

[15] Vern Bullough and Bonnie Bullough, *Women and Prostitution: A Social History* (Buffalo, NY: Prometheus Books, 1987).

[16] I Kings 11:1,3. Tells of Solomon's concubines.

[17] Jan Hutson, *The Chicken Ranch: The True Story of the Best Little Whorehouse in Texas* (Cranbury, NJ: A. S. Barnes & Co., 1980).

[18] Herbert Asbury, *The Barbary Coast: An Informal History of the San Francisco Underworld* (New York: Garden City Publishing Co., 1933).

[19] Pierre Berton, *Klondike: The Last Great Gold Rush 1896–1899* (Toronto: McClelland & Stewart, 1972).

[20] George H. Hicks, *The Comfort Women: Japan's Brutal Regime of Enforced Prostitution in the Second World War* (New York: W. W. Norton & Co., 1995).

[21] K. Connie Kang, "Better Page of History Recorded," *Los Angeles Times*, December 12, 1994.

[22] Sam Jameson, "Japan Apology Goes to WWII Sex Slaves," *Los Angeles Times*, July 19, 1995.

[23] Sam Jameson, "Japan Plans a Fund as Amends for Sex Slaves," *Los Angeles Times*, August 30, 1995.

[24] Hilary E. MacGregor, "Fund for 'Comfort Women' Coming Short in Japan," *Los Angeles Times*, December 30, 1995.

[25] Sally Stanford, *The Lady of the House: The Autobiography of Sally Stanford* (New York: G. P. Putnam's Sons, 1966).

[26] Gloria Steinem, *Outrageous Acts and Everyday Rebellions* (New York: Holt, Rinehart & Winston, 1983) p. 248.

[27] Shawn Hubler, "Did Father Know Best?" *Los Angeles Times Magazine*, April 9, 1995.

[28] John Glionna, "The Usual Suspects," *Los Angeles Times*, November 14, 1995, p. E8.

[29] Laurie Becklund, "Prostitution Arrests Cost $2,000 Each, Study Finds," *Los Angeles Times*, July 10, 1987, p. 1.

[30] Gloria Allred and Lisa Bloom, "Prosecution or Persecution?" *Los Angeles Times*, December 6, 1994.

[30a] Alan Dershowitz, "Why Heidi Fleiss Shouldn't Go to Jail," *Los Angeles Times*, December 20, 1994.

[31] Laurie Bell, ed., *Good Girls/Bad Girls: Sex Trade Workers and Feminists Face to Face* (Toronto: The Women's Press, 1987), pp. 49–50.

[32] Bell, pp. 82–83.

[33] UPI, Baton Rouge, LA, "Prostitution Law Voided," *Los Angeles Times*, February 13, 1994.

[34] UP, Hershey, PA, December 12, 1975.

[35] Associated Press, Hershey, PA, "Decriminalizing of Prostitution Urged by Panel," *Los Angeles Times*, December 10, 1975.

[36] Hilary Evans, *Harlots, Whores & Hookers* (New York: Taplinger Publishing Co., 1979).

[37] "Strong Point Purchase of Bordello Nearly Complete," *Los Angeles Times*, May 29, 1986.

[38] Janice G. Raymond, "Prostitution is Rape That's Paid For," *Los Angeles Times*, December 11, 1995.

[39] Vern Bullough, *Science in the Bedroom: A History of Sex Research* (New York: Basic Books, 1994), p. 256.

[40] Bullough and Bullough, pp. 20–21.

[41] David H. LeRoy,"The Potential Criminal Liability of Human Sex Clinics and Their Patients," *St. Louis University Law Journal* 16 (1972), p. 586 [cited by Aileen Goodson, in *Therapy Nudity & Joy* (Los Angeles: Elysium Growth Press, 1991), p. 150].

Other Readings

Polly Adler, *A House is Not a Home* (New York: Rinehart & Co., 1953).

Kathleen Barry, *Female Sexual Slavery* (Englewood Cliffs, NJ: Prentice-Hall, 1979).

Vern Bullough and Bonnie Bullough, *Sin, Sickness, and Sanity: A History of Sexual Attitudes* (New York: New American Library, 1977).

Vern and Bonnie Bullough, *Prostitution: An Illustrated Social History* (New York: Crown Publishers, 1978).

James Cleugh, *A History of Oriental Orgies* (New York: Crown Publishers, 1968).

Merle Colby, *A Guide to Alaska: Last American Frontier* (New York: Macmillan Publishing Co., 1950).

Xaviera Hollander, *The Happy Hooker* (New York: Dell Publishing Co., 1972).

Otto Kiefer, *Sexual Life in Ancient Rome* (London: Abbey Library, 1934).

Leslie McRay with Ted Schwartz, *Kept Women: Confessions from a Life of Luxury* (New York: William Morrow & Co., 1990).

Robin Morgan, *The Word of a Woman: Feminist Dispatches 1968– 1992* (New York: W. W. Norton & Co., 1992).

Sean O'Callaghan, *Damaged Baggage: The White Slave Trade and Narcotics Trafficking in the Americas* (London: Robert Hale, 1969).

Raphael Patai, *Sex and Family in the Bible and the Middle East* (Garden City, NY: Doubleday & Co., 1959).

Joanna Richardson, *The Courtesans: The Demi-monde in Nineteenth-century France* (London: Weidenfeld & Nicolson, 1967).

Gitta Sereny, *The Invisible Children: Child Prostitution in America, West Germany and Great Britain* (New York: Alfred A. Knopf, 1985).

CHAPTER EIGHT: SAME-SEX SEX

[1] *Bullfinch's Mythology: The Age of Fable or Stories of Gods and Heroes* (Garden City, NY: Doubleday & Co., 1948).

[2] Robert Flacelière, *Love in Ancient Greece* (New York: Crown Publishers, 1962).

[3] Hans Licht, *Sexual Life in Ancient Greece*, trans. J. H. Freese (London: Lund Humphries, 1932).

[4] G. Rattray Taylor, *Sex in History* (New York: Vanguard Press, 1954), p. 95.

[5] Taylor, p. 230.

[6] Lillian Faderman, *Odd Girls and Twilight Lovers: A History of Lesbian Life in Twentieth-Century America* (New York: Penguin Books, 1991).

[7] Otto Kiefer, *Sexual Life in Ancient Rome* (London: Abbey Library, 1934).

[8] Kiefer, p. 186.

[9] Kiefer, p. 282.

[10] Kiefer, pp. 297–298.

[11] Kiefer, p. 299.

[12] Kiefer, pp. 310–311.

[13] Kiefer, pp. 311–314, 312.

[14] Robert Graves, *I Claudius: From the Autobiography of Tiberius Claudius, Born BC X, Murdered and Deified AD LIV* (New York: Vintage Books, 1934).

[15] Kiefer, p. 316.

[16] Kiefer, p. 336.

[17] Leviticus 18:22; 20:13.

[18] Genesis 19.

[19] Judges 19–20.

[20] Genesis 1:28.

[21] I Samuel 18:1.

[22] Taylor, p. 34.

[23] J. Locke, *An Essay Concerning Human Understanding* (Chicago: Henry Regnery, 1956).

[24] Anke A. Ehrhardt and Heino F. L. Meyer-Bahlburg, "Effects of Prenatal Sex Hormones on Gender-Related Behavior," *Science* 211 (1981), pp. 1312–1318.

[25] Simon LeVay, *The Sexual Brain* (Cambridge, MA: MIT Press, 1993).

[26] Gunther Dörner, *Hormones and Brain Differentiation* (Amsterdam: Elsevier, 1976).

[27] Simon LeVay, "A Difference in Hypothalamic Structure Between Heterosexual and Homosexual Men," *Science* 253 (1991), pp. 1034–1037.

[28] Dean H. Hamer, Stella Hy, Victoria L. Magnuson, Nan Hu, and Angela M. L. Pattatucci, "Linkage Between DNA Markers on the X Chromosome and Male Sexual Orientation," *Science* 261 (1993), pp. 321–327.

[28a] "Study Links Homosexuality and Heredity," *Los Angeles Times*, October 31, 1995, p. A8.

29" 'Living in Sin' Is No Longer a Sin, Church of England Report Says," *Los Angeles Times*, June 7, 1995.
30Richard C. Paddock, "S.F. to Allow Civil Ceremonies for Gay Couples," *Los Angeles Times*, January 30, 1996.
31Paula L. Ettelbrick, "Marriage Is Not a Path to Liberation," in *Homosexuality: Opposing Viewpoints*, ed. William Dudley (San Diego: Greenhaven Press, 1993), p. 177.

Other Readings

Dennis Altman, *The Homosexualization of America* (Boston: Beacon Press 1982).

John Boswell, *Christianity, Social Tolerance, and Homosexuality: Gay People in Western Europe from the Beginning of the Christian Era to the Fourteenth Century* (Chicago: University of Chicago Press, 1980).

John Boswell, *Same-Sex Unions in Premodern Europe* (New York: Villard Books, 1994).

Vern L. Bullough and James Brundage, *Sexual Practices in the Medieval Church* (Buffalo, NY: Prometheus Books, 1982).

Vern Bullough and Bonnie Bullough, *Sin, Sickness, and Sanity: A History of Sexual Attitudes* (New York: New American Library, 1977).

Margaret Cruikshank, *The Gay and Lesbian Movement* (New York: Routledge, Chapman & Hall, 1992).

John D'Emilio, *Making Trouble: Essays on Gay History, Politics, and the University* (New York: Routledge, Chapman & Hall, 1992).

William Dudley, ed., *Homosexuality: Opposing Viewpoints* (San Diego: Greenhaven Press, 1993).

Alfred C. Kinsey, Wardell B. Pomeroy, and Clyde C. Martin, *Sexual Behavior in the Human Male* (Philadelphia: W. B. Saunders Co., 1948).

Alfred C. Kinsey, Wardell B. Pomeroy, Clyde C. Martin, and Paul H. Gebhard, *Sexual Behavior in the Human Female* (Philadelphia: W. B. Saunders Co., 1953).

William H. Masters and Virginia E. Johnson, *Homosexuality in Perspective* (Boston: Little, Brown & Co., 1979).

Raphael Patai, *Sex and the Family in the Bible and the Middle East* (Garden City, NY: Doubleday & Co., 1959).

Reuters, "Living in Sin is No Longer a Sin, Church of England Report Says," *Los Angeles Times*, June 7, 1995.

A. L. Rowse, *Homosexuals in History: A Study of Ambivalence in Society, Literature and the Arts* (New York: Macmillan Publishing Co., 1977).

Elizabeth Reba Weise, ed., *Close to Home: Bisexuality & Feminism* (New York: Seal Press, 1992).

CHAPTER NINE: MAKING BABIES

[1]Geoffrey Sher and Virginia A. Marriage with Ean Stoess, *From Infertility to In Vitro Fertilization: A Personal and Practical Guide to Making the Decision that Could Change Your Life* (New York: McGraw–Hill, 1988), p. 48.

[2]Marlene Cimons, "New Life for Old Technique," *Los Angeles Times*, January 10, 1995.

[3]Lord Rothschild, "Sperm Movement Problems and Observations," in *Spermatozoan Motility*, ed. David W. Bishop (Washington, DC: American Association for the Advancement of Science, 1962).

[4]"Guidelines for Gamete Donation: 1993," *Fertility and Sterility*, Official Journal of the American Fertility Society, Supplement 1, 59, No. 2 (February 1993), pp. 1S–9S.

[5]Sir James Gray, "Flagellan Propulsion," in *Spermatozoan Mobility*, ed. David W. Bishop (Washington, DC: American Association for the Advancement of Science, publication No. 72, 1962).

[6]Lori B. Andrews, *New Conceptions: A Consumer's Guide to the Newest Infertility Treatments, Including In Vitro Fertilization, Artificial Insemination, and Surrogate Motherhood* (New York: St. Martin's Press, 1984).

[7]C. Polge, "Increasing Reproductive Potential in Farm Animals," in *Reproduction in Mammals*, Book 5: *Artificial Control of Reproduction*, ed. C. R. Austin and R. V. Short (London: Cambridge University Press, 1972).

[8]The Repository for Germinal Choice (Escondido, CA).

[9]*Vasectomy Reversal: A Second Chance for Fatherhood* (Newport Beach, CA: Hoag Hospital).

[10]Reuters, "Doctor Details Sperm Removal from a Dead Man," *Los Angeles Times*, January 20, 1995.

[11]Henry Weinstein, "Judge Rules Man Can Bequeath Sperm in Will," *Los Angeles Times*, June 19, 1993, p. A18.

[12]Carla Hall, "A Legacy of Litigation," *Los Angeles Times*, November 10, 1994.

[13]Diana Frank and Marta Vogel, *The Baby Makers* (New York: Carroll & Graf Publishers, 1988).

[14]Elizabeth Mehren, "A Controversial Sperm Bank Where the Women Are in Charge," *Los Angeles Times*, February 6, 1983, pp. 1, 10.

[15]The Repository for Germinal Choice: Cofounders 1963, Hermann J. Muller and Robert Klark Graham (Escondido, CA). Robert K. Graham, *About the Repository for Germinal Choice* (Escondido, CA).

[15a]Edwin Chen, "Sperm Bank Donors All Nobel Winners," *Los Angeles Times*, February 29, 1980, pp. 1, 3.

[16]Keay Davidson, " 'Nobel Prize Sperm Bank' Faces Lawsuits, Competition," *Los Angeles Times*, September 25, 1984.

[17]William J. Broad, "A Bank for Nobel Sperm," *Science* 207 (March 21, 1980), pp. 1326–1327.

[18]Richard C. Paddock, "Bill Would Curb 'Master Race' Sperm Banks," *Los Angeles Times*, March 1, 1983, pp. 3, 15.

[19]Personal communication.

[20]Annette Baran and Reuben Pannor, *Lethal Secrets: The Shocking Consequences and Unsolved Problems of Artificial Insemination* (New York: Warner Books, 1989).

[21]C. R. Austin, "Fertilization," in *Reproduction in Mammals*, 1 *Germ Cells and Fertilization*, ed. C. R. Austin and R. V. Short (London: Cambridge University Press, 1972).

[22]S. Fishel and E. M. Symonds, eds., *In Vitro Fertilization: Past–Present–Future* (Oxford: IRL Press, 1986).

[23]Marcida Dodson, "Twins Born From Eggs Implanted in Woman With Early Menopause," *Los Angeles Times*, November 7, 1986.

[24]Huntington Reproductive Center, Newsletter No. 6, Fall 1994.

[25]NBC News Report, January 26, 1996.

[26]Constance Holden, "Perils of Freezing Embryos," *Science* 267 (February 3, 1995), pp. 618–619 (quotation p. 619).

[27]Genesis 16.

[28]Arthur L. Wisot and David R. Meldrum, *New Options for Fertility: A Guide to In Vitro Fertilization and Other Assisted Reproduction Methods* (New York: Pharos Books, 1990).

[29]Leslie Berkman, "Twins, Grandma? She's Pregnant Pioneer," *Los Angeles Times*, October 6, 1992.

[30]Francisco J. Ayala, "The Myth of Eve: Molecular Biology and Human Origins," *Science* 270 (December 22, 1995), pp. 1930–1936.

[31]Jonathon Weil, "CUMC Reports 1st Birth After Embryo Biopsy," *Cornell '93*, Winter 1993, p. 6.

Other Readings

Joel H. Batzofin, "XY Sperm Separation for Sex Selection," *Urologic Clinics of North America*, 14, No. 3 (August 1987), pp. 609–617.

David R. Bromham, Maureen E. Dalton, and Jennifer C. Jackson, eds., *Philosophical Ethics in Reproductive Medicine* (Manchester, England: Manchester University Press, 1990).

Robert Edwards and Patrick Steptoe, *A Matter of Life: The Story of a Medical Breakthrough* (New York: William Morrow & Co., 1980).

Clifford Grobstein, *From Chance to Purpose: An Appraisal of External Human Fertilization* (Reading, MA: Addison–Wesley, 1981).

"Guidelines for Human Embryology and Andrology Laboratories," *Fertility and Sterility*, Official Journal of the American Fertility Society, Supplement 1, 58, No. 4 (October 1992), pp. 1S–16S.

Judith Rich Harris and Robert M. Liebert, *The Child: A Contemporary View of Development*, 3rd ed. (Englewood Cliffs, NJ: Prentice-Hall, 1991).

Richard J. Harrison, *Reproduction and Man* (New York: W. W. Norton & Co., 1967).

Robert Lee Hotz, *Designs on Life: Exploring the New Frontiers of Human Fertility* (New York: Pocket Books, 1991)

[32]"Intrauterine Insemination," *The American Fertility Society: Guideline for Practice*, 1991.

Beth Ann Krier, "King of the Anonymous Fathers," *Los Angeles Times*, April 21, 1989.

David G. Lygre, *Life Manipulation: From Test-tube Babies to Aging* (New York: Walker & Co., 1979).

John A. Robertson, *Children of Choice: Freedom and the New Reproductive Technologies* (Princeton, 1995).

"Through the Glass Lightly," *Science* 267 (March 17, 1995), pp. 1609–1618.

E. Peter Volpe, *Test Tube Conception: A Blend of Love and Science* (Macon, GA: Mercer University Press, 1987).

CHAPTER TEN: TEMPEST IN A TEST TUBE

[1]Robert Edwards and Patrick Steptoe, *A Matter of Life: The Story of a Medical Breakthrough* (New York: William Morrow & Co., 1980).

[2]George F. Will, "Will Man-Made Man Be Next?" *Los Angeles Times*, August 4, 1978.

[3]Ethics Committee of the American Fertility Society, "Ethical Considerations of Assisted Reproductive Technologies," *Fertility and Sterility* 62, No. 5 (November 1994), pp. i–vi, 1S–125S.

[4]Colin Norman, "IVF Research to End?" *Science* 241 (July 22, 1988), pp. 405–406.

[5]Marlene Cimons, "Clinton Bans Funding for Embryo Creation," *Los Angeles Times*, December 3, 1994.

[6]Keith Stewart Thompson, "Research on Human Embryos: Where to Draw the Line?": *American Scientist* 73 (March–April 1985), pp. 187–189.

[7]Jonathan Glover and others, *Ethics of New Reproductive Technologies: The Glover Report to the European Commission* (De Kalb: Northern Illinois University Press, 1989).

[8]Russell Chandler, "Vatican Condemns Human Artificial Reproduction," *Los Angeles Times*, March 10, 1987, pp. 1, 23.

[9]S. Fishel and E. M. Symonds, eds., *In Vitro Fertilization: Past–Present–Future* (Oxford: IRL Press, 1986).

[10] Eliot Marshall, "Rules of Embryo Research Due Out," *Science* 265 (August 19, 1994), pp. 1024–1026.

[11] Richard T. Hull, ed., *Ethical Issues in the New Reproductive Technologies* (Belmont, CA: Wadsworth Publishing Co., 1990).

[12] Abigail Goldman, "Eagle Rock Woman, 50, Gives Birth to Triplets," *Los Angeles Times*, November 12, 1994.

[13] Julie Marquis and Tracy Weber, "Clinic Whistle-Blowers Were Paid to Keep Quiet," *Los Angeles Times*, June 2, 1995.

[14] Richard Stone, "Religious Leaders Oppose Patenting Genes and Animals," *Science* 268 (May 26, 1995), p. 1126.

[14a] Larry B. Stammer and Robert Lee Hotz, "Faiths Unite to Oppose Patents on Life Forms," *Los Angeles Times* (May 8, 1995), p. A1.

[15] "Frozen Assets: 'Twin' Sisters Born 18 Moths Apart," *Los Angeles Times*, April 24, 1987.

[16] H. Graham, *Eternal Eve* (Garden City, NY: Doubleday & Co., 1951), p. 41, cited by Batzofin.

[17] R. J. Ericsson, C. N. Langerin, and M. Nishino, "Isolation of Fractions Rich in Human Y Sperm," *Nature* 246 (1973), p. 421, cited by Batzofin.

[18] Joel H. Batzofin, *Sex Selection—An Overview*, (available from the Huntington Reproductive Center, Pasadena, CA), p. 4.

[19] David M. Rorvik, *In His Image: The Cloning of a Man* (New York: J. B. Lippincott Co., 1978).

[20] Constance Holden, "Random Samples: Embryo Cloners Jumped the Gun," *Science* 266 (December 23, 1994), p. 1949.

[21] Constance Holden, "Random Samples: Perils of Freezing Embryos," *Science* 267 (February 3, 1995), pp. 618–619.

[22] M. Goodman, B. F. Koop, J. Czelusniak, D. H. A. Fitch, D. A. Tagle, and J. L. Slightom, "Molecular Phylogeny of the Family of Apes and Humans," *Genome* 31 (1989), pp. 316–335, cited by Carl Sagan and Ann Druyan, *Shadows of Forgotten Ancestors* (New York: Ballantine Books, 1992).

[23] Johann Wolfgang von Goethe, ed. and trans. Stuart Atkins, *Faust: A Tragedy, Parts I & II* (Boston: Suhrkamp/Insel, 1984).

[24] Aldous Huxley, *Brave New World* (New York: Harper & Row, 1932, 1939; Bantam Books, 1953).

[25] "Through the Glass Lightly," *Science* 267 (March 17, 1995), pp. 1609–1618 (quotation, p. 1609).

Other Readings

Lori B. Andrews, *New Conceptions: A Consumer's Guide to the Newest Infertility Treatments, Including In Vitro Fertilization, Artificial Insemination, and Surrogate Motherhood* (New York: St. Martin's Press, 1984).

Annette Baran and Reuben Pannor, *Lethal Secrets: The Shocking Consequences and Unsolved Problems of Artificial Insemination* (New York: Warner Books, 1989).

David R. Bromham, Maureen E. Dalton, and Jennifer C. Jackson, eds., *Philosophical Ethics in Reproductive Medicine* (Manchester, England: Manchester University Press 1990).

"Guidelines for Gamete Donation: 1993," *Fertility and Sterility*, Official Journal of the American Fertility Society, Supplement 1, 59, No. 2 (February 1993), pp. 1S–9S.

"Guidelines for Human Embryology and Andrology Laboratories," *Fertility and Sterility*, Official Journal of the American Fertility Society, Supplement 1, 58, No. 4 (October 1992), pp. 1S–16S.

Robert Lee Hotz, *Designs on Life: Exploring the New Frontiers of Human Fertility* (New York: Pocket Books, 1991).

"Intrauterine Insemination," *The American Fertility Society: Guideline for Practice*, 1991.

Steven Maynard Moody, *The Dilemma of the Fetus: Fetal Research, Medical Progress and Moral Politics* (New York: St. Martin's Press, 1995).

Richard Stone, "Religious Leaders Oppose Patenting Genes and Animals," *Science* 268 (May 26, 1995), p. 1126.

CHAPTER ELEVEN:
THE COPULATION EXPLOSION

[1] Donna E. Shalala, letter to Ann Landers, "Teen Pregnancy is Everyone's Problem," *Los Angeles Times*, August 19, 1994.

[2] Planned Parenthood Affiliates of Southern California, "When JR Took Mandy for a Little Roll in the Hay, which One Had the Condom?" Advertisement, *Los Angeles Times*, December 8, 1986.

[3]Shari Roan, "The Birth Control Bust," *Los Angeles Times*, July 11, 1995, p. E1.

[4]Eric Harrison, "AIDS Is No. 1 Killer of Young Americans," *Los Angeles Times*, December 2, 1994.

[5]G. Rattray Taylor, *Sex in History* (New York: Vanguard Press, 1954), p. 1887.

[6]Allan Parachini, "Condoms May Get Warning Labels," *Los Angeles Times*, August 24, 1987.

[7]"Condom Testing and Regulations," Carter-Wallace, Inc., Correspondence, February 14, 1995.

[8]"Update: Barrier Protection Against HIV Infection and Other Sexually Transmitted Diseases," *Morbidity and Mortality Weekly Report* 42(30) (August 6, 1993), pp. 589–591, 597.

[9]"Condoms and Their Use in Preventing HIV Infection and Other STDs," *HIV/AIDS Prevention*, Centers for Disease Control and Prevention, July 30, 1993.

[10]William L. Roper, "Commentary: Condoms and HIV/STD Prevention—Clarifying Message," *American Journal of Public Health* 83(4) (April 1993), pp. 501–503.

[11]Roper, p. 502.

[12]Charles Krauthammer, "The Scourge of Illegitimacy: 1. Stop the Subsidy," *Reader's Digest*, March 1994, pp. 49–50, condensed from *The Washington Post*, November 1993.

[13]Charles Murray, "The Scourge of Illegitimacy: 2. Tomorrow's Underclass," *Reader's Digest*, March 1994, pp. 50–53, condensed from *The Wall Street Journal*, October 29, 1993.

[14]Kathy M. Kristof, "Welfare or No, Teen Pregnancy Spells Poverty," *Los Angeles Times*, August 8, 1994.

[15]Frank F. Furstenberg, "Don't Blame Welfare for Society's Ills," *Los Angeles Times*, August 23, 1994.

[16]Wade Roush, "Population: The View From Cairo," *Science* 265 (August 26, 1994), pp. 1164–1167.

[17]Thomas Robert Malthus, *A Summary View of the Principle of Population*, 1830, reprinted in *Three Essays on Population* (New York: The New American Library of World Literature, 1960).

[18]Lester R. Brown, "Population Growth Sets Record," in *Vital*

Signs 1992: The Trends That Are Shaping Our Future, ed. Linda Starke (New York: W. W. Norton & Co., 1992), pp. 76–77.

[19]Roush, p. 1164.

[20]Mary Mycio, "Abortion-Rights Foes Find Few Backers in Ukraine," *Los Angeles Times*, June 6, 1995.

[21]Brown, p. 76.

[22]Kim Murphy, "180 Nations Adopt Population Plan," *Los Angeles Times*, September 14, 1994, p. A1.

[23]John-Thor Dahlburg, "Faith & Practice: A Changing World Puts Abortion in the Spotlight," *Los Angeles Times*, January 24, 1995.

[24]John-Thor Dahlburg, "Faiths Disagree on Morality of Abortion," *Los Angeles Times*, January 24, 1995.

[25]Robin Morgan and Gloria Steinem, "The International Crime of Genital Mutilation," in *The World of a Woman: Feminist Dispatches 1968–1992*, ed. Robin Morgan (New York: W. W. Norton & Co., 1992), pp. 90–101.

[26]Jody L. Jacobson, "Maternal Mortality Takes Heavy Toll," in *Vital Signs 1992: The Trends That Are Shaping Our Future*, ed. Linda Starke (New York: W. W. Norton & Co., 1992), pp. 112–113.

[27]Robert F. Service, "Contraceptive Methods Go Back to the Basics," *Science* 266 (December 2, 1994), pp. 1480–1481 (quotations p. 1480).

[28]Peter Aldhous, "A Booster for Contraceptive Vaccines," *Science* 266 (December 2, 1994), pp. 1484–1486.

[29]David Pimentel, C. Harvey, P. Resosudarmo, K. Sinclair, D. Kurz, M. McNair, S. Crist, L. Shpritz, L. Fitton, R. Saffouri, and R. Blair, "Environmental and Economic Costs of Soil Erosion and Conservation Benefits," *Science* 267 (February 24, 1995), pp. 1117–1122 (quotation p. 1117).

[30]Laurie Garrett, *The Coming Plague: Newly Emerging Diseases in a World Out of Balance* (New York: Farrar, Straus & Giroux, 1994), p. 11.

[31]Stuart B. Levy, *The Antibiotic Paradox: How Miracle Drugs Are Destroying the Miracle* (New York: Plenum Press, 1992), p. 223.

[32]Lester R. Brown, "Overview: Entering a New Era," in *Vital Signs*

1992: The Trends That Are Shaping Our Future, ed. Linda Starke (New York: W. W. Norton & Co., 1992).

Other Readings

Lester R. Brown, *Who Will Feed China?: Wake-up Call for a Small Planet* (New York: W. W. Norton & Co., 1995).

Leon F. Bouvier and Lindsey Grant, *How Many Americans? Population, Immigration and the Environment* (San Francisco: Sierra Club Books, 1994).

Lincoln H. Day, *The Future of Low-birthrate Populations* (London: Routledge, 1992).

Griffith Feeney, "Fertility Decline in East Asia," *Science* 266 (December 2, 1994), pp. 1518–1523.

Paul M. Insel and Henry Clay Lindgren, *Too Close for Comfort: The Psychology of Crowding* (Englewood Cliffs, NJ: Prentice-Hall, 1978).

Hal Kane, "Leaving Home," in *State of the World 1995: A Worldwatch Institute Report on Progress Toward a Sustainable Society* (New York: W. W. Norton & Co., 1995), pp. 132–149.

Richard Leakey and Roger Lewin, *The Sixth Extinction: Patterns of Life and the Future of Humankind* (New York: Doubleday & Co., 1995).

George D. Moffett, *Critical Masses: The Global Population Challenge* (New York: Viking Press, 1995).

John M. Riddle, *Contraception and Abortion from the Ancient World to the Renaissance* (Cambridge, MA: Harvard University Press, 1992).

Michael Tobias, *World War III: Population and the Biosphere at the End of the Millennium* (Santa Fe, NM: Bear & Co., 1994).

CHAPTER TWELVE: CYBERSEX

[1]Michael Schrage, "Why Sonic the Hedgehog Needs to Jump Onto the Info Highway," *Los Angeles Times*, November 3, 1994.

[2]Amy Harmon, "The Oracle of Yahoo Has Internet Surfers Going Gaga," *Los Angeles Times*, April 10, 1995.

[3]Daniel Akst, "Side Roads Leading to the Internet," *Los Angeles Times*, November 2, 1995.

[4]Robert A. Jones, "Pssst! Want to Buy a Dirty CD?" *Los Angeles Times Magazine*, March 19, 1995.

[5]Paul Tharp, "As Computer Porn Mushrooms, Welcome to Cybersleaze," *New York Post*, November 3, 1994.

[6]*Man Enough*, ISBN/DOS: 1-57251-057-4, Time Warner Interactive.

[7]Julio Moran, "Man Accused of Possessing Child Porn from Internet," *Los Angeles Times*, May 18, 1995.

[8]Edward J. Boyer and Abigail Goldman, "Girl Lured From Home by E-Mail Is Found in L.A.," *Los Angeles Times*, June 12, 1995, p. A1.

[9]Murray S. Davis, *Smut: Erotic Reality/Obscene Ideology* (Chicago: University of Chicago Press, 1983).

[10]Quoted by Nadine Strossen, *Defending Pornography. Free Speech, Sex, and the Fight for Women's Rights* (New York: Charles Scribner's Sons, 1995).

[11]Strossen, p. 20.

[12]Strossen, p. 28.

[13]Strossen, p. 67.

[14]Gloria Steinem, *Outrageous Acts and Everyday Rebellions* (New York: Holt, Rinehart & Winston, 1983).

[15]Steinem, p. 223.

[16]*Final Report of the Attorney General's Commission on Pornography*, Introduction by Michael J. McManus (Nashville, TN: Rutledge Hill Press, 1986), p. ix.

[17]*Final Report*, pp. 540–546.

[18]Karen Kaplan, "Germany Forces Online Service to Censor Internet," *Los Angeles Times*, December 29, 1995.

[19]Michael Freemantle, "Instrument Develops Its 'Eye' for Smell," *Chemical and Engineering News*, December 18, 1995, pp. 30–31.

[20]Robert A. Jones, "Pssst! Want to Buy a Dirty CD?" *Los Angeles Times Magazine*, March 19, 1995.

Other Readings

Associated Press, "Senate Approves Plan for TV-Show Blocking Device," *Los Angeles Times*, June 14, 1995.

Lawrence J. Magid, *Child Safety on the Information Highway* (Arlington, VA: National Center for Missing and Exploited Children).

"Modern Anxiety: What to Do When Smut Rides the Internet?" *Los Angeles Times*, June 10, 1995.

Robin Morgan, *The World of a Woman: Feminist Dispatches 1968–1992* (New York: W. W. Norton & Co., 1992).

Kim Murphy, "Youngsters Falling Prey to Seducers in Computer Web," *Los Angeles Times*, June 11, 1995.

Donald Symons, *The Evolution of Human Sexuality* (London: Oxford University Press, 1979).

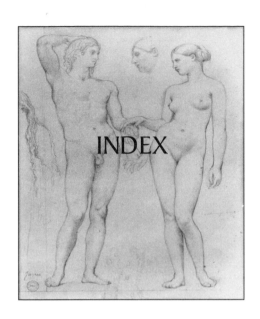

INDEX

WITHDRAWAL

25 10/09
26 1/12
27 5/13
28 14/10